# PRAISE FOR
## *KG: A to Z*

"Kevin Garnett played basketball with unrivaled intensity and eccentricity. . . . Happily, his new memoir is shot through with these qualities as well. Abjuring a standard chronology, *KG: A to Z* tells the author's story . . . alphabetically. . . . The glossary format suits his restless mind."

—Josh Swansburg, *The New York Times Book Review*

"This book shows us how complicated and dynamic Kevin Garnett is. He crushed it in the NBA, and he crushed it with his memoir."

—Trevor Noah

"I love the way this book is set up as an index. Kevin made it simple for dopes like me. Though I have to say, I went to *J* and I went to *K* and I didn't see anything about me."

—Jimmy Kimmel

"This book challenges formal expectations. . . . The narrative of Garnett's life doesn't run straight through the book, but it zigzags intuitively, rendered in candid prose. . . . The text captures the peerless intensity that Garnett displayed on the court. . . . A gift for die-hard Garnett fans."

—*Kirkus Reviews*

"The athlete autobiography is a well-established though often disappointing genre. It's rare for one to truly stand out among the many disposable ones that are released each and every year. Garnett's new book, *KG: A to Z*, co-written with David Ritz, is one of those very satisfying exceptions. One reason is that *KG: A to Z* is not presented as a traditional narrative. . . . The book travels alphabetically through dozens of different entries with Garnett giving his thoughts on disparate topics such as video games, *Family Guy*, Allen Iverson, *Uncut Gems*, the Book of Job, and many more. In a more standard autobiography, many of the detours taken here would be annoying, a distraction from an overarching story, but here, this format works to Garnett's advantage. . . . Readers are certain to come away feeling like they just shared a wonderful time with Garnett as he regaled them with his personal opinions and favorite stories. For any NBA fan, such an experience would be a true delight and this book is the closest most of us will ever have to replicate it for ourselves. . . . Garnett's autobiography captures his large and passionate biography as well as any book ever could, making it one of the rare books by an athlete worth intentionally seeking out."

—Micah Wimmer, Fansided.com

# KG A to Z

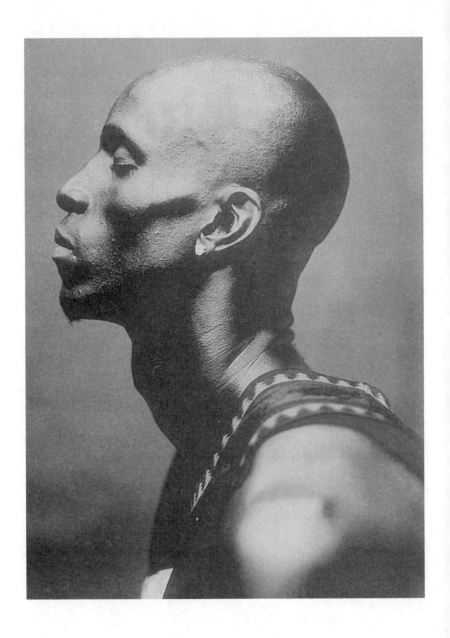

# KG A to Z

An Uncensored Encyclopedia of Life,
Basketball, and Everything in Between

# Kevin Garnett

*with* **David Ritz**

**SIMON & SCHUSTER PAPERBACKS**
New York   London   Toronto   Sydney   New Delhi

Simon & Schuster Paperbacks
An Imprint of Simon & Schuster, Inc.
1230 Avenue of the Americas
New York, NY 10020

First Simon & Schuster paperback edition February 2022

SIMON & SCHUSTER and colophon are
registered trademarks of Simon & Schuster, Inc.

For information about special discounts for bulk purchases,
please contact Simon & Schuster Special Sales at 1-866-506-1949
or business@simonandschuster.com.

The Simon & Schuster Speakers Bureau can bring authors to
your live event. For more information or to book an event,
contact the Simon & Schuster Speakers Bureau at 1-866-248-3049
or visit our website at www.simonspeakers.com.

Interior design by Kyle Kabel

Manufactured in the United States of America

1   3   5   7   9   10   8   6   4   2

Library of Congress Control Number: 2020952154

ISBN 978-1-9821-7032-5
ISBN 978-1-9821-7033-2 (pbk)
ISBN 978-1-9821-7034-9 (ebook)

*I dedicate this book to
my beautiful children and family.*

*He who angers you, owns you.*

—KG

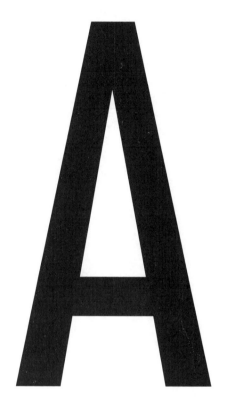

"Anything Is Possible!" / Arm Wrestling /
Arrival / Atlanta / Red Auerbach

# "Anything Is Possible!"

It was 2008, and after thirteen seasons, I had finally won the muthafuckin' finals and helped bring the Celtics their first championship in more than twenty years. When the horn went off and the game was over, time froze. My mind froze. I had halfway been expecting a buzzer-beater; but it was a blowout. We beat down the Lakers by thirty-nine points. Confetti was coming down as I was going up. I'd never been that high or felt so hyped.

I was in the bliss: people grabbing at me, hugging, kissing, crying. I looked over at my wife, saw my kids, my family, my friends, my fans, and then, like a movie, my brain went on rewind, replaying scenes, rushing at me at once: hooping in Billy's driveway when I barely knew how to shoot; waking up the neighborhood at five in the Carolina morning cause I couldn't stop working on my dribbling; a country kid, then a teenager trying to download those badass Chicago streets; wins, losses, bumps, bruises, a million memories, a million hours on the grind, hacking, scraping, clawing to get where I needed to go; and there I was at last. Reporter Michele Tafoya holding up a mic in front of my face. The Boston crowd wildin' out. She gotta shout for me to hear.

"League MVP. Defensive Player of the Year. Now it's time to add NBA champion to your résumé. How does that sound?"

I put my hand to the fresh-out-the-box championship hat on my head.

"Man, I'm so hyped right now."

I take a second to gather myself.

Another rush of images flashing in front of me: sitting at Ruth's Chris Steak House during a family dinner; watching D-Wade playing Chauncey in the Eastern finals; my struggles in Greenville, AAU tournaments, endless games in endless parks in endless neighborhoods, going, growing, never stopping, learning, burning with an energy that gets more intense year by year, wanting this thing, wanting it for all my twelve years in Minneapolis, wanting it for the T-Wolves fans, wanting it for the Celtics fans, wanting this ultimate win, this championship that I've desired more than anything—more than money or fame or sex. And now the reality clicks in my brain, runs down my spine, enters my soul, and I'm taking off my hat and tilting my head straight back and screaming like a madman.

"Anything is possible!"

A few moments later, I add, "Made it, Ma! Top of the world! I'm fucking certified! I'm muthafuckin' certified!"

3

I'm yelling so loud that my voice can be heard beyond those sixteen—soon to be seventeen—championship banners hanging from the rafters all the way up to heaven. Yellin' up there to Malik Sealy and Eldrick Leamon and everyone I loved and lost. Everyone who got me to this moment.

In the middle of the mad scramble I see Kobean. I call him "Kobean" or "Bean" cause his dad is Jellybean. Bean knows what I was going through. I'd been chasing him, been chasing Shaq, been chasing Timmy, been chasing all the legacies, and now the moment is mine.

"Congratulations, man," says Bean. "Enjoy this, cause there ain't gonna be too many more. I'll see yo bitch ass next year."

I have to get in my blows, have to say, "We activated now. This ain't that Minnesota shit."

"We'll see."

"Say hi to Vanessa and the kids," I say.

"Love you, my brotha."

"Love you too, dawg."

Then I give him one of those gorilla hugs around the neck and ask, "Bean, y'all out tonight?"

"Hell, yes," said Kob, "we getting the fuck outta this bitch."

It's beautiful because I know how pissed he is—Bean hates losing more than anyone—but I also know that he has to be a little happy for his OG.

Like me, Bean believes in the unstoppable human spirit. It's that spirit that makes anything possible. Those words come from my heart, from my guts, from the life I've lived. Those words apply to right now, this very second, because here I am, a dude who has ADD and ADHD, and as a result doesn't read a lot of books,

sitting down to write my own book. Ain't that a trip?

Attention deficit disorder and attention deficit hyperactivity disorder. I got 'em both. I also have dyslexia, meaning I see shit backwards. I see things in vision. For a long time, I was believing that I was mentally disabled, until a great friend of mine—shout-out to Torey Austin—said, "Hey, man, maybe that means you have superpowers." Torey's words arrived right on time. Before that, I was dealing with feelings of heavy inferiority, cause my teachers were on me for not reading right. The formal diagnosis happened later in life when I was already an adult. As a country kid in South Carolina, I didn't have access to sophisticated professionals who could figure out what was wrong. I struggled with words on the page.

Yet here I am, writing words on a page.

That's one of the reasons I decided to structure the book this way, like an encyclopedia, with little bite-sized entries. Because of my reading problems and my limited attention span, I'm not the kind of dude who's gonna kick back on the couch with a book for an hour or two. I'm gonna pick up a book, read a page or two, and then bounce. So I wanna write the kind of book that I'd wanna read. I want to change it up, do it differently. I've never been much of a rule follower. I didn't follow the rules when I skipped college and went straight to the draft. Didn't follow the rules when I negotiated what was at the time the biggest contract in professional sports. Didn't follow the rules when I'd bring up the ball or play on the wing rather than plant myself down low like every other big man. So I sure as hell ain't

*Celebrating the 2008 NBA championship.*

gonna follow the rules here. I'm writing a book that, like hoop, is filled with suspense, surprises, high drama, and big fun.

There are a bunch of words and names and phrases that start with the letter "A" that have been important in my life and come before "Anything Is Possible!" Like "AAU" or "Alpha" or "AI." Trust me, we'll get into all that eventually. But I have to start with "Anything Is Possible!" because that's the *most* important. That's what everything you're gonna read about adds up to. Here's one more: "Agenda." Let me say it straight-up: my agenda is to show you how negatives can turn into positives and how positives can change your life for the better. And the only way I'm gonna be able to do that is if I'm fully honest about those negatives. About the mistakes I've made. About the hardship I've experienced. About the pain. I know being honest isn't always comfortable. This is the first time I've ever said anything about my learning disabilities. I never even told the Kobean story before because I know he was dyslexic. And if I'm really being honest, then I also have to say that right now I'm wondering if this is such a good idea. I'm starting to feel doubt creep in.

Doubt will trip you up, turn you back, have you quit. The only thing holding us back from charting new territory is doubt. Gotta understand that doubt. Just can't delete it by wishing it away. Gotta work with it. We all do. We gotta talk to the muthafucka. Gotta say, "I see you, Mr. Doubt. I hear you, Mr. Doubt. I know you wanna keep me from doing what I was meant to do. But I also know that, while you're part of me, I do not intend to allow you to become *all* of me. Because I got no choice, I'm gonna tolerate you. And because I know it's a smart move, I'm gonna try and understand you. The more I understand you, Mr. Doubt, the less you're gonna have to say. So I'm gonna get you out of the driver's seat and put your ass in the back of this car. I know you're gonna try and backseat drive. I know you're gonna tell me I'm moving in the wrong direction, that I'll never reach my destination. So please keep it down back

there. Even though that chatter might go on forever, I'm now the one with my hands on the wheel. I'm doing the driving. And I'm taking myself to where I need to go."

These words I write represent a triumph over doubt. Going at a challenge is the only way I know of meeting that challenge—and beating that challenge. I'm opening up about Kevin Garnett, the man, the player, the person—and what it took to build that human being. Growing up, it was difficult to find love. Maybe that difficulty is part of the reason why a beast emerged. That beast got all over me. Sometimes it looked like the beast would self-destruct. But I thank Jehovah God that at an early age I saw that intensity could be put to purpose. *Had* to be put to purpose. *Had* to be used as a tool. *Had* to be deployed strategically. Intelligently. The beast is an energy that requires refinement and focus. And energy is what rocks the world. Energy is what rocks this book.

Warning: my energy is different. Hard to contain. Impossible to suppress. My energy doesn't move in predictable patterns. I'm all over the place, and it ain't just ADHD. It's something greater than that. Something deeper. Holier. Call it my essence. My spirit. I have a zigzagging spirit. That's how I've lived my whole life. And so this book is gonna zigzag too. That's another reason for this non-linear approach. It's not only the way I live my life, but it is the way I remember and reflect on my life. I don't see a single straight narrative from start to finish. I see flashes, bursts, eruptions, explosions. Just like that night we won the title, when all those memories flooded through my mind. If my story is a ball, the ball is always moving. I'm dribbling, I'm passing, I'm head-faking, I'm lobbing, I'm dunking. One moment I'm thinking about shit that happened ten years ago, the next I'm thinking about what happened ten seconds ago. Yet for all the jumping ahead and laying back in the cut, if you read closely, you'll see that the dots connect.

So let's go on a trip where we break down doubt and bust through obstacles. Let's go where they're telling us we can't go. Let's do what they're telling us we can't do. Let's explode our creativity.

## Arm Wrestling

*see* **Glen Davis**

## Arrival

I was born in Greenville, South Carolina, May 19, 1976. Born with excess energy that needed to be expressed in the worst way.

Moms was my main connection to the outside world.

Shirley Garnett. Resourceful. Smart. Not a hugging mom, not big on holding your hand, but big on you-gotta-learn-to-do-it-for-yourself. Discipline. Determination. Devotion to the Jehovah's Witnesses teachings. Structure. Extreme work ethic. You *will* go to the Kingdom Hall. You *will* do your chores. You *will* do as you're told, or else. "Or else" was too scary to think about. So I did what I was told.

Moms was a lioness who made me a lion.

A few fundamental facts:

I'm a country kid. Carolina is deep country.

I'm a boy in a household of girls. Moms, two sisters—older one is Sonya, younger is Ashley—and me.

I had Moms's work ethic before I was five. Mowing grass. Chopping wood. No bike, so I'm walking and running everywhere, through the woods, jumping over creeks, finding my footing. Clean the house every day. Very tidy. Everything in its place. So orderly and neat that I have a compulsive disorder without even knowing it. Even to this day, come to my house and you'll see every single object in its place. No dust anywhere. No dirty dishes in the sink.

Me and my sisters scrubbing the floors but not minding cause Moms had Stephanie Mills on the radio singing "Put Your Body In It" and "You Can Get Over." Teddy Pendergrass was telling us "Wake Up Everybody," McFadden & Whitehead were shouting "Ain't No Stopping Us Now." Old-school soul music pushing us through those tasks, giving the grind a groove.

Moms teaching me manners. Say "yes, ma'am" and "yes, sir."

Moms working all sorts of jobs. She's working at the 3M plant Monday through Friday and cleaning people's houses on weekends. At another time, she's working the graveyard shift at a hotel—6 p.m. to 6 a.m.—but still has enough energy to come home and get us ready for school. I give Moms big props for getting us through.

Moms's love was tough love. Because she was hard, she brought me up hard. For example: I got in a fight when some bigger dudes jumped me. I ran like hell. Seeing I was running, Moms caught me, grabbed me, and broke a stick over my head.

"Boy," she demanded, "go back out there and fight." I had no choice. Learned to slap box. Learned to wrestle. Learned to fight in many forms.

Moms, one of nine kids, fought her way through life and saw me doing the same. That attitude might be cold, but Moms was right.

Moms could also be wrong. Once I cut my inner leg real bad trying to jump a gate. Moms cleaned up the wound but got all up in my face. "You can't be doing stuff like that." But I knew it happened only because I misjudged the jump. Next day I was there, studying the situation and refining my jump. I cleared the gate by two inches. I *could* be doing stuff like that.

We were crammed into a little two-bedroom in a small, quaint section of Greenville called Nicholtown. I had G.I. Joes. I had He-Mans. Transformers. Those figures talked to me. I made up stories. Always roaming through the woods behind our apartment building, where make-believe adventures came to life. I could envision, conjure up characters. I could entertain myself. My imagination was wild.

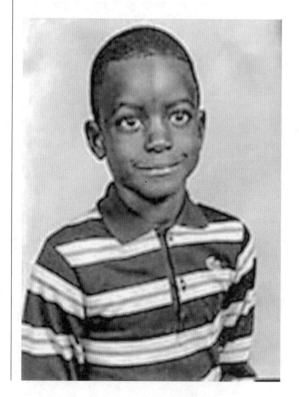

*Me as a little guy.*

# Atlanta

Some weekends, Moms would put us in the car and drive two hours down to Atlanta so we could see things we never saw. Moms was like that. We stayed at the Days Inn, but that didn't keep her from driving through Buckhead. "We going house hunting," she said. We couldn't begin to afford anything in that fancy neighborhood with lawns as big as baseball fields.

"See that house on the hill there?" she asked.

"I see it."

"See how they planted all the pretty flowers? See all those tall trees? See that beautiful landscaping?"

"I do."

Moms liked painting the picture for us. But for all her fanciful talk, Moms was about finance.

"What do you think it's worth, son?"

"Don't know."

"Least a million dollars. Maybe more. Work hard enough, get smart enough, and you can have a house like that."

She went on to say that Black people lived in a lot of those houses. The world of comfort and luxury wasn't restricted to whites. For all her sternness, Moms was a dreamer. She got me to start dreaming.

# Red Auerbach

*see* **Doc**

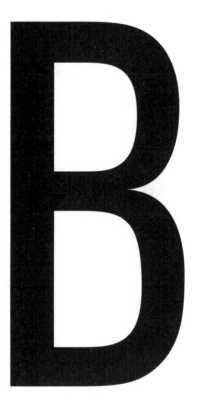

Ball Boys / Charles Barkley / Beauty / Chauncey B-B-B-B-Billups /
Larry Bird / Black and Proud / Blocks / *Blue Chips* /
*The Bold and the Beautiful* / The Book of Job / Booray / Break Dancing /
British Knights / James Brown / Brown Paper Bag / Bug / Bye

# Ball Boys

They call 'em ball *kids* now, but when I came into the league they were only boys, running around, piling up the towels, getting us water, doing all the dirty shit no one else wanted to do. Most of 'em were happy cause they got to see behind the scenes.

These kids fascinated me. I saw how they loved getting hats and shoes, loved rebounding the ball for the players. I also saw how helpful and willing they were to make life easier for us.

I'd ask them a million questions.

"Yo, where you from?"

"How old are you?"

"Where'd you get the job?"

Answer was usually something like, "My dad owns the team" or "My aunt dates the GM."

In Minneapolis, Clayton, the equipment manager, would see me in the locker room talking to nine ball boys and want to know why.

"They're cool kids," I said. "They got interesting stories."

In New York, Portland, Salt Lake City, Houston, Dallas, Miami, I'm still asking these kids all sorts of questions.

The ball boys got great energy. Positive energy. You can always use positive energy. Look for positive energy. Use positive energy. Sometimes positive energy comes from places you'd never expect. That's why you can't look down on no one or feel superior. You'll miss a chance to get energized.

At first, I saw there wasn't much diversity. As time went by, that got challenged. And slowly but surely you had teams setting up programs with the local school systems. Good attendance and good grades might get you the gig. That motivated kids to get to school and do well. Soon I was seeing ball kids in all colors from all walks of life. That made me happy. Diversity always makes me happy.

# Charles Barkley

Love Chuck. One of my favorite people in the world. Extremely smart dude. And also one of the great teachers.

I relate to Chuck cause he's a southern boy like me—coming out of little Leeds, Alabama. Loved watching him play for the Sixers in those shorty-shorts. He was a new kind of player. He could take the ball coast to coast. He could hit the three. And he was physical as hell. Brotha could bang down low. He was one of the few players who seemed to express the energy

I had inside me—one of the few star players, I mean. There had been plenty of superstrong players in the league, but they were role players—guys like Maurice Lucas, Rick Mahorn, and Bill Laimbeer. "Enforcers," they were called. They were hoop's equivalent of the hockey goon. I liked watching them. I admired their fearlessness. But I saw their job for what it was—riling things up and throwing opposing players off their game. There wasn't a lot more expected of 'em than that. If they fouled out or got thrown out, that was fine—and even better if they got a player on the other team thrown out.

Chuck was the first player I saw who'd mix it up like that yet also be the best player on the court. Like the one time the Sixers were playing the Pistons and he and Laimbeer got into a nasty brawl in the last seconds of the game. After he was

*Charles inducted into the Basketball Hall of Fame, 2006.*

done scrapping, Chuck went to the locker room and took out the rest of his anger on a toilet. Broke the damn seat. Craziest thing to me about all that, though, was Chuck had thirty-six points and fifteen rebounds!

When he was asked about his physical style of play, he said: "As long as you don't get arrested for it, it's all right." Other players with that mentality weren't just role guys, they were looked at as villains— the players that fans loved to hate. Not Chuck. Fans loved him. He was so good that you couldn't *not* love him. He was one of the two best trash-talkers I ever played against—him and Gary Payton— but no matter how much trash Chuck talked, he made sure his game had the last word. I looked up to him for that.

Chuck, Shaq, and Hakeem were probably the most dominant post men I played against. And that's no slack against Karl Malone or Timmy Duncan.

But facing Chuck was different. It was like playing chess. There was a mental aspect to it. The more I studied him, the more I was influenced by his psyche.

I also looked up to him because he said I *shouldn't* look up to him. "I am not your role model," he announced in that famous Nike commercial. Damn, that shit was dope! Black-and-white and there wasn't no music. Just Chuck looking into the camera and speaking his truth. It was such a contrast from the happy, smiley "Be Like Mike" Gatorade commercial. That Gatorade commercial wasn't my reality. Chuck's reality and mine were the same.

The commercial was Chuck's idea. He brought it to Nike. Said he was inspired from when he'd go give speeches to schools. He'd go to a mostly white school and ask how many kids wanted to play in the NBA. Only a few would raise their hands. Most of the kids would say they wanted to be doctors or lawyers or firemen. Then he'd go to a mostly Black school and ask the same question, and nearly all the kids wanted to play in the NBA. He got frustrated by the fact that Black kids saw their only career options as athletes or entertainers, and he wanted that commercial to start a conversation about how to change that.

When I played against Chuck, he didn't want no conversation with me—about anything. Chuck denies it, but he didn't like me when I first came up. He was in Phoenix and had been in the league over ten years. He was NBA royalty. And here I come, young brotha eager to prove myself. It was kind of like the dog who's been in the house for a while and then this new puppy runs in and gets all up in the big dog's face, yippin' and snappin' and whippin' his tail. A lot of players back then would come into the league actin' all sheepish and reserved and keepin' their heads down. Not me. I was ready to go. I don't think Chuck was feelin' it. Not at first. But he grew to love me.

We got even tighter when I had my *Area 21* show on TNT. He and I were always bantering, always talking shit. I'd clown him for falling asleep on the air, and he'd rag on me for my skinny jeans—which I still wear unapologetically.

In 2016, North Carolina passed its garbage "bathroom bill," which discriminated against transgender people. The upcoming NBA All-Star Game was in Charlotte, and Chuck said publicly he thought the game should be moved to another city because of the bill. He told his bosses at TNT that if the game wasn't moved, he was going to sit it out. Thanks in large part to Chuck's pressure, the game did get moved, to New Orleans. As Chuck said in an interview with Ellen DeGeneres, "Anytime you're Black, you got to stand up for other people. Cause Black people know what discrimination is like. And if you're in a position of power, you got to always stand up against discrimination. I'm never gonna sit back and let discrimination happen on my watch."

Despite what Charles Barkley says, he most definitely *is* a role model.

# Beauty

The thing about those drives to Atlanta is that they weren't all that necessary. That craving of what I couldn't see wasn't something that Moms taught me. It was something I already felt. I saw beauty early. I saw beauty in a strange way. I saw beauty that washed over my mind and soul and transformed my very being. Ain't talking about a vision of God, but a human vision. I knew it was beauty because it changed how I viewed the world. I knew it when I was a young kid.

Out back of the apartments where we lived is this big, rollin'-ass hill. Before you get to the hill, there are rows of clotheslines where folks be hanging out their laundry. Socks and undies and brassieres flapping in the breeze. Sun burning down from the blazing blue sky. Birds chirping. Wildflowers giving off heady perfume. A mutt chasing a tomcat behind the garbage can.

Squirrels scurrying up trees. Sounds of music—maybe Kool & the Gang's "Celebration," maybe Stevie Wonder's "Master Blaster"—coming from radios and turntables inside the apartments. Walk past the clotheslines and keep looking at that hill that's probably two acres. At the bottom is a creek. Beyond the creek are trees. Almost like a forest. Except the trees are cut off on top. Looks like someone has trimmed them so perfect I can see beyond them, into the distance where there is a road, a highway, with cars racing in both directions.

The clotheslines, the creek, the hill, the trees, and the moving cars on the roadway: the whole scene hits me as the most beautiful thing I've ever seen. I can't tell you why, but something stirs deep inside me. It was a painting, a picture I'll never forget. Looking back at it now, I can see what it represented: the wideness of the world. Even as a know-nothing kid, I knew that the projects didn't define me. I could walk outside and see this expanse, this space, this openness. I could see that in their cars people were going places. That meant I could go places. I couldn't say it then—I didn't have the words or the understanding—but I can say it now: beauty means movement.

The beauty of that scene captivated me to the point where I stood for a full hour just breathing it in. When I was through, I looked up at the sun, staring at that yellow glow of amazing light. I felt lit.

Then I felt Moms's slap.

"Boy," she said, "what you doing staring at the sun? Don't you know it'll burn your eyes to cinders?"

"I like looking at the sun," I said. "It changes all the colors around me to green and black. Everything looks beautiful when I stare at the sun. When I stare at the sun, I feel like I'm in a dream."

"Better to bow your head and talk to Jehovah God."

The minute Moms walked away, I went back to staring at the sun. But this time, I prayed.

"Lord Jehovah God, watch over me. Watch over my mom and sisters. Please protect us. And Lord, please bless me to get out of here someday. Put me in a better place."

I kept staring, kept seeing yellow and green and black, kept feeling the warm glow of light. When staring time was over, I blinked my eyes and looked away. The world came back into focus. That scene remained. The cars in the distance. Me in one of those cars. The beauty of going from one place to another.

# Chauncey B-B-B-B-Billups

That's how the Pistons' amped-up announcer John Mason introduced my man in the D. "B-B-B-B-Billups."

Some called him Mr. Big Shot. I shortened it to Shot. He was one of those hoopers I'd heard about growing up. Wasn't no social media or YouTube mixtapes, but all the hot prospects heard about each other. Shot, Vince Carter, Paul Pierce, Shareef Abdur-Rahim, Jelani McCoy, Robert Traylor. They all had reps. I finally got to see what they could do in person in April of '95 at the McDonald's All-American Game in St. Louis. That shit was crazy. Started even before the

*Dunking in the McDonald's All-American Game and receiving the John R. Wooden Most Valuable Player Award from the legendary coach himself, April 1995.*

game, at the Slam Dunk Contest, when Vince brought down the house. Contest should've been over after the first round. Vince did a nasty 360, a foul-line dunk where he finished crouched in a Bruce Lee pose, and a through-the-legs piece

that brought all of us onto the floor to mob him.

In the game, though, I wasn't tryin' to be friends with nobody. I was there to prove myself against the greatest high school players in the nation. And like any game I ever played in, I was there to win. Wasn't gonna be easy. The East roster was loaded: Vince and Shareef, plus dudes like Antawn Jamison and Ron Mercer, who both would have long careers in the league. The West had me, Paul, Jelani, and Tractor Traylor. Shot was there but didn't play cause of a hurt shoulder.

Didn't matter. Me and P straight tore it up. I knew P from playing with him earlier in AAU, so we already had chemistry on the court. And that game was an early sign of what could happen—what twelve years later *would* happen—when you put us two on the same team. The West won 126 to 115. P led all scorers with twenty-eight—which was just two points shy of the scoring record Jordan set in 1980. I got me eighteen points, eleven rebounds, and the MVP award. But P should have won it.

Maybe the sweetest part of that whole weekend happened when Shot and I got to talking at the airport on our way home. I know he thought I was crazy after seeing how hyped I was during the game, but our talk was much more chill. And deep. We were fantasizing about the future. Where would we go to college? Where would we play in the NBA? Kids dreaming. But Shot was a different kind of kid. Already mature. And not just interested in his own story. He wanted to know mine.

Over the years, we got tighter. Came to love him. Big heart. Generous soul. Family man. Shot and his wife, Piper, had kids early. I'm the godfather to Ciara, one of their daughters. When we'd all go on vacations together, Piper would rent a huge suite at a hotel to accommodate everyone. That's why when I established myself in Minneapolis and added a big extension to my house, I called it the Billups Suite.

Shot learned early in his career that basketball was a business. He'd been picked by the Celtics third overall in the 1997 draft. Then, halfway through the season, he was traded to Toronto. There was a lot of pressure on Boston's coach, Rick Pitino, to make the playoffs that

year, and he thought he'd have a better chance with a veteran point guard. So Shot got shipped to the Raptors for Kenny Anderson. I know it was hard on him. I know he was hurt and felt betrayed. But it was a valuable lesson. Ain't no loyalty in the business of basketball. Loyalty among players, absolutely. But not when it comes to owners and the bottom line. I didn't learn that till later in my career. Most players don't. So it was actually a good thing for Shot to get that reality check early on.

The next couple years didn't get any easier for him. He got traded to Denver. Mike D'Antoni was the coach. He moved Shot to shooting guard. This was another of those blessings in disguise. Some in the media marked it as a demotion—moving Shot off the ball. But it helped him further develop his stroke—develop that deadly accuracy. In Denver, he was back home where he'd grown up. Shot showed his love for Colorado off the court as well as on it, like the time he visited one of the survivors of the Columbine massacre in the hospital. He wasn't home for long, though. After a couple of seasons, he was traded to Orlando, where he sat out the season with a shoulder injury.

By that point, there was a lot of talk that Shot was a draft bust, but that was bullshit. I told him, "Get your ass to Minnesota. Let's get that chance to play together we didn't get in St. Louis. Only thing is, you won't be starting. We got Terrell Brandon running point. TB is one of the smartest point guards in the league. I've learned a lot playing with him, and you will too."

Shot didn't get hung up on ego. He saw this as an opportunity to improve his game and help our team. And that's what happened. TB mentored Shot. Shot downloaded TB. And when TB went out with a knee injury, he told Shot, "It's your turn." Very few dudes in the NBA would've been supportive in that situation—rooting for Shot to succeed instead of seeing him as a threat. Props to TB.

Having Shot in Minnie was beautiful. His dad and mom were real people, his brother, Hot Rod, was a real brotha. Their family adopted me. I loved being around them, eating at their table, having them eat at mine. Shot and I did everything together, including putting on Santa outfits and doing Christmas shopping for charity.

I remember a quote from Shot that made an impression. "Just because someone doesn't play with the same fire as KG, it doesn't mean they're soft," he said. "It also doesn't mean they don't care. But in KG's raving, crazy mind, that's how he sees it. If he sees something one time, that's what he believes in, no matter what. That's not always great for a leader . . . but that's who he is."

I could take criticism from someone like Shot cause he knew me inside and out.

In the summer of 2002, Kevin McHale, the T-Wolves' Vice President of Basketball Operations, told Shot that although he could offer him a long-term deal, he still couldn't start him. He'd still be backup for TB. Shot thought about it

*Christmas shopping with Chauncey Billups for kids in Minneapolis, 2001.*

until Detroit made an offer he couldn't refuse. He'd start for the Pistons. It was another mountain for him to climb. Broke my heart to see him go, but my heart was also happy for his new opportunity.

As the world knows, he crushed it in the D and wound up winning it all in 2004 by beating the Lakers in the finals 4–1. Shot won the finals MVP and, typical of him, said, "I wish I could cut this trophy into thirteen pieces and give a little bit to everybody." He'd changed the Pistons' culture. He'd taken everything he got from Terrell Brandon and multiplied it by four. His body got stronger, he further developed his three-point shot, he got good with his fade, he started slashing inside more. My brotha upgraded every aspect of the game.

Beyond hoop, when Obama started campaigning in Michigan, he asked Shot to introduce him. That's the kind of respect people have for Shot. In my fantasy life, when I think of becoming a multibillionaire and buying an NBA team with my own bread, my co-owner is Chauncey Billups.

# Larry Bird

*see* **Isolation; "King Kunta"; Kobe**

# Black and Proud

"Jet-black skin," Moms once said, "is beautiful skin. Lotion it up so it shines. Don't come out here looking ashy. No son of mine is gonna buy into that lie that

says lighter is brighter cause it's closer to whiter. Ain't nothing better than dark black. You hear me?"

I heard her. Her pride became my pride.

# Blocks

I blocked over two thousand shots in my career. But just as important were the ones that didn't count.

When I entered the league, I started noticing how players would get up a shot after the referees had whistled the ball dead. This was the kind of tactic that made me realize I was playing with the greatest hoopers in the world. That never happened in high school. But pros knew how important it was to find the rhythm of their shot. Sure, you can take shots during the game to find that rhythm, but each miss could mean another chance for the other team to score. And if you don't find that rhythm soon, your ass is gonna be pulled out the game. So taking dead-ball shots was a risk-free way for players to get that stroke. Just seeing the ball go through the net once could give a player the confidence they needed to light it up the rest of the game.

Well, if they could get in a practice shot, that meant I could get in a practice block. When I saw those practice shots coming, my attitude was, *Get the fuck outta here. Ain't gonna let no one get any extra advantage.* So I started ripping those dead-ball shots right out of the air, goaltending like a muthafucker. No easy shots. Not on my watch.

First time I did it was my rookie year in Minnesota. We were playing the Pacers

*Rising up for a block against the Kings, 2006.*

and they had to stop the game for a few minutes to fix the shot clock. Reggie Miller thought he'd get up some shots while we waited. First one, I swatted against the backboard. He tried it a couple more times. Same thing. One of the refs came over and told us to cut it out. He took the ball and walked away. Which was all I cared about—keeping the rock out of Reggie's hands and not giving him any chances to heat up.

From that game on, I kept doing it. It ticked off a lot of players. Like I was going against some unwritten code. I remember Vince Carter saying that when guys figured out what I was doing, they started throwing up crazy shots that had no chance of going in, just to see how high I would jump for it. But now everybody in the league does it.

My life has always been about questioning rules, and blocking dead balls is one more example.

## Blue Chips

*see* **Shaquille O'Neal;** *Uncut Gems*

## The Bold and the Beautiful

Moms's mom was Grandma Mil. She wasn't much of a hugger and kisser. Also like Moms, she wasn't too interested in cooking. She'd reheat leftovers in the microwave and serve up snacks. She lived on Watts Avenue, the hardest street in the hardest hood of Greenville.

"Ain't moving to no posh neighborhood," she said. "Ain't going to no big house. Ain't running from no one."

Grandma Mil was a real woman. Her mother and her mother's sisters had been enslaved. They'd been raped. Grandma Mil carried heavy history. That's why she carried a strap. She went to the grocery store strapped. Wasn't playing no games. Always on edge.

When I went to visit Grandma Mil, I had to be quiet from 1 to 4 p.m. That's when she watched her soap operas. *Days of Our Lives. Another World. Santa Barbara. The Bold and the Beautiful.* Her focus was intense. She'd talk to the screen. "Don't marry that man!" "Child, you makin' a big mistake!" "Stay away from her if you know what's good for you!" She could talk, but I couldn't. During commercials, she might fix a real quick bologna sandwich. She'd cut that bitch in half, grab a glass of milk, and get me to heat up the pork and beans with butter on top. She taught me to make my first little meals. Grandma Mil, like Moms, taught me to stand my ground.

Grandma Mil also taught me history. Through her, I learned about Nat King Cole. She said he was the best singer who ever sang. She also said he was singing what both Black and white people wanted. But he caught hell for breaking down boundaries. He got his own TV show only to have it canceled when white sponsors didn't like how white chicks were grooving on his good looks. Long live King Nat Cole.

Grandma Mil also talked about how Elvis took his shit from cats like Chuck Berry and put a twist in it. She said that Elvis came out of Memphis funk. He studied Black musicians we ain't ever heard of.

Through the older generation, I learned about James Brown. JB is taking it to a different place than Chuck Berry. He ain't hiding who he is. He ain't afraid of looking greasy, sounding greasy, singing greasy. When I get old enough, I see Bobby Brown the same way. He's all the way Black.

The older generation also helped me through my fears. In Carolina, for example, storms can be scary. You'd see the flashes of lightnin'. You'd hear those huge booms of thunder. You'd think the world was coming to an end.

"Just go into the bedroom," Grandma Mil would say, "and lie down. All that noise is just the Lord doing his work. He's spraying the land with water. Making the plants grow. Giving us another day. Praise the Lord."

I'd do it. I'd lie down, get quiet, listen to the storm, think of the power of nature, think that the world wasn't coming to an end. The world was being replenished. I'm able to deal with the world because of women like Grandma Mil.

Moms also wanted me to know the world I came from.

It took her a while, but she located her long-lost father in LaGrange, Georgia, south of Atlanta, way back in the woods. She takes me and my sisters to visit him. This is red-clay, thick-swamp Georgia. They killing raccoons and squirrels and possums, they killing anything in the forest and cooking 'em up for dinner. My shoes are covered in mud. Take off the shoes and walk around barefooted. Swim in the water hole. Watch out for the snakes. Go there every other summer to hang with Grandpa Ed.

# The Book of Job

Moms was devoted to Kingdom Hall. That's where Jehovah's Witnesses hold services. I had no choice but to attend. I wasn't naturally drawn to religion. But it was out of the question to question anything we were taught. And though as soon as I left Carolina I didn't attend Kingdom Hall anymore, some of the lessons learned there have lasted.

At the time, I didn't realize it. What kid does? But looking back, I see that in every experience we go through, there's something to absorb, something that helps get you over it. As I already said, it took me forever to learn that I had dyslexia and all those other disorders. That shit wasn't diagnosed till the last years of my NBA career. As a kid, all I knew was that reading was tough and focusing was even tougher. Moms didn't help, but, in a weird way, Kingdom Hall did. Here's how I'd break it down:

My sisters were super A students. I wasn't. I was seeing sentences backwards and didn't know why. Moms would crack jokes about my inability to comprehend a book or read it right. That brought on shame and crushed my confidence. At the same time, I was a little genius at math. When my sister Sonya saw me using my fingers to count, she said, "No, put your hands down. See it. Envision it."

I could! I caught on quickly. I could calculate, I could see numbers in my mind. They weren't jumbled up. Words were.

Then came the moment when I had to put together the right words. At Kingdom Hall, every kid had to give a speech before the entire congregation. The speech had to be backed up by scripture. When it came time for me to give my speech, I was scared out of my mind. But I had no choice. Moms wouldn't let me out of it. Kingdom Hall wouldn't let me out of it. So I did it. I studied scripture and stood up explaining something that stuck with me forever: the Book of Job.

Understanding that portion of the Bible helped me in every chapter of my life. But the act of facing an audience also added to my confidence. I saw I could do it. In spite of my shyness, I could address a crowd of people. I didn't cop out or run

out or pass out. I stood and said what I was prepared to say.

Here's my understanding of the Book of Job:

The Devil and God are in serious conversation. God gives his man Job props for devotion. Devil says Job is only devoted because his life is cool. Take away the cool and Job will curse God and start digging the Devil. God says, "Never." Devil says, "Wanna bet? Let me at him and I'll mess him up to where he'll be calling you a dirty dog." God agrees, as long as the Devil keeps Job alive.

Bet on. Devil kills Job's animals, servants, and every one of his ten children. Job's devastated, shaves his head, tears up his clothes, but still praises God.

Now the Devil's doubly determined. Goes back to God for the okay to put more of a hurtin' on Job. God is game. This time the Devil covers Job's body with horrible sores. The pain's unbearable. Even Job's wife says it's time to damn God.

But no sir, my man Job keeps up the praise. Four friends come over to commiserate. They're silent for six days. On the seventh, they start chopping it up. Everyone, including Job, has his own interpretation of why God is messing with Job. But none of these explanations are good. Job thinks his friends' reasoning is twisted. He goes off on his brothas and sends them packing. Job sees this is a matter between him and God.

The story switches up to where Job is challenging God. He wants to know why some good folk suffer while some bad folk live large. No answers are coming—God ain't talking—but Job keeps asking. Finally, God shows up to say man can't really understand him, but Job should know that his devotion will be rewarded. For standing strong, God gives his servant thousands of animals and ten new kids. Job lives to 140.

The point?

Patience. Fortitude. Faith.

Even when the pain is unbearable.

Patience. Fortitude. Faith.

Even when you know you've been scammed.

Patience. Fortitude. Faith.

Even if your own friends or family seem to be turning on you.

Patience. Fortitude. Faith.

Even when you're tired of taking the lumps.

Patience. Fortitude. Faith.

Patience keeps you on your feet. Fortitude gives you the strength to move forward. Faith has you believing that there's more to this fucked-up world than what we see with our eyes.

There's a divine order that's working undercover. Nothing is greater than spirit. Like Job, you can try to break it down with your friends and talk your head off until you turn blue in the face. But this spirit, this order, this goodness of God, can't be explained. It just is. You accept it or you don't. I believe if you do, you'll get through. If you don't, you'll suffer even more.

## Booray

Can also be spelled *bourre*. The most famous card game in the league. I didn't learn booray till my rookie year. First thing I learned was can't no broke brotha play booray. You gotta know what you're doing. It's cash money on the line. A variation of spades where the stakes get high in a hurry. Rajon Rondo is the king of booray. Can play two separate booray games at once—and be winning at both. He's got him a booray-wired brain that can figure the shit out before anyone. Don't play booray with Doe.

## Break Dancing

Michael said Billie Jean was not his lover. I didn't know what Michael was talkin' 'bout, and I didn't care. The groove got me. The moves made me move. My sisters and I watched the video on a little TV. We watched every Michael video, the old ones from the Jackson 5, the new ones from *Thriller* and *Bad*. I could do it all. I was agile. I was slippery. I was loose. I could do the wop. I could pop and lock. I could slip and slide. I could spin. I could flip. I had me my own bop. Had me some serious choreographic creativity. When it came to footwork, Michael was my coach.

I got hooked on break dancing. Would jump in dumpsters, pull out the boxes and spray-paint 'em. Then take 'em to Blythe Elementary, where I'd put 'em down in the yard and start break dancing. "It Takes Two" by Rob Base & DJ E-Z Rock was my go-to song. I'd have my little name on the back of my shirt, Members Only jacket, Airwalk high-tops. Airwalks were skateboarding shoes. I loved skateboarding too. It was a huge part of my life. Had me a Nash and rode it everywhere. Skating and dancing were similar in that they were both about footwork and balance.

And the way the treads on those Airwalks were designed to help grip a skateboard also helped on the cardboard boxes. I found basketball to be a lot easier just because the footwork was very similar to dancing. I'd mimic players' footwork the same way I'd done with dancers. Footwork was always one of my great strengths. A lot of players have a hard time with footwork, especially in the post. I never had that issue.

# British Knights

*see* **Shoes**

# James Brown

*see* **The Bold and the Beautiful**; "King Kunta"; WNBA

# Brown Paper Bag

"Get a job, boy," Moms says, "and make some money." I already got a job cutting grass—that's how I paid for my Nash. Also worked the grill at Burger King. Bagged groceries at the supermarket. But Moms wants me to find a better-paying job and there ain't no arguing with Moms. "Yes, ma'am, I'll look for something else."

I find me a dishwashing job at a local bar named after the TV show *Cheers*. (I never watched *Cheers*, by the way, but I loved *MacGyver*.)

"Son," says the Cheers manager, "we're paying you three bucks an hour. We need you here six p.m. to two a.m. Take it or leave it."

I take it. I walk into a kitchen where all hell has broken loose. It's mainly Mexican cats, but the brothas are up in there too. One brotha's got his shirt off. He's tatted and fresh out of prison, three gold chains hanging down his neck. He's smoking a cigarette while cooking with one hand, the smell of cut-up onions so strong my eyes start tearing, pancakes flippin', bacon fryin', grease poppin', water boilin', coffee percolatin', steaks sizzlin', one cat bragging 'bout his pimping, another cat dealing weed. So many different voices, so many moving parts. But no time to think or slow down, cause in the midst of the madness I gotta get my groove on, I gotta get these dishes washed, scrub these pans, clean these knives, find my way into this system, because believe me, there *is* a system, and if any part of it breaks down, the whole joint collapses. I gotta slide into the mix, into a matrix I've never seen before, a matrix that's always switching up because a party of ten has just arrived and is ordering everything on the menu. So break into double time, soap up those pots and wipe 'em down super fast, see how the brothas and Mexicans are picking up their game—the man at the grill, the man at the stove, the man at the cutting board, the man seasonin' the meats, the vegetable man cutting carrots and sprinkling parsley. It goes on and on, faster and fiercer, cats get funnier, talkin' much trash, having much fun, the grimiest and coolest people I've ever seen.

At the end of the night, drained as a muthafucka, I get handed a brown paper bag with twenty-four one-dollar bills stuffed inside. I'll go on to learn to be a busboy and even a waiter. I'll learn things about dealing with people that'll last me a lifetime. The brown paper bag will get fatter.

One thing, though, I didn't know then but know now is that the brown bag—and the kitchen where I sweated so hard to learn the system—was a true-life paradigm of things to come. Everywhere you go there's a system you gotta download. A matrix you gotta learn. A mix you gotta slide into. Don't matter if it's the funky kitchen at Cheers or Boston Garden. There's always a flow. Go with the flow and you'll be fine. Fight the flow and you'll be stuck. And if you're stuck, that small brown paper bag is only gonna get smaller.

# Bug

When I was a kid, we were always moving. Moving doesn't always make for happy times. But there were happy times, especially when we lived at the Lake Shore apartments with another family. They had one bedroom, we had the other, and we all shared the living room, bathroom, and kitchen. I was three or four years old.

The other family was headed by Mr. James Peters. He had a beautiful wife named Pam and a son my age, Jamie, called Bug cause he was small and compact. Mr. and Mrs. Peters and Bug became my fantasy family.

Like Moms, Mr. Peters worked in a factory and was gone most of the time. On weekends, though, we'd watch him clean his prized possession—his Maxima. Me and Bug weren't allowed to touch the car. All we could do was watch him wash it, wax it, clean the tires, vacuum the inside, and dry it like it was a precious jewel. It was Mr. Peters who got me to fall in love with cars. When I got into the NBA and Bug came along with me to Minneapolis, I bought twin Lexus GS 300s, one for Bug and one for me to drive around Greenville. When the second season began and I headed back to Minnie, I left my Lexus with Mr. Peters, who wound up driving it for years. Fact is, I believe he still is. I know he's taking better care of that car than anyone.

Bug and I became brothas. That brotherhood helped keep me from going off the deep end during so many hard times. Bug was a thinker. The most supportive person in my life. I was ying to his yang. Big spirit. Big smile. Big spirit. Big brain. A quiet Gemini who kept to himself. Chess player. Always color-coordinated. Wore a Flintstones watch with a tan band. Loved that watch. Loved Bug.

Seemed like it happened in the dead of night when I was sleeping. Maybe Bug didn't want to tell me cause we'd both wind up crying. All I know is that one morning I woke up and they were gone.

"Where's Bug? Where are Mr. and Mrs. Peters?" I asked.

"Moved," said Moms.

"To where?"

"Don't know."

Man, my brotha disappeared and there was no one to console me. Moms wasn't the consoling type.

Bug would be back, but at the time I had no idea how or when.

# Bye

Actually the full nickname is "Bye Bye." That's what they called my real father. It was Uncle Pearl who told me that. Uncle Pearl was witty. He was street. He knew all the brothas making all the noise. That's how he knew my dad. He was the one who told me that my father went by Bye Bye. He also said my father had hooped for his high school. They tagged him "Bye Bye 45" cause he was fast on the breaks. I never got to see any of this. When I hit the streets, some of the OGs be saying, "Hey, you must be Little Bye. You must be Bye's son. You got his little head. You got his fiery eyes."

I didn't know what to think. Didn't know what to say. Rather than sound stupid, I stayed silent. I was a quiet kid. A shy kid. But a kid who always wondered about this man called Bye.

Then here come some strange events, like something out of a storybook.

My older sis, Sonya, walked me to nursery school every morning before making her way to Beck Academy Middle School. Every day we passed by these two people standing outside their house. They'd wave at us like they knew us and called out, "Hey!"

I waved back. "Hey!"

They were always smiling. I was smiling, but I never knew why. Something about them felt familiar. But I was a four-year-old kid. What did I know? It was just a vibe I picked up. Sometimes it'd be raining, but rain doesn't keep kids from walking to school. And rain didn't keep these old folks from always standing in front of their little place and waving.

Don't ask me why, but I noticed they were both left-handed. Watching them wave at me became the highlight of my day. It went on for a year.

Three years later, my daddy showed up. He had moved to Goose Creek, five hours from Greenville. That's why he said he hadn't been around. No matter, I was glad to see him. Who isn't glad to see their father? First thing he does is put me in his car and drive me to his folks' house.

His parents—you guessed it—are the two old kindly people who'd been waving at me every day when I went to nursery school. Suddenly, I got me a new grandma and grandpa. They hug me. Tears are rolling down their cheeks. I start in to crying.

"We always knew who you were," says Grandpa. "But we knew things weren't right between our son and your mother, and we didn't want to get in the way."

Dad's mom, Granny McCullough, cooked up a storm. She fed me pork chops and corn bread and apple pie. Grandpa told me stories, said I was named after one of my uncles, Kevin Mark McCullough. I got to meet him. A short dude who reminded me of Eddie Murphy. Funny as shit. Joking all the time. He and his beautiful wife, Geneva, had a great family. Met another aunt on my father's side, Pam, who, swear to God, looked like Pam Grier. She was tall—6 feet 3—sexy, kind, and loving. She had these huge hands with rings on. Her nail polish was poppin'. Smoked these long Virginia Slims cigarettes. Lots of style, but also lots of warmth. Aunt Pam was dope.

That week, Moms let me hang out with my father and his family. I fell in love with his family. They became my family. Love everywhere.

But in the midst of this love, I saw another side of my dad, his violence. Minute I saw it, I knew I never wanted to be that way. I didn't ever want to do anything like that. That incident changed my life. It turned my stomach. It also made me understand that I had to treat females as queens, not possessions. That applied to everyone, even my sisters, who, by the way, were strong like Moms. If they wanted to, they could knock out a dude with one punch.

I understood why Moms went around strapped. She had to deal with powerful men. Yet, among these men, she was just as powerful, even more so. She wasn't gonna let no one abuse her. I didn't blame her. I respected her for respecting herself to where no one was gonna fuck with her without getting fucked over himself.

My days with Bye were brief. After that short week, he left and never looked back. When he ghosted me, I used to think, *Fuck him. He's an asshole. He's a coward. He's afraid of being a daddy. If he don't wanna have nothing to do with me, I'll never have nothing to do with him.*

And I never did.

That didn't stop Uncle Pearl from telling me about him. He said my dad wasn't always rough. He could be smooth. Ladies liked him. Uncle Pearl said I inherited that good quality from my father. I could see that, cause even as a shy kid, I was more comfortable talking to girls than boys. I saw my friends be uneasy when a girl approached. They'd get tongue-tied and back off. I never did. Given the fact that I had such a scary mother, you'd think otherwise. You'd think women would make me nervous.

But I lucked out. I got enough of my father to offset my mother. Or maybe those two parts just merged inside my soul in a way that let me chat up any female. I'm not talking about sex. I don't mean that this comfort I feel with women is something I use as a line. It's not about hitting on women. It's about seeing them as fascinating human beings. Women excite my curiosity. I wanna hear where they come from; how they got to be who they are; why they feel the way they feel.

Strange part is that for much of my life I was outright enraged at both my mom and dad. That rage can still be stirred up. But as I got older, I did something I think we all need to do: control the energy. Took me a long time, but I learned that both my female energy and my male energy came from mighty powerful people.

The more I've lived out my story, the more apparent the challenge becomes to balance those parts from my past. To avoid hurting others based on the hurt inflicted on me as a kid, I need to harmonize those parts.

There's another crazy twist about meeting my dad and his family.

The Boys & Girls Club had a summer camp for young kids. That's where I caught up with a host of different characters. Cute girls. Cool guys. But also foes. One kid in particular had an alpha about him. If we were splashing in the pool, he'd splash me hard. We'd get into it. We'd fight. One day he beat my ass; the next day I beat his ass. Wasn't that we hated each other, but somehow we got into a brawl every single time we wound up in the same space.

After meeting Aunt Pam, she said to me, "I got a son your age."

"You got a picture?" I asked.

"Sure."

But before she could get it, he walked through the door.

We looked at each other with amazement.

This was the brotha I'd been fighting at the Boys & Girls summer camp!

Shammond Williams.

Rather than fight, this time we hugged.

"I know this nigga!" I shouted.

"What'd you say?" said my new grandma, not liking my language.

"My bad, Granny. I apologize." That's the first time I used the word "Granny." It felt so good to say it.

"Boy, you gonna have to wash out your mouth with soap," she said. "I know that y'all in the streets be talkin' crazy. Just don't be talkin' that way up in here. You hungry?"

*Playing against my cousin Shammond Williams of the Seattle Supersonics, 2001.*

Here comes a plate of macaroni and cheese while I'm still trying to digest the fact that my former foe is a first cousin.

Like me, Shammond Williams winds up playing in the league. Before that, he graduated from North Carolina, where he was a star hooper. Shammond was respected throughout Greenville. His dad was Schoolboy. Legendary cat whose street dreams came alive. Remember Nicky Barnes, the Black godfather of Harlem? Well, Schoolboy was the Black godfather of Carolina. Schoolboy was one of our heroes.

There were crews everywhere. Greenville brothas. Southside brothas. Travelers Rest brothas. Anderson brothas. If you were looking for a badass, you'd find him at the Cleveland Street Y, where shit could pop off. But if Shammond was there, he could chill it out. He moved like a street politician without giving up anything. I was proud to be his cousin.

# C

Carnation Evaporated Milk / Vince Carter / Sam Cassell / Chalk /
Mark Clayton / Derrick Coleman / Cynthia Cooper-Dyke /
Cosmetology / Kevin Costner / The Courts / Crews / Mark Cuban

# Carnation Evaporated Milk

Carnation. Spam. Sardines with crackers. Got two pieces of bread? Put anything in between. Ain't got no bologna? Just slather on some mayonnaise. Ain't go no mayo? Just use maple syrup or molasses or just plain sugar. When the heat was off, Moms had to open up the stove so we could all warm up. Or you had the kerosene heaters that you had to get up and refill in the middle of the night. You didn't really know that was the bottom. You didn't really know that you were going through it. This was life. Hanging clothes on the line. Hurrying to get the clothes in before it rains. Make do with what you got. Survive.

# Vince Carter

*see* **Chauncey B-B-B-B-Billups; Block; Dunk; Isolation; LeBron James; One-and-Done; Gary Payton; Shoes**

# Sam Cassell

*see* **Glen Davis; Allen Iverson; MV3; Paul Pierce; Flip Saunders; Showdown**

# Chalk

It started with Jordan. When he came into the league in '84, he had this ritual. Right before tip-off, he'd dump some chalk on his hands to help with his grip and dust it off at the scorer's table. That's where the Bulls TV and radio broadcasters sat: color man Johnny "Red" Kerr and his play-by-play partner Jim Durham. Well, the first time Jordan did it, Johnny made some remark about how the stuff was flying everywhere. If Johnny hadn't said anything, who knows if it would've become a tradition. But he did, and after that Jordan hit the chalk every game to mess with Johnny and Jim. It became a good-luck charm. It also became a gag for the TV audience watching at home. Johnny and Jim would put on surgical masks and respirators or open umbrellas to protect themselves from the flying chalk.

Well, when I got to the league, I took that move and put a different spin on it.

I never took to the sportswriters. I saw how they liked to stir up controversy. If they could get you to say shit against an opposing player—or, even better, bad-mouth one of your teammates—that made their day. Not all of them were pricks, but many saw their job as a way

*Tossing chalk, 2004.*

to make misery. I avoided them as much as I could, but you gotta give interviews, and when I did, I followed one simple maxim: Less is more. In fact, not long after I got to Boston, Paul Pierce, Ray Allen, and I made it a policy that we wouldn't do interviews unless it was all three of us together. That way they heard everything that was coming out of my mouth, and I heard everything that was coming out of theirs, and there'd be no chance for writers to twist our words and use them against us. Not that I ever read what they wrote. My focus was on the game, not the so-called experts on the sidelines analyzing the game. I got

coaches—brilliant coaches—to critique me. I got my own sense of self-evaluation that's harsher than anyone's. Don't need nothing else.

Though I never read that stuff, other people did and would tell me about it. It always got back to me. So at the start of the game, when I'd get ready to roll out there, I would go over to the area along the sideline where the writers were sitting. I'd load my hands up with chalk, way more than I needed. I'd fling it at them and then clap my hands—but the clap was really just to hide the fling. The stuff would go everywhere, all over their computers. It wasn't no joke like between

Jordan and Johnny and Jim, but it made me smile to see how pissed the writers got, see them holding their papers up in front of their faces. Wasn't no Twitter or Instagram back then. If they wrote something nasty or straight-up false about you, you couldn't come back at them online. What was I gonna do? Write a letter to the editor? That was the time when the media expected the players to just sit there and take it. Not me. The chalk was my response.

Later on, LeBron would take the move and put his own spin on it. Load up even more than I did before flinging it high in the air. People love it. It gets the fans hyped. But me? Whenever I see that I think, *What a shame. All that chalk and not a single pissed-off writer to show for it.*

## Mark Clayton

I was eleven or twelve when Moms took the money she'd been saving up from all her different jobs and bought us a house in Mauldin. Nicer neighborhood. Well-maintained houses with lush green yards and blooming flowers. Better surroundings, but life inside our crib was scary. Moms got remarried. Now I got a stepdad, Ernest. He's a street dude. In the beginning, me and him ain't cool. He was hard. Had him a team of brothas who moved appliances for an appliance store. Had other action he wouldn't talk about. Be gone for months at a time. Never knew why. Then, boom, he's home, ranting and raving about some shit. A couple of situations are rough. Very aggressive and heavy-handed. No police come around. The hood is my police, and the hood is staying out of rough family stuff. Confusion. Fear. Uncertainty. Pain. Get me out of this. Lemme run outside and play.

Back in the old neighborhood, before we moved to Mauldin, football came before basketball. I studied the way Tony Dorsett cradled the ball as he busted through the line. Fell in love with Walter Payton. Wanted to be Mark Clayton catching Dan Marino's passes. I could fly. I could see myself outracing the defenders and catching everything in sight.

Imagine this scene: A huge football field behind Hughes Middle School with fifty brothas running every which way. That's how we played—twenty-five on twenty-five—with one quarterback. It was a free-for-all. A delirium. A blast. And me, well, I was in the middle of the mix. I had to be, cause these were all the dope brothas in the neighborhood. Those wild-ass games were where I built up a little rep.

If I play forcefully, if I play with anger, hell, if live with rage, that's because rage and pain are first cousins. Pain leads to rage. But given the times and the household where I'm raised, rage can't be expressed. Kids can't talk back. And none of us kids are saying anything that will trigger Ernest's rage. Moms's rage too.

Moms had many sides. No smoking, no drinking—that's fine. That's good. That keeps me on the straight and narrow. Sometimes she goes off on her Jehovah's Witness raps. Jehovah telling you to do this, Jehovah telling you to do that. Then she'll turn around and come after me for breaking one of her rules.

*Mark Clayton, 1986.*

When I was getting my ass whooped by Ernest, I'd fantasize that my real father would come rescue me and, like Batman or Superman, bust through the door and fuck up my stepfather. "You can't do that to my son! You can't touch that boy! He's my child!"

But the fantasies didn't last long. My real dad remained a ghost. Ernest kept on me till I put on some size and showed him I was willing to give back what I was getting—and then some.

Those are bad memories. The good memories have to do with Bug. Moving to Mauldin meant reuniting with Bug.

When I first saw him after so many years, I was shocked. And thrilled. Bug and his parents, Mr. and Mrs. Peters, were nearby. The reunion warmed my heart.

Bug had him a beard, hair growing all up and down his legs and arms. He was walking bowlegged. Meanwhile, I was shooting up in height while he was no taller than 5 feet 5.

It was Bug, by the way, who introduced me to all the cats who were hooping hard. It was in Mauldin where my basketball mania began.

## Derrick Coleman

When I experienced my growth spurt in my early teens, that brought on some insecurities. That might sound strange. I know being tall is something usually seen as good. But for a kid, it also means you're always gonna be noticed. You can't hide. You're the focus of attention. And if you don't feel good about yourself to begin with—as many kids don't—you don't wanna be noticed. You can feel awkward. You can even feel like a freak of nature. Being shy, the last thing I wanted was attention.

When I shot up out of nowhere to become a full-sized adult, the adjustment from normal to abnormal wasn't easy. In that regard, the person who helped me most was Moms. I've already talked about Moms's rough side. First time I ever saw anyone shoot a gun, it was Moms doing the shooting. Ask me the one person I was scared of all my life, and the answer is Moms.

Yet Moms had wisdom and courage and could set me straight.

Sometimes, when Moms saw my spirit sinking low, she'd stop and talk to me.

"What's wrong?" she'd ask.

I'd hem and haw and finally say something about feeling weird.

"About what?"

"About being so tall."

"Boy," she'd say, "ain't no reason to feel weird about nothing. You got every reason to feel good. Every boy wants to be tall. Every man wants to be tall. That means you get to look over everyone. That there is a blessing. Now, I seen you slouching, and I seen you slumping over. Don't wanna see no more of that. Wanna see you standing up straight. Straight and erect. Straight and proud. Proud to be tall. Proud to be who you are."

As I shot up in height, hoop seemed like the more appealing sport than football. I was growing so fast that my height got ahead of my coordination. So the first thing I focused on was dribbling. I became a dribbling fool. Mornings before school, I would get up at five, get dressed, grab my books and my ball, and creep out the house so I didn't wake anyone. I'd drop my books at the bus stop, take my ball, and go to the top of Basswood, which was a long-ass street. I'd dribble to the bottom, and then dribble right back to the top. Wouldn't stop until everybody started showing up to the bus stop. First I started with one hand. Then the other. I'm sure the neighbors got sick of me. The sound of nonstop dribbling must've

*Derrick Coleman pushing the ball for Syracuse, 1987.*

driven 'em crazy. Either they were heavy sleepers or were just good-hearted people, because they never told me to knock it off.

There was one dude, my homie Wes, who liked to sit on the front porch in the morning and watch me. "Pick your head up!" he'd yell out to me. "You see how Coleman brings it up? That's how you got to do."

"Who's Coleman?"

"Derrick Coleman. He plays for Syracuse. You need to know this shit."

This was around the same time ESPN was coming on strong. They got all the Big East tournament games. So now I'm seeing Derrick. He becomes my favorite player and the Syracuse Orange becomes my favorite team. I'm also seeing Alonzo Mourning, I'm seeing Malik Sealy. Studying them. Learning from them. Soon I'm skating to the park, looking for whatever pickup games I can find.

## Cynthia Cooper-Dyke

*see* WNBA

## Cosmetology

Before we moved to Mauldin, Moms went into cosmetology and began working in a shop called Guys and Dolls. Soon she set up her own business. Next thing you know, Ernest and a little crew of Mexicans were fixin' the garage into something else. Before long she had herself a couple of dryers, shampoo bowls, the whole operation. A going business.

I worked in her beauty salon for two years.

"Come over here, boy, and help out. Take the rollers out of Miss Maybury's hair."

Being obedient, I'd do it. Take out the rollers. Sweep up the floor. Wash down the sinks.

"Now go wash Miss Washington's hair and do it right."

Plenty of her clients were from Kingdom Hall. They had a gym over there where some of the boys would hoop. Naturally I joined in. But competition brings out what they call worldly energy, and during church games, worldly energy isn't welcome. Word gets back to Moms. Moms tells me to tamper it down. Moms also says if worldly energy is coming out when you play, stop playing.

Moms was more than firm. Moms could get physical. I understood that. I also understood that my job was to listen to her. But this was when passion overwhelmed fear. I had to play. And to get better, I had to play with the baddest dudes. That got me to sneaking out the house to hoop. Because Moms was so busy with her customers, I could pretty much roam around as much as I wanted to.

Moms didn't care a thing about basketball. Her thing was education. Learn my lessons. Get through school. Go to college. When I got to Mauldin High and made the team, I didn't even tell her. For all of ninth and tenth grade, she didn't even know I was playing. It wasn't until the eleventh grade, during a game when I scored forty points, that I saw her sitting in the stands. I swallowed hard.

That was a Friday night. I didn't go back home till Sunday. I stayed with friends. I knew Moms would be pissed. In fact, she was so pissed she found my uniform I'd hidden in my closet and tore it up.

"You ain't playing basketball," she said, "you're concentrating on your studies."

I knew enough not to argue. I also knew that, no matter what, I had to hoop.

That Monday I went back to school and the coach gave me a new uniform. I kept playing.

**Favorite Movies**

1 *Serendipity*
2 *Life*
3 *Harlem Nights*
4 *American Pie*
5 *Sherlock Holmes*
   (the Robert Downey Jr. version)

## Kevin Costner

Costner was cool with Whitney in *The Bodyguard*, but my favorite film of his is *For Love of the Game* where he plays a baseball pitcher trying to throw a perfect game. I related.

Kevin's character, Billy Chapel, is at the end of a professional career that lasted nineteen years. He's an old-school competitor. Plays through injuries. Loyal to his team. Loves his teammates. The title says it all. He's playing for love, not glory or gold.

When he gets out on the mound and starts to pitch, the sounds of the roaring crowd—the hecklers, the haters, the screamers, the crazies—all that noise stops. Nothing but silence. That silence allows you inside the zone. That happened to me more times than I can remember. Might be MSG or Staples or the Boston Garden. Might be regular season or a hyped-up playoff game. Decibels could be off the chart, but it wouldn't matter.

I walk on the floor and don't hear a thing. For a few seconds, I'm in a bubble

*Kevin Costner in* For Love of the Game.

of quiet. That bubble lets me focus. That quiet brings me back to myself.

I still go back and rewatch the movie to remember that in the middle of a hurricane, there's always an eye. With the screaming winds surrounding it, the eye is quiet. The eye is peaceful. The eye is letting us see that, with the right focus, we can proceed in silence and accomplish feats the world considers unachievable.

# The Courts

A hot spot for hoop in Greenville was the Springfield Park courts. Kind of like Kronk in Detroit, Emanuel Stewart's funky gym where he trained the fiercest fighters like Thomas "Hit Man" Hearns, the Motor City Cobra. If you could survive Kronk, you could survive anything. Same with Springfield Park.

The king of the courts was Reggie Goldsmith. Looked like everything came easy to Gold. He was the first superstar outta Mauldin. All of Greenville respected him. He was a 5'8" guard, slippery as hell. The street dudes gave him props because he had nice hands. He could fight. He was good with the ladies. Gold also had him a gold Nissan 300ZX. In my younger days of going to the park, I saw him and said to myself, "Oh, shit, that's Gold." Or if we were already playing and he showed up, it was like, "Muthafuckas, get ya asses off this court. Don't come down here no more." With that easy attitude, he alpha-ed up the park. Controlled the scene. Stepped in when kids were getting bullied. He

ran things right. The cool bro everyone gravitated to.

Even though Gold never came close to the NBA—he wound up at a small-town college—he became a role model. He was also a dude whose personal history meshed with mine. Turned out that Gold's stepfather was best friends with my real father. He also dated a few of my older cousins.

When he was seven, Gold came over to my crib and met my mom, who, at the time, was pregnant with me. That's when my parents were still together. He remembered my sister Sonya being there and being chased out the house cause the big folks were getting high and didn't want the kids to know.

Gold was also the first trash-talker who made a mark on my mind. When he was on the sidelines watching me, he'd be saying, "Give it to him, big fella. Don't wait on him. Bust his ass." Even without being in the game, his mouth controlled the action. When he was in the game, he was a finesse player who'd dunk the brick, turn to the defenders, sneer and say, "You didn't see that shit coming, did you?"

Gold talked a hundred miles an hour. I saw the speed of his speech had a lot to do with the rhythm of his game. The speed of his speech was another reason why he was able to command any situation. His tone took over the park. It was from Gold that I learned that rapid-fire talk to the point where eventually I could take over that same park with my own motormouth.

Some dude I didn't know might be fixin' to get in the game, but before he did, he'd be shouting in my face, trying to throw me off. "You ain't doing that shit to me, big fella."

"Well, come on in," I'd say. "You're next."

He got in. *Boom!* Game on! Here I go, rip his ass, fake his ass, dunk on his ass, humiliate his ass.

"You ain't talkin' shit now, are you?" I'd ask.

Besides Reggie Goldsmith, the big boys on the court were the Frank brothers, Baron and Paul. Baron, called Bear, was 6'6", 295 pounds, a bald bully, sweating, grabbing your neck, picking you up, throwing you on the ground. Paul was also a knockout artist. Loved him some Charles Barkley. Bear was our Patrick Ewing, our Olajuwon. He became part of my crew along with Bug and Will Valentine. We became known as the Basswood Boys. We were something like a family. We clung tight and had our fun, but one thing you gotta know about country brothas is that we gonna fight before we shoot. Now everyone's shooting cause everyone's got guns. Even back in the day, kids in Chicago, LA, and New York had more guns than candy. Not so in Carolina. In Carolina, the stick, board, and bat were the basic weapons. And of course the hands too. Fuck with one of us, you gonna have to fuck with all of us.

# Crews

The principle is deep. It goes all the way back to the tribes of the Bible days. Wolves run in packs. So do dogs. And so

do we. Depending on the culture, crews are different. College kids join fraternities and sororities to get a feeling of belonging. When they're adults, rich people join country clubs.

In the hood, we start forming crews early. Sometimes those crews are pretty innocent, kids who just enjoy each other's company. But in other instances, crews morph into gangs. Different historical moments require different reactions. To my mind, the motive behind all this crew-forming is a feeling of safety. Safety in numbers. Safety in surrounding yourself with brothas who got your back. Safety in stepping out knowing you ain't stepping out alone.

I was born in the second half of the seventies and raised up in the eighties. The eighties were murderous. The eighties traumatized much of Black America. I'm not saying everyone, but millions of brothas and sistas got fucked up, not just those who got cracked out, but those who had cracked-out friends and relatives.

The South did not escape the crack era. Crack washed over my people like a tsunami. Crack killed the harmony in the hood. It turned the eighties into a suicide nightmare. Some of my uncles, some of the coolest cats I knew, blew their cool on crack. Man, if one family on the block didn't have someone who touched crack, sold crack, or got cracked out in some form or fashion, I'd be shocked. It was a pitiful thing to witness. A population being devastated by an evil drug. Where did it come from? Who was behind the scourge? Who was profiting? It felt like premeditated genocide. To this day I keep wondering what forces were behind it.

All I know is that it fucked up Black America and added to the buildup of crews.

When I got into the league, I brought a crew from home. You could call the nineties a posttraumatic version of the eighties. We were all still in shock of what we went through to survive. Our crews surrounded us, comforted us, protected us. The bigger I got in the world of hoop, the bigger my crew got. At one point it felt like I was rolling with an army.

Then a strange thing happened. In the second half of my career—say, a decade in—the crew started thinning out. The more I matured, the less I needed company. Fast-forward to today, where I'm sitting here in an empty house writing a book. Ain't no party. Ain't no crew cheering me on. Just looking out at distant mountains, scribbling and thinking and gathering my thoughts. Solitary. Solo. Enjoying my own company.

That's not to bad-mouth crews. I needed them when I needed them. In the mad-scramble hood or in the mad-scramble corporate culture or in the mad-scramble NBA, crews can help you stay sane. When you're riding high, why not spread the joy and take a crew on the ride with you? But at the end of the day, when the glory passes and the cheering stops, it's all about taking care of business. Thinking straight. Making sound decisions. Thinking it through on your own.

Being alone is different than being lonely. Lonely means you're missing something. But if I spend an hour or a day or even a week by myself, chances are I'll be learning something I never knew before. And although I don't speak to my crew every day and party like we used to, we're all still connected by heart. What happened to us is what happens to all real crews. We grew up.

For now and forever, we are OBF. Official Block Family.

## Mark Cuban

Love the guy. He was the first to finesse the league. Showed the league how to treat players. Cuban came off as the fantasy fan who'd won a team. He put video on huge monitors in the locker rooms when you weren't supposed to do that. Big ol' comfortable chairs. Massage rooms with candles and New Age music. Treated his players like kings. Also fed 'em like kings. The visiting teams got post-game four-course gourmet spreads. Can only imagine what the Mavs got.

I had to give him props. After my first meal at the American Airlines Center, I went to his office and said, "Mr. Cuban, excuse me for interrupting, but I gotta say something. When I was a rookie, I was the guy who had to run to Taco Bell and McDonald's and grab bags for everyone. Just so you understand that I appreciate what you're doing."

"Thanks, KG. Good game tonight."

Before long, you could see Cuban changing the culture. Practice facilities getting a 24/7 chef. Nutrition becoming a big item. The right kind of juices. State-of-the-art showerheads hitting you with maximum pressure. Jet-spray tubs big enough to house seven-footers. Now they're hiring barbers and players can get a haircut before going home.

The history of the league is the history of more than a few cheap owners looking to beef up profits at the players' expense. Cuban turned that around. He put in benefits—health and comfort benefits—that, if they came out of a player's pocket, might cost him $200,000. I believe he did it not only cause he's a fan who loves his team but also because it was the right thing to do. Not to mention how it motivates hoopers to wanna play for the Mavs. In my book, Cuban's cool.

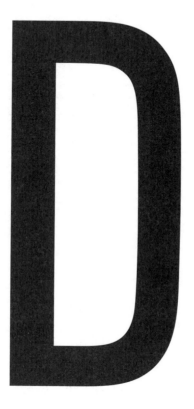

# D

Glen Davis / Depression / Dissecting / DMX / Doc /
Double-Team / Dr. J / Dr. Jekyll and Mr. Hyde /
Duke vs. Michigan / Tim Duncan / Dunk / Kevin Durant

# Glen Davis

Being a rookie in the league is hard no matter what team you're on. It's a huge adjustment. You gotta get used to the travel and hotels. You gotta get used to everybody you've ever known—or even just met one time—coming outta the woodwork looking to score some tickets or wanting you to invest in some business or just straight-up asking for cash. And you gotta get used to not being the shit.

Before you turn pro, you've been the shit on every team you've ever played on. But as soon as you come into the league, you get humbled real quick. You've just joined the inner circle with the best players in the world. You're swimming in a sea of history. Ain't like college, where the talent divide is as wide as the Grand Canyon. Everybody in the league got serious game. And everybody in the league is trying to *stay* in the league. They got families to take care of. Mouths to feed. Everybody out to keep their jobs. Rookies can be viewed as a threat to that job security. Terrell Brandon mentoring Shot is the exception to the rule. Rookies in the league are like minnows in shark-infested water. They gotta fight to stay alive and prove they belong.

So then just imagine being a rookie on the 2007–08 Celtics. You got me, P, and Ray uniting with the goal of winning a championship.

My first encounter with Glen Davis when he got to Boston was a nasty altercation. We had words about something I can't even remember. All I do remember is that we were both pissed. Next day we didn't even talk to each other. But twenty-four hours later, here comes Glen talkin' 'bout "Look, Ticket, about the other day. I was outta line. Sorry."

That was the first time a player in the league apologized to me for anything. That touched my heart.

"I ain't here to fuck with you," he said. "I'm here to learn from you."

"Hey, man," I said. "I'm sorry too. Sorry we got off on the wrong foot."

And that was it. Going forward, we became brothas for life. Turned out he had an even rougher childhood than mine. Others called him Big Baby. I called him Funk.

I had some stuff to teach Funk—how to guard bigger players; in-depth post moves; how to utilize his mobility. For a big man, Funk had great mobility. He was also smart.

If I gotta go into a foxhole, I'm taking Funk with me.

Funk was originally drafted by Seattle, which packaged him in the deal for Ray. The Celtics had traded a couple of their big men—including Al Jefferson—in the trade that brought me there. So we were relying on Funk to make more of a contribution than you'd expect of a typical rook. He stepped up.

In December, our starting center, Kendrick Perkins, had to sit out because of a sore toe. That wasn't so strange. Dudes get banged-up toes all the time. But Perk didn't hurt his toe hoopin'. He'd assembled his bed wrong and it collapsed on his foot. The media made a joke of it, and looking back, it's pretty funny, but at the time none of us were laughing. Half the roster was different from the season before, and we needed every game to help us adjust to playing with each other and build our chemistry. We'd had the same starting five every game so far—myself, P, Ray, Doe, and Perk—and we were cooking, seventeen wins and just two losses so far. But we weren't satisfied or taking anything for granted. Nope, we were thinking, *Damn, Perk, you an NBA player making NBA money. Why you gotta be assembling your own furniture? Why you buyin' IKEA?*

So, Funk finally gets his first career start. Was nervous as hell. Damn near hyperventilating. But he played his heart out. Had sixteen points—including ten out of ten from the free-throw line—and nine rebounds. That's when I knew this dude was gonna be integral to our success. That's why I rode him hard, pushing and challenging. He and I worked out every day together. No better workout partner than Funk.

Then came that night against Portland in December 2008. We'd built a twenty-five-point lead late in the third quarter, so all us starters came out. Well, by the middle of the fourth quarter, the Blazers had cut it to thirteen. What was

great about that Boston team was our ability to check ourselves. Didn't need the coaching staff to tell us when we weren't playing up to our ability. So, during a time-out, I gathered together the group of bench guys who were out there and told 'em what was up. I wasn't nice about it. Wasn't polite. And Funk got pissed. Not pissed at me. Pissed at himself. Pissed that he hadn't played better and that he'd let the team down. Now the starters had to go back into the game. He stormed out of that huddle and sat at the end of the bench in tears, the TV cameras catching it all.

Sam Cassell was sitting near him on the bench and threw a towel over his head to keep people from seeing. And I understand that instinct. He wanted to protect his teammate's privacy. He knew the media would make a big deal of it, which of course they did. But Funk had no reason to be embarrassed by those tears. The opposite—should've been proud of those tears. Cause it showed just how much he cared. All of us on those Celtics teams were like that. We were all super passionate. We all wore our hearts on our sleeves. And I will always take a more passionate player who ain't that skilled over a more skilled player who ain't that passionate.

Funk was both—passionate and skilled.

During the four years I played with him in Boston, he had some clutch moments. Like Game 4 of the 2010 finals against the Lakers when he had eighteen points—half in the fourth quarter.

"I felt like a beast," he said at the press conference after. "Really. I'm gonna just be honest with you. I felt like I couldn't be denied."

*Celebrating a win against the Jazz with Funk, 2011.*

I was so proud of him after the game, and so proud when I heard what he'd said—talking with that swagger I'd worked hard to help instill in him. The student had become the master.

Yet there were still times when I had to remind him he would never out-alpha me.

We were in Toronto, where we were gonna play the next day. We always went out to eat as a team, so we jumped in the Sprinter and rode over to invade Ruth's Chris like an army of barbarians. They gave us a private room and shut the door, but you couldn't shut out the noise we were making. Beats had just come out with portable speakers that had us blasting Lil Wayne and all the hottest shit. We started shootin' dice and getting louder until the manager came in and asked us to tone it down. We were incapable of toning it down, so we decided to get the fuck out.

Next day the game with Toronto was a dogfight. We ended up winning at the buzzer. We were gassed but amped. We got on the plane. It was like *Soul Plane*, that movie with Kevin Hart and Method Man and Snoop Dogg, where, thirty thousand feet up in the air, brothas go wild. Well, we made *Soul Plane* look like *Mary Poppins*. Brothas shooting dice, playing booray. The energy was crazy. No one could calm us down. Doc had to close off the curtain between the front and back, where there had to be at least six different gambling sets poppin' off at the same time. We called it Little Las Vegas. Meanwhile, Funk had his shirt off, arm wrestling nonstop. He was layin' everyone down. He'd also got himself some cheerleaders, like Tony Allen, behind him. So when Funk slammed Leon Powe, who's strong as fuck, TA was screaming, "Oh shit! Yo, you knocked his ass down!"

I just sat there, watching. I was playing the Robin role. Don't gotta be Batman. Paul Pierce was also watching and, wanting to have some fun, said some shit about betting on me against Funk. Funk was ready. Funk screamed, "Let's go."

"Who the fuck you talkin' to?" I asked Funk.

"Your punk ass," he said.

"Calm your ass down."

"Ain't nothing to be calm about. I'm the man up in here."

"Fuck you."

Funk wasn't taking it lightly. We headbutted.

P shouted out, "I got my money on Ticket. Ain't no one can beat Ticket."

P laid down a big piece. Now everyone was placing bets. It was the young guys versus the OGs.

Before we locked up, I told Funk, "I seen you grabbing the table with your left hand to get leverage. I see how you had to deal with that young bull."

I said that cause it was true, and I also said that to worry him.

"That ain't got nothing to do with it," said Funk.

Funk kept talking greasy, and I kept reminding him that without that leverage he couldn't whip no one.

"Shut the fuck up," he said, "and just lock up."

We did just that. But when we locked, he saw my arm was longer than his. I had the tall leverage on him. And while I'm not bulky, I'm stronger than most people give me credit for.

To drive Funk a little crazy during the lockup, I waved my left hand around like a conductor conducting an orchestra.

"Don't need this hand to be grabbing nothing," I said. "How 'bout you, dawg?"

"You going down, Ticket," he said.

I said, "I ain't going nowhere, nigga. I ain't no Leon Powe."

I saw his forehead break into a little sweat so I goosed up my gab.

"You best be grabbing that table even harder, cause this shit ain't working out the way you figured it would."

Funk started grunting, I started waving my free hand around even more, teasing him with every motion. The guys were screaming loud.

Funk's eyes got bigger. The sweat ain't just a trickle. The sweat's a stream. I could feel he was hurting.

I kept waving that free hand.

Kept telling him I ain't going nowhere.

And then, I felt the slightest break in his lock. That break was all I needed. I let out a holler and slammed his hand down—*boom!*—headbutted him and said, "Don't you ever in life disrespect me. I'm the silverback in this muthafucka. Monster up in here."

We all got up to hug and laugh like the fools we were.

# Depression

*see* **Illmatic**; **Silence**

# Dissecting

I see dissecting other people's games as the crown jewel of my legacy. I'm talkin' about geometry and angles and makin' a dude spin, and when he spins, being there for a rake and a rip. My gift for mathematics. My third eye. I see him gettin' ready to pump fake, I ain't goin' for it. The ball right here, I'm gonna just rip the ball out of his hand. The better I played, the more the game slowed down. I'm talking *Matrix* shit. Yes, I had physical skill—some God-given and some earned through thousands of hours of hard work. But that dissecting is a fine finesse. It's where physical and mental come together.

# DMX

When DMX hit, I was already in the league. I wasn't out there robbin' or stealin', but I *was* experiencing different shit in the street—some of the same shit DMX was spittin' about.

DMX barked the same way I barked. His voice wasn't smooth. His tone was harsh. His texture was rough. I liked that. His music resonated. His beats represented me. I played like his beats. What if Magic Johnson came from the hood? What if Magic had a DMX attitude? That's how I thought of my game. I played like the music I was listening to. I played in your face. In-your-face music, in-your-face hooping. Hip-hop heads putting a hurtin' on hoopers and, come to learn, hoopers putting a hurtin' on hip-hop heads. It's going back and forth.

*DMX performing at Woodstock '99.*

I was also living like what I was listening to. My crew and I would go somewhere other brothas might be afraid to go. We were deep as fuck. We strapped. That's how you had to travel. That was the culture back then.

DMX gave us our anthems.

# Doc

Could've saved him for "R," but he's too important to wait that long. I'm bringing him into the story early. I'm bringing him in right now because I'm feeling him. Without Doc, I'd have never made it to that mountaintop.

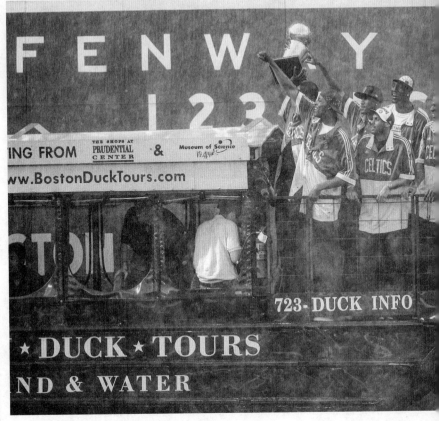

*Celebrating the 2008 championship on a duck boat, just like Doc envisioned.*

It was summer 2007. After twelve seasons with the Minnesota Timberwolves, I had joined the Boston Celtics for five players and two first-round picks in the biggest trade for one player in league history. I was stoked.

Before the start of the season, my new head coach, Doc Rivers, came over to Paul Pierce, Ray Allen, and me—the three players he saw bringing a championship to Boston—and told us to meet at a certain dock in the harbor at 6 a.m. the next day.

We all groaned.

"Okay," he said. "Make it eight a.m."

We arrived 8 a.m. sharp. All we saw was Doc and a big ol' boat. The boat looked like a bus on the water.

"What is this?" I asked.

"A duck boat," said Doc.

"What are we doing?"

with the people cheering. We're going around this dam. We're going under this bridge. We're stopping in front of this building. And all the while, fans are going crazy because you took the team from last year's lousy season to this year's winning season. They're going crazy because you will have forged the biggest turnaround in the history of basketball. They're going crazy because you, Kevin, are gonna be Defensive Player of the Year. They know all about your offense, but they've never seen you play defense like this before."

I couldn't keep my eyes off Doc. He had a huge presence. His gravelly voice made you wanna listen to him even more. He was forceful. But it was the soul under the force that got to me. Some people are good planners; others are visionaries. Doc's a visionary. He manifests what he's feeling; and what he's feeling gets you reeling with motivation. Doc is no one you wanna disappoint.

In February that season, we were in the locker room after a game with the Lakers at Staples. It was our last game against them in the regular season. Doc took an envelope and said, "I'm passing this around and I want everyone to put a hundred bucks inside."

*What? Why?*

"If you trust me, just put in the money."

We trusted him. Everyone gave, including the coaches and equipment managers.

"Okay," said Doc, "I'm sealing this envelope and hiding it in the ceiling. If you ever want to see this money again, you'll have to come back here to face this team in the finals."

When we did face them in the finals, Doc didn't forget. He took the envelope

"Getting in the duck boat. We're going for a ride."

Paul was looking at me, Ray was looking at Paul, and then all of us were looking at Doc as if to say, *What the fuck?*

We climbed on the boat where Doc, in his hoarse but always upbeat voice, said, "We're going on a water tour of Boston. When you win the championship, this is the boat that will take you around the city

*Doc congratulating me on our way to a playoff win against the Hawks, 2008.*

he'd hidden and gave us each our hundred back. A beautiful moment.

When the Clippers fired Doc after the 2020 season, I was mad. The stats were in his favor: In seven seasons the Clips made the playoffs six times. Doc's winning percentage was .631. Beyond the stats, though, are the spiritual facts: he maintained the franchise during hostile times. For that, the franchise should have given him another chance. They prematurely killed the dream.

In 2014, the Clips' owner, Donald Sterling, was revealed as a racist. They caught him on tape. Doc's players were understandably crushed. The team morale was in a free fall. That's when Doc stood in the locker room and said,

"My name is Glenn Rivers. I'm from Chicago and I'm Black and I'm pissed. Our owner's a racist and I don't want to do anything for that man." Then he pointed to the bigger story. The story was about more than Sterling. Sterling was shit, but Sterling was history. Excellence in any activity—sports, politics, business, whatever—can be achieved during trying times. Trying times are what tests a man's character.

When hell broke loose in Kenosha, Wisconsin, after the police shooting of Jacob Blake, Doc used a post-game press meeting to say, "It's amazing why we keep loving this country and this country does not love us back."

Facts.

I'm looking up at a Mount Rushmore of coaches. I see the chiseled images of Gregg Popovich, Phil Jackson, and Red Auerbach. I see Larry Brown and John Thompson. But I also see Doc. Doc is high up there.

He's the father who made me a complete player. He pushed me harder than anyone. Doc made it okay to make mistakes. He said it was okay to be tired, okay to mess up. He got me to rest. Before Doc, I didn't really know how to turn it off. Doc was the kind of coach who would take the team to the movies just to get our minds off hoop. He knew obsession could have us overplay, overreact, take us out of the zone. Doc also had deep-down wisdom about family and kids and how to conduct yourself as a man of integrity.

Ain't but one Doc Rivers.

shut that off. You add a third playmaker, though, and it renders a double-team just about useless. You swing the ball enough, there ain't no way the defense can keep up on their rotation. The ball always moves faster than feet. So then the other team has to forget the double-team and just play straight-up. And that's when the playmakers can really go to work.

It might sound obvious, but it ain't. There are a lot of players who see the double-team as a challenge. Their eyes get wide when they see those two defenders converging. Rather than just quickly give up the ball to their suddenly open teammate, they want to show off how good they are by trying to dribble around it. So having a Big Three isn't only about having three playmakers. It's about

## Double-Team

Everybody always talks about the Celtics being the first Big Three and how that changed the game—set it up for LB and D-Wade and Chris Bosh in Miami and Steph and Klay and KD in the Bay. But not many people talk about why having a Big Three strategically works so well. It wasn't just about having three superstar players. It was about how having those players on the court at the same time forced the other team to react. It was about the double-team.

When you got two playmakers you gotta worry about, it's difficult. You run a double-team at one, he looks to get it to the other for an open look. But a good defense can rotate quickly enough to

*Double-teamed by the Spurs' Sean Elliott and David Robinson, 1999.*

having three *unselfish* playmakers who are willing to buy into the system and are okay with maybe not getting off as many shots as if they were their team's primary or secondary playmaker.

How you handle the double-team is a lesson for life. Which option will you choose? The selfish decision that satisfies your own ego but makes victory more uncertain? Or the selfless decision that makes someone else look good and is likelier to guarantee victory?

# Dr. J

*see* **Dunk; Shoes**

# Dr. Jekyll and Mr. Hyde

*see* **Tim Duncan**

# Duke vs. Michigan

If you were a kid in the early nineties, no matter where you were growing up in America, you were most likely either a Duke or Michigan fan. Duke had the clean-cut boys with the *90210* style out of an Abercrombie & Fitch ad—Bobby Hurley and Christian Lacttner and Cherokee Parks. Michigan had the Black kids with the shaved heads and the baggy shorts and black socks—the Fab Five that included Juwan Howard and Jalen Rose and Chris Webber. The way the two teams represented the racial divide in America wasn't

100 percent fair or accurate, because Duke had plenty of Black players who could ball, like Grant Hill and Antonio Lang. But the most famous name on Duke's team didn't belong to any of their players. It was their head coach, Mike Krzyzewski.

Michigan's Fab Five represented a shift away from the white patriarchal structure of basketball and helped introduce the player empowerment movement that I further advanced when I skipped college for the draft and later negotiated a record-breaking contract. Of course, back in the day I didn't think about any of this. I just loved the way C-Webb would throw down on the rim with a ferocity I'd never seen before. All my life I'd been a devoted fan of the Big East, but Michigan instantly became my favorite team.

One day a white kid on the block asked me over to play one-on-one. This was when we'd moved to Mauldin. His name was Billy. He was 6'5" and a Duke fan. His favorite was Laettner—whose NBA career would, like mine, jump off in Minnesota. Billy was the only kid with a hoop in his driveway, a glass backboard, the whole bit. He was cool. He let me be his practice bait. He worked his Laettner moves on me to where I felt like a fool. Didn't like that feeling. Didn't like getting my ass kicked. Got tired of being a stick man. That's when you put up your hands during a game and no one's passing to you. Before long, I got to where I was holding my own against Billy. I imagined I was C-Webb, refusing to let Laettner back me down. I imagined we weren't in Mauldin at all but in Ann Arbor's packed Crisler Center. The clock ticking down. The crowd going crazy. Never imagined how close that dream would get to becoming a reality.

*C-Webb flying high for Michigan, 1992.*

# Tim Duncan

Timmy is Mr. Hyde to my Dr. Jekyll. We were opposites in so many ways. I skipped college. He stayed at Wake Forest all four years. I was loud. He was quiet. I played with furious energy. He played with calm collectedness.

And yet we were more similar than we were different. He played nineteen seasons. I played twenty-one. We both valued loyalty and stability. And what we shared most was the way we were humble students of the game. Like Timmy, I put in the work. His work ethic was incredible. So were his moves. Damn tough dude to guard. All his finesse. The way he could back you down or face you up, do those jab steps and feints, swing the ball low and dare you to reach, take you off the dribble or kiss it off the glass or flip up that baby hook.

Over all those years, we played against each other more than fifty times, and every one felt special. He always forced me to play at my highest level. (There was only one other cat I got so hyped up to play against: Rasheed.) Unfortunately, that hype could work against me. I'd be

*Dr. Jekyll and Mr. Hyde, 2000.*

talking all my shit, and where it would psych out most players, it only locked in Timmy tighter. He fed off it. That pissed me off. I'd be spending all this energy trying to get him off his game, I wouldn't realize that he'd gotten me off mine.

And he'd talk shit too. You wouldn't know it if you watched him on TV because he'd do it real subtle. He wouldn't even talk in sentences. He'd just hit you in phrases. "Gotchu." "Ooh, almost." "Nice try." No gangsta shit. Nothing hard-core. Which made it sting even more. Like he couldn't be bothered to spend more than a couple of syllables on your ass. Like you were a little gnat he just shooed away.

*Dunking during an exhibition game against the Raptors in Rome, 2007.*

# Dunk

I view Jordan as the all-time greatest dunker. But Chris Webber is right up there up with him. C-Webb turned layups into dunks.

Dunks give you status. If you dunk that brick, ain't no one jumpin' on you. You set a tone. Make a mark. Here I am!

The greatest dunk I've ever seen in person? Several come to mind. One was Kobean at the 1998 All-Star Game. The other was in Sydney during the 2000 Olympics. Before the Olympics began, the US team—which included Vince Carter, Shareef Abdur-Rahim, Ray Allen, Tim Hardaway, Alonzo Mourning, and Gary Payton—had a bounty out on Yao Ming. We bet on who'd be the first brotha to dunk on Yao. Each of us failed. Yao's size and blocking stopped us cold. We beat China anyway and ultimately faced France in the final.

During that game, Vince stole the ball and drove to the basket. Standing between him and the hoop was a 7'2" monster. Vince leaped over the monster and dunked with the force of Satan. Later, the French writers called it *"le dunk de la mort"*—the dunk of death. I got so excited that in my mind I saw the monster as Yao Ming. Turned out the cat was Frédéric Weis, a player for France. Because of my confusion, I let out one of my ear-piercing screams and pushed against Vince, thinking he'd won the bet. Vince was so surprised he almost punched me in the face by accident, as if to say, "Dude, what the fuck is wrong with you?" All I can say is that I live on hype, and sometimes hype trips me up.

*Vince Carter unleashes* "le dunk de la mort" *in the 2000 Olympics.*

Not many people know about the dunk contest at the Deerfield, Illinois, Nike camp in 1994. Never made it into the major media. It was quiet and cool, like a secret legendary event. The three main brothas were Melvin "Helicopter Man" Levett out of Ohio, Vince Carter from Florida, and my man Ronnie "Air" Fields of Illinois. Ronnie won it but Vince and Helicopter Man were still off the chain. To let you know how spectacular Ronnie was, Vince dropped out after Air executed his mind-blowing 360 windmill. Vince knew he could not outdo that dunk. Vince, of course, would go on to the NBA to become half man, half amazing. And when he won the dunk contest at the 2000 All-Star Game, he did it by re-creating that same Air Fields dunk, only in reverse.

For all the competitive fire, Ronnie, Vince, and I were always cool with each other.

During my senior year at Farragut Career Academy in Chicago, Ronnie was my teammate. During a regular-season game, I witnessed a dunk I still can't believe. On a fast break Ronnie had the ball. I was waiting to get the brick back so I could feed him a lob. Instead he just jumped. He didn't even look to see where he was. He took off with both feet. He flew. He was in the air for what felt like forever. *Boom!* When our coach showed us the film the next day, he slowed it down so we could see Ronnie's point of departure was outside the free-throw line!

As for my dunks? I've had my share. Don't know the exact number. Dunks weren't counted on NBA stat sheets until 2000. But I ain't the kind of guy who's gonna list all my dunks. Don't got that brand of ego. I am gonna say, though, that when I dunked, I had DMX in my head. I was dunking to a DMX track.

You can categorize dunks by the situation: put-backs and alley-oops, baselines and breakaways. You can even distinguish them by the sound they make. I love that sound. The way the rim acts as a kind of musical instrument. The way you can hit it with the ball just right so it creates this note unlike anything else you'll ever hear. This deep bass *ca-chunk* that echoes throughout the arena and just lingers there, reverberating for a few seconds before it fades out, like a dropped stone splashing at the bottom of a well. When I think back on my dunks, I not only see them, I hear them.

But my very favorite dunk? That would have to be my very first. Seventh grade. After classes were over, I'd wait in the gym for my bus to come. All the basketballs had been put away, but someone had left out a volleyball. I grabbed it and stared up at the hoop. Like millions of kids the world over, I'd been watching players dunk since I went from crawling to walking. Hakeem. Kareem. Dr. J. Jordan. Dominique. I always wondered whether it felt as good as it looked. And as I inched up in height, I kept hoping I'd be able to do it.

At 5'10", I was a guard. No one was telling me I was a star, but, at the same time, no one was throwing me off the court. I was holding my own. And on that particular afternoon, with no one looking, I took a deep breath, took that volleyball, jumped with all my might, and—hell, yes!—stuffed it! I was instantly hooked. I turned into a dunk addict. I started dunking everything in sight: soccer balls, tennis balls, ping-pong balls, you name it.

I'm not trying to be cute by using that word "addict." I know too many people who've struggled with and succumbed to addiction to ever be flippant about it. But straight-up, there is a legit chemical euphoria that comes from dunking a basketball. I don't know if scientists have ever studied what receptors in your brain light up when you dunk, but I bet they're similar to the ones stimulated by any mind-altering substance or circuit-overloading behavior. The sensation of dunking that volleyball immediately hooked me, and though I would keep chasing it for the next three decades, the thrill and satisfaction of that first time would never be eclipsed.

# Kevin Durant

*see* **Double-Team; Negotiating**

Education / Ego / Ejection / Eminem / Escort / Euros /
"Everything Is Everything" / Patrick Ewing

# Education

The difference between Mauldin High and the other schools I'd attended wasn't just the affluence but also the emphasis on academics, which is the main reason Moms moved us there in the first place.

Studies weren't easy for me due to my learning disorders, but luckily I had some great teachers. Shout-out to Miss Willoughby, little white lady, cool as fuck. Never demanding or scolding. Unlike Moms, who got pissed when I couldn't comprehend my reading assignments, Miss Willoughby was patient. She taught geography, which, along with math and science and social studies, was my favorite subject. That was another way the world opened up to me. I could read a map better than I could read a book. I could focus on the seven continents, the great oceans—the Atlantic, the Pacific, the Arctic, the Indian—I could see the planet, imagine different cultures, different languages, different climates, valleys, deserts, and jungles. Geography represented mystery and majesty, snow-covered mountains that soared above the clouds, tiny villages in Africa, sprawling cities in South America. My imagination came alive. My imagination went wild.

Miss Willoughby also got me into history. When she told the story of the Boston Tea Party, for example, she said, "One foggy night in the winter of 1773, at a wharf in Boston Harbor, enraged American colonists disguised as Native Americans secretly boarded English ships and threw hundreds of chests of tea overboard. These were the Sons of Liberty whose mantra was 'no taxation without representation.'" Man, the whole scene came alive, like a movie. She and I connected from day one. I aced all her tests. I felt her passion for teaching and watched her sparkle when my hand was the first one up to answer the tough questions.

Miss Willoughby, together with two other teachers—Mrs. Seidel and Mrs. Cook—encouraged me. Man, did I need encouragement! I'm not sure they were able to identify my ADD, ADHD, and dyslexia, but they sure knew that I was struggling with disorders. And because of that, they didn't ridicule or humiliate me. They helped me with kindness. Without their kindness, I wouldn't have respect for education and righteous teachers. Education and righteous teachers can sometimes do more to change the world than the most powerful politicians. That's because they actually change hearts and mold minds.

# Ego

A strong ego—not an oversized ego—is a must. A strong ego is a right-sized ego.

It helps get you where you need to go. It supplies the fuel required to get you off the ground when it's time to soar. On the court, ego is necessary. But off the court, I would only be egotistical to people using their egotism to bully.

Example: One time in Boston, I go into a bar to pick up some chicken wings. I'm waiting at the bar. Bar is packed. All the seats taken. This girl is sitting next to me, just trying to enjoy a drink. In comes this dude who throws $100 in front of the girl, like, "Fuck you, I'm sittin' here." That's some ugly shit. I can tell the girl is bothered by it but doesn't know what to say. Well, I take that $100 and toss it back at him. I say, "She was here." Should've seen the look on his face. There's this flicker of excitement at seeing me, followed by his sudden realization that he done fucked up. He mumbles some meek-ass apology then quickly disappears into the crowd.

My wings arrive a couple minutes later and I leave. If the dude would've just been patient for a couple of minutes, he could've had my seat. He could've told all his pals who he saw and maybe even struck up a conversation with the chick. Instead, he let his ego get in the way. He headed out hungry and alone.

## Ejection

*see* **Rasheed Wallace**

## Eminem

*see* **The N-Word**

## Escort

The wealth and academics weren't the only difference between Mauldin High and the schools in Greenville. Greenville was all about football and wrestling while in Mauldin hoop was the thing.

I had entered Mauldin High as a 6'6" ninth grader and was named a starter on the varsity basketball team. I wanted #32, Magic's number, but it was taken. So I took #21 for my jersey, thinking of Dominique Wilkins with the Hawks and Malik Sealy

*Junior year at Mauldin High, 1994.*

with St. John's. Malik was the first dude I saw playing at that level who looked like me—skinny and dark-skinned. Back then it wasn't cool to be dark-skinned. It was all about light-skinned dudes. Malik's look helped my own self-esteem.

Freshman year I held my own. I was still developing my offensive game—I'd only average about twelve points a game that year—but I could defend. Pulled down fifteen rebounds and blocked seven shots per game. Sophomore year I doubled my scoring average to around twenty-five points per game. But it was during my junior year, the 1993–94 season, that I really broke out.

The Beach Ball Classic was a highlight, a high school tournament held every year in Myrtle Beach between Christmas and New Year's. It was founded in 1981 by Dan D'Antoni, older brother of Mike, the longtime NBA head coach. Dan is also a basketball lifer. For thirty years he coached at Socastee High School in Myrtle Beach, and he started the Classic to bring attention to South Carolina high school hoopers. By the time I got to Mauldin, it was one of the nation's premier tournaments. Our team went 1–2 before getting knocked out, but I scored 101 points over those three games—including forty in a five-overtime thriller that we pulled out against Los Angeles's Loyola High School.

Bug wasn't at that tournament—it was a four-hour drive from Mauldin to Myrtle—but that was the only game of mine he missed. His parents bought him a stickshift Ford Escort that became our main ride. Loved that car. Didn't matter where I was playing, Bug drove that Escort forty, fifty, sixty miles and got to the game on time. I wasn't bothered not having family in the stands. If Bug was there, all was well.

# Euros

My all-time favorite was Arvydas Sabonis, born in Lithuania. I had tapes of him playing for the USSR. He was a beast. Stood his ground against Ewing and Robinson in the '88 Olympics. He let us

*Arvydas Sabonis, 2002.*

know Americans weren't the only ones who could hoop. Cat was 7 feet 3. Could jump. Play all five positions. Use either hand. Flexible. Fluid. And also cerebral.

In 1995, I met Arvydas in the locker room at the Alamodome in San Antonio. He was back there with his wife as well as one of his sons, who had a headful of crazy hair. Talking in his thick accent and forceful manner, Arvydas had us all enchanted with his stories of taking on the greatest in the game. I just sat there. Could have listened for hours. His own professional story ended sadly cause he blew out both Achilles tendons. Anyone will tell you that after that, you're never the same. You lose your explosiveness. On a happier note, his son with crazy hair was Domantas Sabonis, who made it into the NBA in 2016 with OKC. I consider Domantas's dad one of my heroes.

Other Euros were stupendous. German Dirk Nowitzki. Spanish Pau Gasol. Argentine-Italian Manu Ginóbili.

Did I like how they brought the flopping and the flailing to the game? Sure, why not? It gave them an identity. That Euro step-back move, that one-legged fadeaway off the backboard—all major contributions to NBA style. I loved it when other cultures integrated their skills with ours. Everyone benefited. The internationalization of basketball is one of the great stories in sports history.

The more I traveled, the more I appreciated the European approach. European players don't go to college. They start playing professionally as soon as they're good enough. Ricky Rubio started playing pro at fourteen. Compared to him, Dirk and Luka Dončić were old men when they started at sixteen. Playing pro at that age means ain't nobody got time for immature bullshit. You're playing with grown-ass men who need the money to feed their families and ain't interested in putting up with no prima donnas. That'll make you grow up quick. Not like the American system of basketball, the hype-machine culture of yes-men that starts in AAU. Everybody wanting to cash in on you, everyone kissing your ass and saying things they think you want to hear rather than the things you *need* to hear. So when American players finally get into the league, they gotta overcome all that ego-trippin' in a way that European players don't. Exceptions to the rule exist, obviously. There are some American players who come into the league really mature, and some Euros who can be dicks—think cause they're hot shit abroad that's gonna translate to the NBA. But for the most part, the European model seems better designed to set a player up for success.

Some say the Euro style is soft. Bullshit. What do you think we were doing in Boston? Swinging it around the arc trying to get an open look for Ray or P. What do you think the Warriors were doing during that championship run? That was straight Euro ball. It ain't soft. It's *smart*. And once everybody realized that, once everybody saw all the success a team could have playing like that, everybody started imitating them. Everybody rocking the Eurostep now. If that ain't a part of your game, your game is incomplete.

What you're starting to see now, of course, is the NBA beginning to swing back the other way. Now, after a few years of all these teams going smaller and focusing on wing play and shooting threes, there's a resurgence of big men like Anthony Davis, Joel Embiid, and KAT. Teams are all so small now that nobody can guard the bigs down low or keep them off the glass. Don't be surprised to see big men reassert themselves even more in the coming seasons. That's just how the game goes: it's cyclic, always changing. And that's what makes it beautiful. But the basic principles of the Euro game? Those are here to stay.

## "Everything Is Everything"

I heard this song on *The Miseducation of Lauryn Hill*. This was the late nineties. It was something different that caught my ear. I dug the Fugees, and when Lauryn went out on her own, I paid attention. I heard her say that what's meant to be will be. She was talkin' 'bout the certainty of change but also questioning the rules. She

| Favorite R&B |
| --- |
| **1** S.O.S. Band |
| **2** Luther Vandross |
| **3** Alexander O'Neal |
| **4** New Edition |
| **5** Jodeci |
| **6** Stephanie Mills |

was slick, telling us to hear her "mixture where hip-hop meets scripture." Made me think. Made me look at my own mixture, the mixture of life changes. She was rappin' 'bout adaptin'.

"Everything is everything" also means that hip-hop, R&B, break dancing, jazz all melds together. Just like sports. Just like hoop. Different forms of art, different forms of expression, but all of them based on life experience. And none of it is possible without understanding improvisation. No matter how prepared you may be, no matter how tight your game, once you're on the floor, everything changes. You hear things, see things, feel things you never felt before. You fly without a net. You make it up on the spot.

*Lauryn Hill performs at the Billboard Music Awards, 1998.*

## Patrick Ewing

*see* **The Courts; Euros; LeBron James; John Thompson; Zero Fucks**

Facts / *Family Guy* / *Family Matters* /
Fans / Father Figures / Ronnie Fields / Steve Fisher /
Fists / Aretha Franklin / The Fun Police

# Facts

If you're going to be a hothead, be a factual hothead. Be an about-information hothead. When you speak, speak with conviction, speak with facts, and back your facts up with even more facts.

## Family Guy

Big game coming up. Maybe even a playoff game. Night before I'm obsessing like a muthafucka. Can't think about nothing 'cept how I gotta strategize, who I'm going up against, how I'm gonna play this player, how I'm gonna work it different, gonna be creative, surprising, strong, crafty.

There comes a point, though, where you can think about something too much. When you gotta shut your mind off and get some rest. That's when I'd switch on *Family Guy*.

Something about the silliness of that show got my mind to stop racing. Beyond being some funny shit, *Family Guy* also comes up with the kind of smart-ass sarcasm that draws me into its make-believe world. There are other pregame rituals I'd come to embrace, but that cartoon was definitely one of the secrets to my success.

As Peter Griffin, the family guy himself, would say, "Heeee heeeee heeee heeee!"

Family Guy *always helped me unwind during the season.*

## Family Matters

*see* **The Go**

## Fans

In another player's book, this entry might fall under other "F" words like "fickle" or "fair-weather." And it's true: fans can be nasty. Look how they did LeBron when he left Cleveland, burning his jerseys. Look at the racist shit that Utah Jazz fans were spewing at Russell Westbrook. Ain't no need for that. Danny Green misses a shot in the finals and he's getting death threats? Ain't no place for that kind of behavior.

I'm not one of those cats who's gonna say "It's only a game." It was never "only a game" to me. For me, basketball truly was life or death. If I didn't have the game, there's a good chance I wouldn't be here right now. Without the game, I could have easily wound up a lost soul. I know a lot of sports fans also need their games in the worst way. Maybe you're experiencing some real hurt and heartache. Maybe you had a parent who you couldn't communicate with, but the one thing you could

always talk about was sports. Maybe your parents passed away and you see your team winning the championship as the ultimate way of saying goodbye to them. Or maybe you or somebody you care about is going through an illness, and every game your team wins gives you another jolt of inspiration and another game to look forward to, something to distract from the sickness. I understand why a fan can get so wrapped up in a team's success that they don't behave rationally. That's the power of sports— and hoop in particular. Like poetry and music and art, hoop gives fans the opportunity to transcend their rational selves, to bask in an otherworldly beauty and let themselves be overcome with emotion. Yes, hoop is absolutely more than a game.

*Waving to the 'Sota fans during my first return to the Target Center since joining the C's, February 2008.*

But not to the point where fans should abandon all sense of human decency.

I don't count booing in that. Fans pay their money, they got a right to boo. If I play like shit, I deserve to get my ass booed out of the building. Actually I loved it when the opposing team's fans booed me. That just drove me more. Better for them if the whole arena just went silent when I touched the ball. Booing me makes me stronger.

But I gotta say that I've been lucky with fans. On every team I've played, fans have shown me much love. Never will forget the first time I came back to Minnie after getting traded to Boston. February 8, 2008. I had an abdominal strain. It was my sixth game in a row where I couldn't play. I decided not to watch the game from the bench because I didn't want to distract the C's from business. Besides, my injury made it hard for me to maneuver. Walking wasn't easy. Easier to sit the whole thing out.

"Don't," said Doc. "You gave twelve years of your life to those fans and they want to have a couple of minutes with you. Give it to 'em. You deserve it. They deserve it. It's the right thing to do."

So, before the game, I came out from the tunnel in my street clothes to quickly wave to the fans. Then the public-address announcer, Rod Johnson, came over the house speakers and introduced me just like old times: "At this time we would like to extend a very special welcome to a player making his return to the Target Center. Ladies and gentlemen, at six foot eleven, number twenty-one, out of Farragut Academy High Schoooool, please welcome Kevin Garrrr-nett!" Puttin' the stank on that last syllable like he always did.

With me gone, the T-Wolves had not been drawing the kind of crowds they were used to. But that night the place was sold out, and the nearly twenty thousand in attendance gave me a standing ovation. Doc was right. It was a beautiful moment. On a chilly Minnie night, I suddenly felt warm all over.

# Father Figures

Before James "Duke" Fisher, coach at Mauldin High, most of my coaches were low rent. Coach Fisher was different. He was rough. He was intense. Country. Stubborn SOB. Half his white skin was partially peeled off because of a motorcycle accident. He looked like burn victim Fire Marshall Bill, played by Jim Carrey on *In Living Color*. Coach Fisher coached basketball and football, but football was his first love and it was with a football attitude that he approached hoop. He was a drill sergeant. I didn't complain then and I ain't complaining now. I needed discipline. I responded to discipline. I liked it. Early on, I saw how discipline on the court was giving my life direction. Didn't give a shit that Coach Fisher was a redneck and always on my case, screaming, "Get your ass moving!" even when I thought I was moving as fast as I could. He knew I could move faster. One other thing about Coach Fisher: he had a good heart. I could feel that. We came from radically different backgrounds, but I never picked up a racist vibe. If he got in my face, it wasn't cause I was Black. It was cause I wasn't working hard enough.

Shout-out to one of my first AAU coaches—Bull. He was a white guy who treated Black kids like his sons. Bull would get all the misfits who didn't get chosen for the big tournaments and take us under his wing. Knowing that a lot of the young dudes were hungry, he'd take us to Carolina Fine Foods that had those big wedgy fries and juicy old-school burgers. If we playing another team and they playing dirty, watch Bull go after their coach. He'd fight for us. You got a problem with your dad or stepdad, Bull went home with you to try to straighten it out. Bull was the confidence. Bull would outbully the bullies who be bullying you. Bull was one throwback brotha you could count on. Another father figure for a kid like me who could use all the father figures I could get. Mainly cause my real father and stepfather were figures I was happy to forget.

My first big-time camp was 1992. First time I got on a plane. First time I was traveling far for basketball. I'd been invited to the Nike camp and man, I was stoked. There were two camps for high school players—Nike and Adidas. Adidas got guys like Shareef and Tractor Traylor. Adidas was in New Jersey; Nike was in Indianapolis. Both camps were loaded with talent.

Three men ran the Nike camp. They were all brothas. First was Horace Brown. He was the god, the recruiter, the guy who let you in. He loved my humbleness and my respect factor.

"How you doing, young man?" he asked when I first arrived.

"Fine, sir."

"Where are you from?"

"South Carolina, sir."

"What's your name?"

"Kevin Garnett, sir."

"Well, I'm Horace Brown and I run this thing and I have my eye on you. I like your game."

The assistant coach, Ron Eskridge, was an older cat from Philly. He was rocking a small puffy afro, a velour Nike suit, gold chain, cool gold watch. Manicured to the T. Looked like Teddy Pendergrass. Smooth cat. But as a former Marine, Coach E also had a discipline that could put off a lot of people. But I figured that mentality was good for me.

"Yo, K," he said. "I seen you on tape. You might think you're hot stuff, but in the Marines you wouldn't last a day."

Maybe not, but when I got on the floor and launched my shit, he decided that maybe I'd last after all. His approach was all about dunking.

"Don't lay nothing back up," he demanded. "Dunk everything in."

"Yes, Coach E."

I locked into everything he said. But, me being me, I had to do more. I had to do my pump-faking.

"No pumping," Eskridge screamed. "Just dunking!"

So I dunked and punctuated the dunk with a "Fuck you!"

"That's what I'm talkin' 'bout!" he hollered.

He liked me cussin' and getting more vocal. He also taunted me.

"This kid you up against today is gonna pound you," he said. "No way you can grab twenty rebounds."

I grabbed twenty-four.

Coach E was a motivator, but the motivator in chief, the man who changed me forever, was William "Wolf" Nelson.

He became my basketball father. I owe him the world. He had a kindly face, wore black-rimmed glasses, and spoke fast, bursting with ideas. Our connection was steely strong. I saw he had information. He saw I had talent. I gave him respect that he gave back to me threefold.

You gotta remember that up until Wolf, with the exception of Duke Fisher, I had dealt with a lot of over-the-hill, rundown coaches. Wolf was a proud Black man committed to bringing out the best in his players. At the time, I didn't know about his great reputation as the coach of Farragut Career Academy in Chicago. Wolf wasn't someone who talked about himself. He talked about you.

There were great players on our Nike team. Ronnie Fields, who played for Wolf at Farragut, looked like the next Air Jordan at 6'3". Andre Patterson was unbelievable. Dre was a supercool dude. The Bailey Brothers—David and Martell—were cold. Ricky Price was a monster. All these stars, and yet Wolf found time to focus on me. He saw my insecurities and knew how to lay them to rest.

Wolf: "Hey, K, bring up the ball."

Me: "What?"

Wolf: "You heard right. Bring up the ball."

Me: "Damn. You want me to play point?"

Wolf: "Hell, yes, play point. Play everything. Do it all."

And then he'd walk off the court to leave me to my own devices.

After practice, he'd come over and say, "Look, I see you dribbling every morning. I know you can handle the ball. No reason not to branch out. Scouts are scouring this joint, and they need to see your versatility. Don't be afraid of what you can't do. Believe in what you can."

Like Coach E, Wolf brought out my boisterousness.

"If it's in you," he said, "let it come out. When you dunk, I want you swingin' on the rim, I want you growlin', I want you sweatin' and smellin', I wanna see that beast."

# Ronnie Fields

*see* **Dunk; Father Figures; Fists; Getaway; Michael Jordan**

# Steve Fisher

The summer before my senior year, I was named South Carolina's Mr. Basketball. Scouts and coaches started coming around in droves. I saw them pulling up on me in weird places. I might be walking down the street, and suddenly some dude was next to me talking up his college. I also learned about the bag men. Guys with bags of money from schools interested in keeping you happy and interested in them. I didn't fool with any of that shit. I wasn't looking for money.

At Springfield Park, some dude might drop off a bag full of Adidas gear. Another cat might drop a Converse bag filled with bread. I saw those bags as traps, so I didn't fuck with 'em. I'd tell the dawgs hanging around the courts, "You take 'em." And they did.

College recruitment was always weird. Cats showing up at restaurants, at football games, following me around. They'd be wearing a Clemson shirt or a South Carolina Gamecocks hat or some other school gear. The way they looked at me and nodded gave me the creeps. I stayed away.

That doesn't mean I wasn't impressed when more legit cats like Steve Fisher, the coach at the University of Michigan, first invited me to visit the campus at Ann Arbor. I refused the initial invitation, but I went later.

"I have this routine, sir," I told Coach Fisher. "You're welcome to come down and see me go through it."

Fisher got in his car and drove the seven hundred miles to South Carolina.

The routine was simple: I went to the park at 10 a.m. and coached the little kids till noon. Then I had lunch and came back to the park and played with dudes my own age. That went on for three, four hours till dinnertime. After eating, I'm in the park again taking on the OGs. That's more brutal and more fun. They looking to slap me down and I'm looking to win their respect. By the end of the day, I've hooped nine or ten hours.

Coach Fisher liked what he saw, but I wasn't ready to sit down for any serious discussion. Fisher wasn't the only one who came calling. Here's Jerry Tarkanian of Fresno State. Here's Bobby Cremins of Georgia Tech. I loved college basketball; Bug and I watched it all the time, followed the stats, and knew these men were the best coaches in the country. As each of them approached me to say nice things, I was polite but distant. Meanwhile, my head was spinning, my mind jumping ahead to college. It was all being laid out there for me. The big picture. The big future.

*In 1994, when I was still dreaming of playing college ball at Michigan.*

During those recruiting days, one recruiter made a big mistake. I was at Grandma Mil's house when he came over. He thought he'd make headway with me by buttering her up. He started to charm her—or so he thought—saying how great his college was and what he'd do for her personally. He even put a bag of money on the floor. Grandma Mil didn't say a word. Just got up and went to her tiny bedroom. Her whole house was tiny, so tiny I could hear the creak of the closet opening and then a click. I knew what that click meant. She was messing with her shotgun.

"Tell your friend he's got thirty seconds to get the fuck outta here," she shouted from her bedroom.

"What are you talking about?" said the recruiter. "I've brought—"

"Don't care what he brought. I'm gonna spread his ass all over the front lawn."

"Mister," I said, "this is for real. Run." And he did, grabbing the money bag before he split.

Grandma appeared with her shotgun in hand.

"Glad he's gone," she said, "cause, Kevin, I don't want you taking money from someone like that. I believe he was trying to get you to do something you shouldn't do."

"Yes, ma'am."

Grandma Mil taught me a lesson I'd never forget: Don't ever make money your major motivation.

# Fists

I realize that the civil rights movement that lifted up Black folks was based on nonviolence. Dr. King preached nonviolence. And, given that moment of history, nonviolence worked. Bills got passed. Changes got made. But in the life of a tall skinny kid with some hoop skills looking to survive and thrive in the environment of high school, nonviolence was not an option. Fighting was required. Moms had taught me that. The playgrounds and streets said Moms was right.

A huge fight marked the end of life in South Carolina. The fight was a turning point. It was a choice I made. It's the biggest thing that ever happened to me in high school. At the time I thought it was the worst thing. Looking back, though, I see it might have been the best thing. I certainly didn't see it coming. Maybe you never see these things coming. I'm talkin' 'bout events that overturn your life and threaten your peace of mind. Events that bust you in the gut till you ain't sure you'll ever recover.

One school day followed another. High school was high school. Mainly hoop, but also a few dope classes with Miss Willoughby.

It was the afternoon. I was walking down the hallway at Mauldin. Heard some noise. Looked over and saw a scuffle. Turned out that my homeboy Trey was in trouble. Trey was always kicking the soccer ball around the streets. He's the educated Black kid on the block. He was also the only Black kid on the all-white soccer team. Not a rough guy. Regular guy. Nice guy. Had both his parents and a dope sister. But for reasons I didn't know, some white kids had jumped him and were beating him down. Bullying ain't something I could stand around and just watch. I'm going after the bullies. Me and my boys separate Trey from the bullies, but then there's pushing and shoving and suddenly all hell breaks loose. It's a melee. Fists are flying. Bones are cracking. We tearing up the hallway like the Tasmanian Devil. I'm getting hit. I'm hittin'. I'm getting cracked. I'm crackin'. Fuckin' mayhem. Blows to the head. Kicks to the groin. Going so fast, knockin' out muthafuckas, getting wilder by the minute. The escalation is fierce. After the damage is done, we back off. We make a point. We have protected Trey, but in the process, we've inflicted serious injuries.

I knew it was a big deal, but what I didn't know was that the father of one of the kids who got beat up went to the law. The law came to school and suddenly we were being accused of mob action. The law said that lynching is part of mob action, even though no one was lynched. South Carolina law was fucked up. The original lynching law was to keep whites from lynching Blacks, but then the powers turned it around and interpreted the statute as any action of violence by two or more people against anyone. Instead of being reprimanded for plain ol' fighting, getting detention, or at worst suspension, we were being arrested for lynching.

When it came to the investigation of how it all went down, some of my boys turned on me. Not Bug. Bug remained loyal. Bug knew I wasn't the instigator, but for the other brothas looking to lighten their punishment, pointing me out as the main culprit helped their case. Until then, I knew nothing about betrayal. I was stunned and hurt. Facts were twisted so they could get off and I couldn't. Not only was I eventually expelled, I was facing jail time. From then on, I was on probation.

This fucked me up bad. I had never faced such a situation. Until then, the road ahead was clear. Senior year at Mauldin, hoop my brains out, get a scholarship to Michigan or North Carolina. Make my mark with the college big boys. Now, forget all that. Deal with a new reality. Now I'm inside the so-called criminal justice system, where everyone knows there ain't no justice. I have to deal with lawyers and court hearings.

At the time I was living in a friend's basement because the recruiters were chasing after me so hard. I didn't want to deal with those crazy recruiters.

Then came the day I was sitting in Miss Willoughby's class when police officers entered. They were looking for me. I was set to bolt. Just jump through the window and run like the wind. Miss Willoughby stopped me. I don't think anyone else could have.

"No, Kevin, you let these men do their duty. Don't make it worse for yourself. It'll all work out. You'll see. Just stay calm. I'm going to vouch for you. I'm going to support you."

I was taken away in handcuffs. I was arrested but released until trial. The charge was lynching. They said I started a race riot.

Making matters worse, there were rumors that said redneck boys were out here looking for me.

Before the incident, I was still a goofy kid. Other than hoop, I didn't take life seriously. Now everything was serious. Miss Willoughby was serious about keeping her word. Even though I'd been expelled and couldn't go to school, she brought me homework. She wanted to make sure that if I transferred out of Mauldin, I'd get credit for the courses I was taking.

That summer I was granted special permission to make a quick trip to Deerfield for my second Nike camp. No chance to see any of the city cause the camp was a bubble. I nearly didn't make it into the camp, not cause of my skills but because of Moms. She had no interest in taking me there. Because a legal guardian was required for a kid to gain admittance, I had to give the illusion that I lived in the area with my parents. That meant cutting bureaucratic corners. Shout-out to Ronnie Fields, who actually did have his home around there and let me use his address on the forms.

It was great to see Wolf again. Great to see Ron Eskridge. I played my heart out; got mentioned in the *Chicago Tribune*, along with Ron Mercer and Schea Cotton, as a high school standout. All good.

Back in Carolina, all bad. My legal situation was still looming. Even though that charge of lynching was bullshit, they had me on assault. I was given parole, but the South Carolina penal system was rigged to the point where I could have been put away for sneezing in front of a cop. Moms didn't want to take any chances.

By then my older sister, Sonya, was out of the house. It was just me, baby sis Ashley, Moms, and my stepdad.

What to do?

# Aretha Franklin

*see* "King Kunta"; One-and-Done; Prince

# The Fun Police

*see* Shoes; *Uncut Gems*

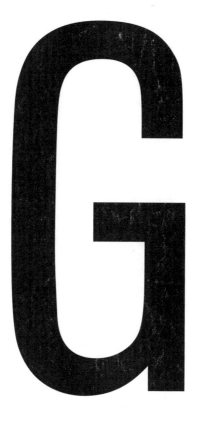

Kenny G / Gatorade and Coffee / Getaway /
The Go / The Great Kabuki / Growing Up

# Kenny G

Maybe because I get off on DMX, Snoop, 2 Live Crew, and Wu-Tang you might think I don't get Kenny G. You're wrong. I love me some Kenny G.

When the trade to Boston came down, I knew the switch would have to do with more than hoop. Doc Rivers helped me out in that area.

"Kevin," he said, "you're intense, and I love your intensity. You're competitive, and I love your competitiveness. But sometimes intensity can be too intense. Sometimes competitiveness can be too much. In order to be effective, sometimes you gotta turn down the heat, because rather than helping you, the heat can hurt you."

Made sense. I thought I ingested Doc's insight, but when we were in the 2008 finals and had a chance to knock out the Lakers in Game 6, I was so hyped up before the game that he made me come to his office. While he went over last-minute reports on his desk, I sat across from him.

"Just sit, Kevin," he said. "Just breathe."

To keep from moving, I had to tell myself, *I'm in a time-out; I'm in a time-out.*

Later Doc said in an interview, "You think about a guy who's been in the league that long and still that jacked up for a game that you literally have to calm him down. That's KG, and that's my favorite KG story."

I was blessed that Doc had a profound understanding of hyperactive hoopers. He also had a profound understanding of me. Before I even got to Boston, he had called my old coaches—every single one—for long discussions. He got the deepest download on me possible.

"Every coach says the same thing about you, KG," he told me. "You play hard as anyone, you love the game, you work tirelessly, you're the best teammate on the squad, and you're stubborn as fuck."

Doc also saw that my stubbornness went with restlessness and over-the-top energy. Through my time in Boston, he helped me tame that energy. Doc helped me with everything.

But recognizing wisdom and enacting wisdom are two different things. I couldn't just tell myself to chill. I had to find ways to create that chill. Watching *Family Guy* was one way. Music was another. It wasn't that I gave up on hip-hop. I was way into Kanye. Kanye and Kenny G were the only music I was bangin' when I first got to Boston. The combination of the two reflected the way I was playing—rugged but smoothed out. My hoop style was being remolded by those two musical modes. You might compare it to a wooden floor that, even though it was sanded once, gets another sanding to get rid of all the splinters.

*Kenny G, 2008.*

I heard Kenny G as a snake charmer. Listening to his soprano sax, I'd sit there and close my eyes and see my thoughts. Kenny G got me to a different place, a new realm of relaxation.

So there I was, checking in to the hotel suite the night before the game. I light a few scented candles. Sit and just breathe. Breathe for five, ten, fifteen minutes. Remember how breathing don't require effort. We're all born to breathe. Now, once I'm into the ease of breathing, I switch on the quiet storm station. Sade. Old-school smooth jazz like George Benson. Soft ballads. Gentle grooves. Before you know it, the chill is there.

Take the wooden mallet and strike the chiming bowl. Listen to the vibrations fill the room before they go silent. Sip a little herbal tea. Call up the masseur to do some cupping on my back. Welcome relaxation. Value relaxation. Understand that deep relaxation is the key to de-stressing my system.

Call the experts to find the best hyperbaric chamber out there. Install it in the crib and use it all the time. The hyperbaric chamber is a natural healer. Does wonders for the body as well as the mind. Dial up new synergy to release toxins. Discover New Age, new waves, new ways to ride my waves, new ways to clean my chakras.

The mind is all about manifestation. Looking back, I realize that I manifested this move to Boston. I saw it before it happened. The mind's powerful. But you can't command it like it's a soldier. It don't obey demands. It don't do what you want just cause you yell at it. You gotta respect it. You gotta let it find its own peace. And if you wanna manifest—if you wanna see your life move in a different direction—that manifestation is a subtle thing. Hit your mind with a hammer and your mind turns to mush. Treat it like a precious jewel and, like a jewel, it'll give off light in a thousand directions. Choose which direction you wanna follow. Let the mind manifest but do it tenderly. Without tenderness, you ain't going nowhere.

They call the greatest hoopers—Jordan, Wilt, Shaq, Bean, Bron—beasts. Well, can a beast incorporate tenderness into his life? If he can, he'll expand his greatness. If he can't, he'll go nuts. It's all a matter of finding true balance.

## Gatorade and Coffee

see **Insomnia**

## Getaway

After weeks of wondering what would happen after being expelled, I was on edge. Now I was finally facing the big court date in Greenville. Moms picked me up at the friend's house where I'd been staying. She had Ashley with her. What I didn't know was that Ashley's bags and mine were packed up and sitting in the trunk of her car. At court they gave me probation. My hired lawyer argued for the probation to be transferred to Chicago. Chicago considered this so-called lynching a misdemeanor that carried a $50 fine. In Carolina it was practically a capital offense. The court allowed the transference. We got back in the car and headed straight to the airport.

We boarded the plane, the three of us squeezed in the last row of coach. I had the aisle seat, but there was still no room for my long legs.

I had questions, but Moms was close-lipped. Better leave Moms alone. The energy she was giving off was firm and standoffish.

Heavy turbulence. Thunderstorms and lightning knifing through the East Coast and following us west. The sky felt angry. I know I was angry. Angry that I was getting no explanations. Angry that my life looked like it was spinning out of control. But what to do with the anger? Moms wasn't about to put up with anyone's anger. Moms was sleeping. Turbulence got worse. Turbulence didn't bother Moms, but turbulence got Ashley scared and grabbing on to my arm. I was supposed to act brave for my little sister. I faked it. But inside I was as scared as her.

Plane plopped down at Midway Airport. Hard landing. But at least we were all in one piece. Took forever to deplane. Moms still wasn't talking, still not giving even a small hint of what would happen next.

We followed her to baggage claim. Waited there for twenty minutes until the suitcases came down. I grabbed Ashley's and mine.

"Okay, kids," said Moms. "Let me give you a hug."

She gave me a half-assed hug.

"Take care of your sister, Kevin."

"Where you going?" I asked.

"Back home."

And before either of us could stop her, Moms turned around and headed back into the departure part of the terminal where, that very day, she caught the next plane back to Carolina.

Ashley and I were standing there, our bags in hand.

I was eighteen, Ashley fourteen.

It was the wrong time for me, the big brother, to break down and cry, but, brother, that's just what I did. I cried like a baby. At that moment, Ashley had to mother me.

"We gonna be okay," she said.

I finally caught my composure. I realized that Moms had trained us.

"Y'all aren't dumb kids," she used to say. "Y'all been working since you were little."

Moms was cold, but she realized her coldness was one of the reasons we could survive.

My instincts kicked in. Who did I know in Chicago? Wolf. Wolf lives in Chicago. Get some change. Go to the phone booth to call Wolf. See the phone book hanging off a chain. Pick up the book and search for Wolf's number. But Wolf's name is William Nelson. You know how many William Nelsons live in Chicago? Hundreds. I didn't know where to start. Besides, I didn't have enough dimes to keep calling.

Next I looked up Ron Eskridge. There were less Ron Eskridges than William Nelsons, but too many to call. Finally, I caught an idea. I'd call Farragut Career Academy, where Wolf coached. I remembered Wolf mentioning the principal, and I asked for him by name.

"Mr. Guerra, this is Kevin Garnett."

"Oh yes, Kevin. Good to hear from you. Coach Nelson's told me a lot about you."

"He has?"

"Yes, indeed."

"Well, sir, I need to speak to Coach Nelson."

"Of course. Let me give you his cell number."

*Cell?* I didn't even know what a cell was. He gave me the number. I dialed. Rang once. Rang twice. On the third ring, he picked up.

"Wolf? It's Kevin."

"Hey, man, what's up with you? Where you at?"

"Midway."

"Midway?"

"Here with my sister Ashley."

"Go out front and stand there. I'm coming for y'all right now."

No more than thirty minutes passed before Wolf showed up in a Cadillac sedan. I've never been so happy to see anyone. As he drove us to where he lived, my eyes were bugging out of my head. Chicago. Nothing like Greenville. Nothing like Atlanta. Spread out. Giant skyscrapers. Dilapidated buildings. Broken glass storefronts. One neighborhood funkier than the other. War-torn country. Too much to take in. My mind about to explode.

"It's all good," said Wolf as we got to his apartment. "Y'all can stay here until I find you a place of your own."

That night he called Moms to tell her he had us.

"What did Moms say?" I asked Wolf when he got off the phone.

"She said she hated to put all this on me, but she knew I was a good man. She knew you'd come looking for me. And she knew I'd get you to where you need to be. You need to be at Farragut. I've already made the arrangements."

At the time, Wolf had no children, girlfriend, or major responsibilities. He really had no life except the kids he coached.

Ashley slept on Wolf's couch. I slept on the floor. That was the start of the most important year of my life.

# The Go

Mauldin didn't prepare me for high school in Chicago. Not even close. Carolina is country, Chicago is concrete. The geography of Carolina is simple. Chicago geography is scrambled. I'd dreamed of going to Chicago, a city that some brothas liked calling the Go.

That quick trip to Deerfield for the Nike camp didn't give me time to see the large landscape. But in my boyhood dreams I had seen the Sears Tower. I wanted to see where they filmed *Family Matters*, my favorite show, which of course was filmed in Hollywood, but what did I know? I took make-believe Chicago to be actual Chicago. I lived in that illusion. Lived in that naiveness.

But when I actually found myself in brick-building, bust-your-ass, real-life Chicago, I saw that if I didn't hurry up and figure it out, I'd either break down or get put down. I remember Nas, the rapper's rapper, saying, "You have to keep your vision clear, cause only a coward lives in fear." I worked hard to keep my vision clear.

Hoop was the healer. The Go was hoop crazy. I could always heal my wounded heart by hooping. In Chicago, everyone wanted to play all the time. Hoop was the great escape. My emotional survival was all tied up in getting to some court, no matter how run-down, and giving it all I got. That's the shit that kept me sane.

But keeping sane and keeping alive in the Go are two separate issues. The gang geography of the Go is not sane. It's nuts. The grid isn't made of straight angles that are easy to decipher. I was living in a Vice Lord neighborhood. That's one gang. But then you got the Stones, you got the BDs, GDs, you got the Latin Kings. Where are the borders? The boundaries? Wolf helped me understand the setup, but the setup was always in flux. Say the Latin Kings won a battle and suddenly enlarged their territory. You got to know about that. You gotta read the streets, and read 'em right, every single day. Wolf pushed me out on the streets, figuring I'd find my way.

"Everything's gonna work out," Wolf told me. "Can't nothing stop you now, son; you here, you here where you need to be, you got your eyes open, you got your nose open, you got a brain in your head and a pep in your step, you getting where you need to go, you doing what you need to do, you a quick learner, quick study, ain't nothing you can't figure out."

I see dudes from Mississippi running some neighborhoods. Mississippi brothas take to Carolina brothas. We get to choppin' and they see I'm humble, I'm quiet, I'm to myself. I'm very chill, but man, when we start hooping, I light up. The animal comes out. Some brothas love that. Some don't.

*The Chicago skyline.*

Played ball every single day. Saw that as a West Sider you can't go just anywhere and play. You can't go to the Wild Hundreds and hoop. Can't go to Kennedy-King and not have no problems. Stay outta Coffin Corner. That's the most dangerous shit in the world. K-Town is rough. K-Town is the serious hood. Split up in different blocks. Sixteenth Street is the holy city. Everything coming through Sixteenth Street. Ridgeway is our street, where the brothas be chillin'. Other streets ain't chilled. Learning the rules. South Side rules ain't West Side rules. You best know the difference. You best be on alert.

Up here big men could handle the ball, do a lot of agile shit. Brothas in the street that didn't go to college are just as good as brothas in college. Met so many ill brothas in the street. Nick Irving. Playing against ex-NBA players like Big Alvin Robertson and Derrick "The Band-Aid Man" Chievous. Legendary cats. Talent at every turn. Meeting new characters every day.

Here comes Dad Woods. He has his own gab. He has his own bop. He's cool people. Dad Woods got him a bunch of hair. He's respected in the streets. He's super friends with Ronnie Fields. The ladies love him. He's another guide who walks me through the maze. Dad Woods takes his time to school me right. He don't gotta do that. He takes me under his wing just because he's cool people. He loves Farragut with all his heart. Older cat who runs the neighborhood. Beautiful cat who gets killed before his time. Rest in peace, Dad Woods.

Bug came to Chicago that summer to visit me. I couldn't have been happier. Having Bug around lifted my spirits. Showed him the Sears Tower. Showed him the lake. Showed him where the Bulls played, where the Bears played, where the L ran around the Loop like a roller-coaster ride.

Thought Bug would stay the whole summer, but after five days his mom showed up in the city and didn't like what she saw. I had dreams of Bug attending Farragut with me, but Mrs. Peters wasn't playing that. She was protective. I understood. But I also knew that sooner or later Bug would be back in my life.

After Bug left, I kept moving through the Go. One day I moved from my Vice Lord hood to the Village that was run by the GDs. My passport to that territory was Mike "Black" Wright. He lived there and secured me permission to play on the Village court. I stayed humble and respectful. That attitude saved my life, cause in the middle of a game things got rough. Gangbangers ain't your typical fans on the sideline. If they think you committed a dirty foul, they might break out their artillery and aim it in your direction. Like anyone else, I get nervous when a gun is pointed at me. But fortunately, I'd learned the gift of gab from both Moms and Grandma Mil.

I said something like, "We hooping hard cause that's all we know. If we came here and didn't play hard, if we took it easy and didn't take your game seriously like it deserves to be taken, we'd be disrespectin' you. And we ain't about that. We about respect. You feel me?"

After several moments of nervous silence, the brothas backed off.

In the Go, my gab got better. It had to. It was a matter of life and death. It also helped being a chameleon. I could change according to changing circumstances. I figured out how to fit in and, no matter how great the danger, I kept my cool. I avoided violence in a city where violence seemed unavoidable.

## The Great Kabuki

As a kid I was obsessed with break dancing, skateboarding, and wrestling. Especially wrestling. Saturday at noon. Don't turn the channel. If you do, I'll fight you. I'll wrestle you. I'll put you in a figure-four leg lock or a sleeper hold. After the show, I meet my boys outside and we go over the moves. We start making our own belts. Go through the garbage to see if someone threw out some old carpet, cardboard, or even pizza boxes. Cut it up in the shape of a big-ass belt like Tully Blanchard wears. Take a marker and write "World Heavyweight Champ" all over it. Wear that joint around the neighborhood like I earned it. Wrestle the other brothas in the neighborhood. Keep it to wrestling, but if someone throws a punch, throw a punch back. Thin line between wrestling and full-out fighting.

I followed the TV wrestlers cause they represented strength. They also had storylines. They were characters out of comic books, except they weren't drawings. They were real. And also fake. We knew they were fake and didn't care, cause fake was part of their entertainment. Fake was funny. Fake was exciting. Fake had 'em body-slamming, choking, poking, kicking, picking a brotha up over his head, twirling him around, and throwing his ass over the ropes into the screaming crowd.

I loved the WWF. Jake "the Snake" Roberts opening up his burlap sack and pulling out a twenty-foot-long python. But I also loved the wrestlers who came before, guys like Dusty Rhodes and The Great Kabuki. Before the WWF went national, pro wrestling was a bunch of regional outfits scattered across the country. They were shabby, small-budget productions, but to a little kid like me they were mind-blowing. Kabuki especially—the way he painted his face white and sprayed poison green mist in his opponents' eyes. Him as well as Bruce Lee movies got me curious early on about Asian culture—a curiosity I'd get to

explore in my travels many years later. (Quick fact about Bruce: I'd later find out that before he became the greatest martial artist of all time, he was a champion cha-cha dancer growing up in Hong Kong. That made me smile, thinking of how my own dancing as a kid influenced my life path.)

Kabuki and those other wrestlers taught me about showmanship. How to get the crowd on your side, or how to turn the crowd against you—which can give you even more energy than when the fans have your back. A lot of the way I expressed myself on the court was inspired by what I saw watching wrestling as a kid.

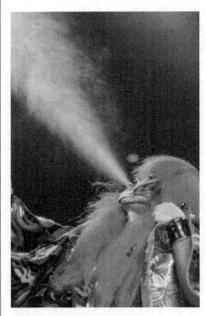

*The Great Kabuki with the iconic mist spray.*

When I got to Boston, for example, I remembered thinking about Kabuki's green mist. For a second, I wondered if I could incorporate that into my pregame ritual. Something like the chalk. Spray green mist in the air and get the crowd hyped. No way to do that without making a mess, though there was one time in the 2012 season when I did a version of it.

We were playing the Wizards. It was a close game late in the fourth. I came to the bench for a time-out, grabbed a cup of water, threw it in my face, and sprayed it into the air Kabuki-style. By that point in Boston, nothing I did surprised my teammates. But Doe was sitting next to me, and he gave me a startled look like, *What was that, bro?*

That was me bringing out my inner Kabuki.

## Growing Up

I had the responsibility of caring for Ashley and making sure her schooling was set up. Learning the train system. Hoppin' on the L, droppin' her off, pickin' her up. Making sure she's okay in the crib. Then headin' out to hoop.

I also had to make enough money to put food on the table and a roof over our heads. That meant odd jobs. That also meant something called the infamous Midnight League. Turned out to be the most competitive league I'd ever played in. That was where all the shenanigans were going on. Midnight League was strictly a Chicago institution. No outsiders allowed. I joined Solid Gold, my one and only Midnight League team.

We had jerseys and coaches and played to win.

It was a whole wild scene: folks of all ages came out to watch. Electric. Exciting. Big fun. Big noise. Boom boxes blasting. Fine chicks flashing. Side bets over here, side bets over there, yelling and screaming and laughing, trash-talking, pot smoking, beer drinking, and, you better believe, brothas bangin' hard on the court. Anything might happen. Dice games. Dancing. Cats breaking out in fights. But overall, the carnival vibe was positive. The league had a beauty all its own.

Keep in mind that these games, at the midnight hour, came after I'd already played four or five hours during the day. Yet I never saw them as burdens. I embraced them with gratitude. If you're a young hot hooper living in the Go, you wanna build up your rep. And the Midnight League provided another stage where you got to prove yourself and also make some change.

What a city! The hooping, the gang hierarchy, the ever-changing street scene: sometimes it scrambled my brain. My head was on a swivel. Got your hat on wrong, get your head blown up. Hike up your pants wrong, get your leg shot up. If Carolina moved at twenty-five miles per hour, Chicago moved at two hundred. I learned that gang life is every day. It ain't no stop-and-play. You can hoop all week and maybe take off Sunday. But gang life is 24/7. It's a true lifestyle. And it may not be you. It might be the brotha sitting next to you who's on the wrong side of a gang—and you know nothing about it. Or you might be mistaken for some other dude who's 6'6" or 6'7". With everyone wearing hoodies, it's easy to make a mistake. And in this world, a mistake can be fatal.

Slick-talkin' muthafuckas everywhere. Hustlers. Pimps. Brothas trying to swindle you outta bread. Brothas bettin' on you. Brothas bettin' against you. Who to believe? Who not to believe? Who to trust? Who to challenge? Who to go to? Who to run from? Cutlass pulling up bumpin' the latest Crucial Conflict. Who's inside? Friend or foe? Make it a point to make no foes. Make points on the court. Keep it on the court. No need to affiliate with any one crew. You a freelancer. You loose. You playing at Kennedy-King only on Saturday. You going to Malcolm X. You going to the Boys & Girls Club on Roosevelt. You at Argyle Park. Wild Hundreds. De La Salle. You everywhere.

By the time September came round, I'd downloaded the Go enough to know how to move through the city. Now it was time to move through my senior year. Time to get down.

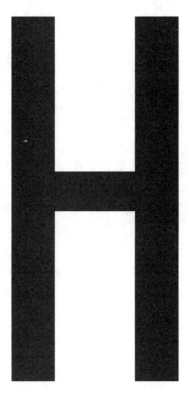

Happiness / Headphones / Heart /
Chamique Holdsclaw / Hollywood / Home Run Inn Pizza /
Homework / Hot Dog / Hyperbaric Chamber

*Rocking the rim for the Farragut Admirals, 1995.*

# Happiness

That year at Farragut was one of the happiest.

Coach E—Ron Eskridge—would take our team out of Chicago to his house in Lombard. He wanted us to experience suburban Illinois life. Here's Applebee's. Here's Dave & Buster's. Here's a county fair. Here's Six Flags.

While Coach E liked the burbs, Wolf went the other way. He'd pile us in his car and drive out to the North Side and have us playing at DePaul with college kids. Wolf had rapport with the streets. The streets respected him because he got so many brothas off the streets. Wolf loved taking us to every street imaginable. Play on the South Side. Play the GDs in the Village. Shout-out to the Village. Hit the LeClaire Courts near Midway Airport. Play the grown men, run back to Farragut, get a snack, hit the Evergreen Mall, check out the crews from Carver High, go home, grab a shower, hit the bricks again, hoop till 9 or 10 p.m., rest an hour, and then give it all you got as a Solid Gold in the Midnight League. Struggle to turn off your mind and fall asleep. Ringing alarm wakes you out of a deep dream. First thought that runs through your brain: *Where am I gonna hoop? Gotta get out there and hoop.*

# Headphones

Headphones nowadays are crazy. Got the noise-canceling joints where you put 'em on and can't hear somebody standing right next to you. I did a Beats by Dre commercial that illustrated that idea. All these fans going ape shit outside the team bus. I put on my Beats and block it all out.

Back when I came to the league, there wasn't no such thing as noise canceling or Bluetooth. We had the portable compact disc player with the little rinky-dink headphones you could only turn up to nine or ten. Had to carry a backup set of double-A batteries just in case yours died. And that cord you were constantly having to untangle. Get it all loose and two minutes later it's knotted up again. And you gotta carry that big-ass Trapper Keeper–style book of CDs around with you.

Sounds like some old-fashioned shit now, but back then? Compared to a regular cassette Walkman? That was futuristic. I remember rolling up in the locker room, blasting those garbage headphones, rapping out loud, using my hands, bumpin' the vets in the chest. They'd be like, "What is he doing?" They're in the middle of their pregame ritual and here I'm interrupting their focus. We were a new generation, man. We were the first hip-hop hoopers. Jordan tried to dabble in it a little, kickin' it with Kris Kross in Michael Jackson's "Jam" video. But MJ was always an R&B fan. To pump himself up before games, he'd listen to Anita Baker's "Giving You the Best That I Got." Rumor was that he'd be singing to opponents when he was working 'em, though I never heard it myself.

Thing about generations, though, is that there's always another one comin' up behind you. And the day I realized I was getting to be a vet happened in Boston when Tony Allen came in the locker room with his Beats on. That was back when they first came out and they didn't keep the music from leakin' out. And they didn't have no max volume. You could turn that shit up to like fifty, which is what TA did. The whole locker room could hear it.

I was in the middle of my pregame routine. I don't let nobody fuck with my pregame routine. I went and tapped him on the shoulder.

"Hey, bro, could you turn them things down?"

"Huh?" he said.

"I asked you to turn it down."

"But it's the new Gucci Mane mixtape," TA said.

Well, I didn't know Gucci. Was listenin' to Jeezy back then. So right away I felt twice as old—looking at this young cat doing the same shit I was doing more than a decade ago *and* not staying up on the latest music. Shit, man, when'd that happen? When did I turn into the vet who'd have looked at young

me swaggering into the locker room and said, "What is he doing?" It made me check myself.

I was fine with being a vet. Being a vet just means you got experience. But being old? Oh, hell no. Being old means you've lost your passion and curiosity. Passion and curiosity are the real Ponce de León fountain of youth shit. Keep curious and pursue your passion and you'll stay young.

So instead of getting all curmudgeonly at TA, I instantly copped that Gucci album and played the hell out of it. And TA, to his credit, turned his headphones down and started paying attention to and emulating my pregame routine. That's the beauty of generations: the one comin' up can always learn from the one that came before, and vice versa—as long as your mind stays open and your heart stays hungry.

*At the 2000 Olympics in Sydney.*

# Heart

A good heart comes from goin' through shit. First off, I'm not a hateful person. Two, I was able to take negative energy and flip it over on a positive tip. Re-form and refocus energy. Channel energy so that it's moving toward construction, not destruction. The way you channel energy determines the course of your life. Your heart has to lead your head. If your head leads your heart, your heart loses power. The power of the heart—the power of love—is the primary power. The head is for thinking, and smart thinking is indispensable. You need to think straight. You need to think clearly. You need to discern good ideas from bad ideas. But it all has to start with the heart. The heart is the miracle muscle.

# Chamique Holdsclaw

*see* **WNBA**

# Hollywood

In an earlier time, before Farragut, I flew out west for an AAU tournament in Vegas to play on a team from Inglewood. The thing was set up by a coach named Thaddeus who I'd met through Bull. Thaddeus had seen me hoop and thought I'd fit in.

"You've heard of Inglewood, haven't you?" he asked.

"Sure. It's where the Lakers play."

"So can you come out?"

"Gotta ask Moms."

I could never tell about Moms. She didn't like her life disturbed. She was moving in so many directions at once that distractions bugged her. She didn't like stopping her world for me. I had to find the right time to ask, hoping she was in the right mood. This time, though, she was willing to give me a week or two.

I was happy. Not only would we fly first to LA, which I'd never seen before, but Moms would get to see me play in a big tournament. I wanted her to ingest my passion for the game. Wanted her to see that hoop was a serious commitment for me and how other players gravitated toward me.

More than anything else, LA meant meeting Paul Pierce, the star of Inglewood High. This is where my brotherhood with P jumped off. Once we met, that was it. P later said, "We were meant to play together in the NBA. It's just too bad it took so long to happen."

He was the brotha who downloaded LA for me. A newspaper wrote about our budding brotherhood, talkin' 'bout me as a down-home country boy, all jittery and wired, and talking so fast that P understood only half of what I was saying.

At the same time, P was brash and loud, "Yeah, baby, yeah!"

I was the country mouse, P the city mouse.

P had LA dialed up. "This is the Fox Hills Mall. This is where the girls are at. Here you buy Cinnabons. Ever had a Cinnabon? Try a Cinnabon."

Cinnabon had enough sugar to fly me to the moon.

P went on. "This is Crenshaw, the main drag. We call it the Shaw. Lose that red Bulls jersey. We Laker fans out here."

So I took off my Scottie Pippen joint and now was cool with just a black T-shirt.

I'm looking out at the Shaw on a Saturday night. A thousand brothas out on the street, brothas crackin', brothas with Jheri curls, low ridin', throwin' down, fine chicks with biker shorts, swagged-out pimps. Never seen nothing like this before. It's on and poppin'.

We pull over for some tacos. Tastiest tacos ever. Keep rolling south. P shows me Inglewood where the Lakers play. Up the freeway to Hollywood. Check out the Walk of Fame. Look for Michael Jackson's star. Look for Prince's star. Drive through Beverly Hills, mansions lined up like museums. On the radio they blastin' Biggie's "Juicy." That was before the East Coast/West Coast feud. Back when Big first dropped *Ready to Die*, LA played the hell out of that. Though not as much as *Doggystyle*. Heard that rattling the trunks of so many rides during that trip.

Flying with P on this private tour of the LA landscape, I'm thinking that the wide, wide world is wider than I ever thought.

We bunked at his house, where our moms became friends. Ms. Lorraine Hosey, a nurse, was also a single parent. Like me, P didn't know his dad. His mother was from Chicago and knew how the city had been overrun by gangs.

"Maybe Kevin would be better off in LA," she told Moms.

Maybe. Playing at Inglewood High with P would be the bomb. More I thought about it, better it sounded. P

also loved the idea. He saw us winning every high school tournament in sight. It would also help us both to get into an elite college basketball program.

Miss Hosey made it clear that P would be going to a good university. Moms said the same about me. College was a definite. P's future was to become a Big Eight superstar at Kansas. My future was to go to Michigan and create a new version of the Fab Five. And if not Michigan, North Carolina.

Next day P started showing me all the hoop spots. Rogers Park. Venice Beach. We wound up in a practice game in Inglewood when one of the brothas got to talkin' shit to me. That zapped me into a zone. I'm dunkin' the muthafucka, blocking shots, shootin' that bitch, runnin' the floor, jumpers, threes.

"You could be killin' LA, KG," says Paul.

When we got to his high school gym, his boys are like, "Oh shit, they got a big brotha from South Carolina comin' in here. We wanna see him. We wanna see what he can do." So naturally I gotta step up, grab the rebound, stuff the rock in the rim, windmill it, get myself crazy, get the whole gym crowd crazy.

Me and P were on an adrenaline high when he, our moms, and I go to Vegas for the AAU tournament, where I'm going to be playing with Paul's team. First time in Vegas, I'm learning how to jump out of cabs and finesse the casinos, grabbing my little pocketful of quarters, pulling dozens of slots as I run up and down the aisle, hitting maybe one in twenty, running back to collect my coins, not knowing whether I'm ahead or behind, not caring.

*Me and P in high school.*

We stay at Circus Circus, where they got ladies bustin' out of their tight little costumes, walking the tightrope, and doing acrobatics right there in the lobby. I'm liking everything I see.

I'm also liking the AAU tournament. Me and P are on the K-Swiss team that always gets beat by a Nike-sponsored team. P and his boys are frustrated. It's some *Bad News Bears* shit. Me, I don't give a fuck. I don't have a history here, so I can play it loose.

"Man," says P, "they kick our ass every year. Wait till you see Jelani McCoy. Wait till you see Schea Cotton. Wait till you see the Collins twins, Jason and Jarron."

Schea was LeBron before LeBron. He was *the* brotha. Weighed at least 260. Yo, he could go. Left-handed, strong as fuck, crazy attitude, steppin' on brothas, fightin', grabbin', playing mad. Balls-out furious. And he's only in the eighth or ninth grade! Talkin' grown-man shit.

Didn't mind. Liked the challenge. And couldn't be happier when I helped P and the K-Swiss crew finally give Schea and Jelani a whipping. Me and P had magic chemistry on the court. That solidified our relationship.

We flew back to LA with our hopes high. High school in Inglewood seemed real. I'd stay in California while Moms would fly back to Carolina.

All good until Moms spent a Saturday on the same Crenshaw Boulevard that Paul had shown me. She didn't like what she saw. The gang bangin' was out in the open.

No arguing with Moms. No LA for me. P wasn't happy, but P knew the power of a single mom. P knew there wasn't nothing to do except hope we'd bump into each other down the road. A lifetime later, it was Shaq who said it best. It was 2001. The Lakers had beat down the Celtics 112–107. But Paul had forty-two on thirteen of nineteen shots. After the game, Shaq grabbed a Boston reporter and said, "Take this down. My name is Shaquille O'Neal and Paul Pierce is the muthafuckin' truth. Quote me on that and don't take nothing out. I knew he could play, but I didn't know he could play like this. Paul Pierce is the truth."

# Home Run Inn Pizza

My favorite pizza in the whole wide world. And I ate *a lot* of pizza that year in Chicago. Tried it all and most places twice. Picking Home Run Inn Pizza in Cicero as my number one pie will probably be controversial because it isn't that deep-dish style the city is famous for. It's more New York–style. They got the crust perfect—not too doughy and not too crispy. My fav was sausage—those fat greasy sausages, so big you could've folded the slice in half and called it a sausage sub.

Cicero had a deep history as a racist hotbed, but that didn't stop Wolf from taking the team there. He wanted us to know that we could eat wherever we wanted. And though he knew the bad stuff that had happened in Cicero, he reminded us there were cool people everywhere.

At the same time, first time I got pulled over was in Cicero. We asked the cop what we had done wrong.

"You're in the wrong neighborhood," was all he said. "Now get the hell out."

*Fuck that shit.* I thought it but didn't say it. After all, I was still on parole and couldn't afford to get my ass locked up. But I could see that Cicero police were a gang all their own.

# Homework

Mr. Clark was my favorite teacher at Farragut. Dark-skinned man with cocaine-white hair like Kenny Rogers, plus a big-ass white moustache, and a face that combined Uncle Ben of Uncle Ben's rice with Frederick Douglass. He wore jeans and a collared shirt and carried a briefcase. He had a little belly and correct posture. Talked proper English. But proper English with soul.

"Class," he said in his stylish charming way, "I wish you good morning. Good morning, ladies. Good morning, gentlemen. Today I'd like to challenge you with several intriguing theories."

Mr. Clark, who could also sing, taught math, scientific theory, and music. And because I loved math and science, I could follow. Other teachers were boring. Mr. Clark was theatrical. Big gestures. Big booming voice. Demanded attention.

Made all kinds of references that I loved. Talked about Sir Isaac Newton, who figured out gravity. Talked about Alexander Graham Bell, who figured out the phone. Talked about Albert Einstein, who figured out relativity.

Mr. Clark was an intellectual and also a brotha. He taught about the civil rights movement. Didn't teach from a book but spoke from real-life experience. He marched. He went down South and took the blows.

"I didn't grow up with privilege," he said. "I was embedded in the mud."

I loved how he used the word "embedded."

"I came up out of the mud," he added, "because I was determined to grow my mind and my spirit. That's my hope for all my students. May your minds and spirits never stop growing."

Those words touched me.

Farragut was definitely a funky school—you might see a guy getting sucked off by a girl in the bathroom—but I took the learning side seriously. I listened. I participated. I raised my hand. Because of those talks I was forced to give at Kingdom Hall, I had confidence as a speaker. When I was the first to figure out the algebra problem, I let out a shout. In science, I loved learning about cell walls, cell membranes, photosynthesis. When Mr. Clark talked about Darwin's theory of evolution, I asked questions until I understood the concept.

"Curiosity," said Mr. Clark, "is what keeps us stimulated."

Mental stimulation helped not only my mind, it also helped me with girls. I'm more than a hooper. I'm someone who can help 'em with their homework.

# Hot Dog

Farragut had a serious gang problem. Race riots were an everyday thing. Now I'm coming from Carolina, carrying this parole for supposedly starting a race riot, so I gotta be careful. But being careful ain't gonna change the culture. Gangs be fighting every day. This fighting was going to spill over to everyone, including me.

During lunchtime I'm with Ronnie Fields and some other teammates when, from out of nowhere, someone throws a hot dog in my face. I snap. I look across the cafeteria and one of the Latin Kings, the gang that dominated the school, stands up and says, "Whassup, homes?"

I go after him. This is the first time my brothas see me brawl. Like I said before, Chicago brothas ain't brawlers. They shoot guns. But my country ass reverts back to what I know best, and I give Hot Dog Man a bad beatdown. Next thing I know, I'm sitting outside the principal's office, waiting to get called in. Along with Hot Dog Man, sitting next to me is a gangbanger I'll call Seven Gun.

Seven Gun points to Hot Dog Man and tells me, "You know he's one of my guys."

Come to learn Seven Gun is the Hispanic gangbanger who runs the school. Farragut is at least 85 percent Latino.

Seven Gun lifts up his shirt. Two straps. I look at his shoe. Another piece strapped around his ankle. Another tucked in the back of his pants.

"I see you the big hooper," says Seven Gun, "but I be hooping too. I want you to get me on the team. I play guard. I shoot threes."

"That's dope," I say.

He daps me.

"Talk to your coach. Make it happen."

"Word," I say.

"One other thing," says Seven Gun. "I see you walking down Christiana Street every morning. And cats be messing with you."

He's right. Every day, four gang-bangers taunt me when I pass by. They talk in Spanish so I don't understand. But I get the idea. I cross the street to avoid them. Seeing them sneering never helps my peace of mind.

Sitting there with Seven Gun, I play it off.

"It ain't no thing," I tell him.

"So far. But the shit can turn ugly if you don't know the shake."

He teaches me the secret shake. The shake is the secret sauce that, given some circumstance, can save my life. In return, I change up things by asking Wolf to put Seven Gun on the team. It's the right move. Seven Gun shows up for all the practices. His heart is in it. He loves the game and winds up holding his own. More importantly, his presence on the squad helps bring Farragut together. As we get into the regular season, journalists write that I'm the one unifying the school. But I'm giving the props to Seven Gun. He was a ballsy brotha willing to jump into a basketball culture dominated by dudes like Ronnie Fields and me.

Turns out beautiful. Our team kills it. Ronnie Fields jumps higher than anybody. Air Fields is an up-and-coming superstar. Farragut has an unbelievable year. For the first time, the Latin Kings, GDs, and Vice Lords all put their hands up, we all dap each other, we hug. The team hits the road and does damage wherever we go. We wind up ranking number one in the *Chicago Tribune*'s ratings and number three in *USA Today*'s national poll.

That season, Farragut went 28–2, led by Ronnie Fields and me. I averaged 25.2 points, 19.9 rebounds, 6.7 assists, and 6.5 blocks, and I shot 66.8 percent from the field. *USA Today* named me National High School Player of the Year.

Before that, Antoine Walker had been king of Chicago. He ruled Mount Carmel High School and went to the University of Kentucky, where his star shone even brighter. Now the whole town was talking about Farragut, Ronnie Fields, and me.

*Ronnie Fields, 1996.*

Jordan would always be Jordan, but Mike was off playing baseball. We high school kids were more on the minds of hoop fans than the NBAers.

In addition to the *USA Today* award, I was named Illinois's Mr. Basketball. This was my second Mr. Basketball in two years in two different states. But the achievement that meant the most was the team winning the Public League championship for the first time in Farragut history, going all the way back to 1901, when the Public League championship began. To give you an idea of how much the game has evolved in all these years, the score of that game was 23–22—in overtime. Winning in the Go got you bragging rights. And nothing felt better.

Then it was on to the McDonald's All-American Game, where our West squad got the win, I got the MVP, and I made a friend for life in Chauncey B-B-B-B-Billups. Meanwhile, I kept studying for the SAT and ACT tests so I could get into Michigan or North Carolina. Because my dyslexia and other learning challenges hadn't been diagnosed, I still didn't know what I was up against. That meant getting tutors, and, just when I thought I was through studying, studying some more.

Everything was dope.

Everything movin' in the right direction.

Wasn't nothing throwing me off course.

# Hyperbaric Chamber

*see* **Insomnia; Kenny G**

*Illmatic* / Insomnia / Invitation /
Isiah / Isolation / Allen Iverson

# *Illmatic*

Nas's debut came out in the spring of '94, right around the time I was dealing with that bullshit at Mauldin and the lynching charge. That was a dark place in my life. The depression was deep. I'd get up in the morning, take a shower, and head back to bed. Kept my window shades drawn so the whole room was black. Stayed in my room all day. Wouldn't eat.

One of the things that got me through was *Illmatic*. It was seven hundred miles between my bedroom and the Queensbridge projects that Nas was rapping about, but it felt like he was writing about my life and speaking directly to me. I'd just listen to that shit over and over.

Even the album cover moved me—the photo of him as a seven-year-old boy superimposed on those grimy buildings. I'd look at the kid and see myself—see how innocent I was back then. I longed for that innocence now that I was starting to understand how cruel and unfair the world could be. *Illmatic* helped me endure emotional pain and realize that my best days were ahead of me. *Whose world is this? It's mine, it's mine, it's mine.*

Around the same time, I had that first Biggie bangin' in my head. And way before, as a kid, I had all the old-school joints. Fact is, music was as important to my makeup as sports. I remember my

Nas, 2010.

Grandma Mil and Grandma McCollough going around the house humming. That humming came from a deeply soulful place. Almost like an ancient hum. I heard it as a hum of hope.

I'm also a whistler. During dark days, whistling is another way of keeping your spirit light. Ain't no harm in whistling your way through life.

But whether it was whistling or humming or listening to the radio or the record player, ours was a musical household to the absolute max. There was so much music you'd think a musician lived there. I saw music—I *felt* music—not only as a source of energy but as a source of pleasure. Music made me feel good. Music made me wanna move. Music made me believe—as I still believe—life is worth living.

## Insomnia

I've never been a good sleeper. Back in the Midnight League, getting home at 3 a.m., I was so hyped sometimes I'd be up till dawn. When I got into the NBA, my insomnia got even worse. Just imagine: The T-Wolves finish a seven-game road trip in Seattle. Game ends around 9:30. By the time we get to the airport and our flight takes off, it's about eleven. Four-hour flight. We land at the airport. Then I gotta drive home. But it's snowing. There's a blizzard. I can't drive too fast. So by the time I get home it's four in the morning. But my body thinks it's earlier. It takes a while to get comfortable being back at home after a week away, takes a while to unwind. But practice starts at nine. I gotta be in the locker room at eight. Which is less than four hours from now.

Sleep science wasn't a big thing back then. Now players are taking daily naps and sleeping in hyperbaric chambers. By the way, I was the first one in the league to get that bad boy. Back then we just pushed through. Red Bull hadn't caught on yet. I had to get creative. I'd pour Gatorade into black coffee and drink

that. Do that two or three times a day. Needed the caffeine to get me awake but poured in the Gatorade so I wouldn't get dehydrated. Nasty as hell, but it works. Wakes your ass right up.

## Invitation

When I got my SAT and ACT scores, I was crushed. I'd tried my hardest and still failed to make the mark. Michigan wasn't gonna let me in. Neither was North Carolina.

But count on Wolf to adjust my attitude. Wolf was always Mr. Positive.

"Keep studying," he said. "You'll take 'em again, and next time you'll make it."

I always followed Wolf's advice, but I wasn't sure I'd ever pass those goddamn tests. No matter, I hit the books and went back to work. Every once in a while I'd look up and see that familiar dark cloud over my head.

That same day the scores came back, a friend drops over with an invitation I'd usually never turn down.

"Let's go hoop," he says.

"Not today, bro."

"Why?"

"Don't wanna talk about it. Just not feeling it."

"Fuck that shit, K. I know you. You need to take your mind off negative shit. I know you. Once you start hooping, you'll feel better."

No arguing with that. So I jump out the crib and we go looking for a game.

"The real dope," he says, "is to go sneak into the Bulls practice. Maybe we'll get a peek at MJ."

MJ had quit basketball to play minor league baseball. He'd been gone for twenty-one months and later returned to the Bulls in March 1995, a month before the McDonald's All-American Game.

"You know where they're practicing?" I ask.

Brotha just smiles at me. Brotha knows everything there is to know about who's hooping where.

"Let's go down to the Hilton where they got the really nice gym, K."

"Cool."

When we get in through a side door, Mike Jordan is in there. Scottie Pippen is in there. We watch them play a couple of practice games. I'm just looking at them. I'm just studying them. I'm focused like a muthafucka.

*Scottie, 1996.*

An hour goes by and a security guy yells at me. Looks like he's waving me down to the court.

"Hey, you!" he screams.

"Me?"

"Yeah, you, big fella. Get down there."

"Throw me my shoes," I tell my man.

I tie up my joints and hurry down to the court.

Pippen says, "You too young to be out here. You just a high school kid."

Jordan says, "Let's just go." Then he points to me and says, "You guard Scottie."

I'm thinking, *Damn, I'm playing against my idol. I'm playing against a guy who's coming off one of the best years of his career.*

Right off, Pippen calls for the ball and does a stutter move before launching a big-ass three.

I'm like, *That's crazy, no way he could have made that shot.*

But then my natural reflexes kick in. I launch my shit. *Boom!* I dunk. *Boom!*

Scottie and I have a word. That just fires me up more. I'm thinking, *I'm holding my own against one of the greats.*

As the game goes on, I'm gaining confidence. Ain't backing down. No one's making a fool of me. I'm competitive with these muthafuckas. I'm playing Scottie close, hard and tough. I'm in his face. I'm acting like every moment of my life has led me to this. Scottie may be Scottie, but right now he's just a hooper I gotta beat to the ball. I'm on fire.

Looking back, I wonder how it all happened. Was the security guard thinking he'd get in good with Jordan and Pippen by tossing them what he figured was some young and tender red meat to feast on? Or maybe the security guard gave me the invitation out of kindness and was putting his job on the line to give me a chance to live out a dream. Either way, I got one thing to say to that security guard: Thank you.

# Isiah

"Then I heard the voice of the Lord saying, 'Whom shall I send? And who will go for us?' And I said, 'Here I am. Send me!'"

This is from the Book of Isaiah in the Bible. Isaiah was a great prophet.

It amazes me to think that on this same day that I played a pickup game against Jordan and Pippen, I met another Isaiah, who spelled his named differently but who prophesized on my life.

During a break in the game with me, Scottie, and Jordan, here comes Isiah "Zeke" Thomas, who'd been watching the whole thing. Ain't crazy enough to be playing with two of my heroes. Zeke is up in that bitch too. I was trippin'.

Understand this: To me, Isiah was the real president of Chicago. He was a hood politician. Loved by everyone. Zeke knew the hard streets. He knew the hard history. He never flinched, fled, or faded. Brotha came up outta concrete. He was a West Sider but wasn't no place in the Go where he couldn't hoop. He knew the grit and grime. The baddest boys in the Go gave Zeke maximum cred. Surviving the Go ain't like surviving nowhere else. And when you do survive—and thrive—the way Zeke did, you don't go around talking about it. You keep that knowledge to yourself. Or if you do share that knowledge, it's only with other brothas who came up in Chicago before or after you.

Because Zeke came before me, he had stories I'd never heard. At the same time, we knew a slew of street brothas in common. Hood tales. How some brothas made it out and others didn't. Zeke always had some jewels. We could chop it up for hours. Another fact: When I saw him in the gym that night in 1995, he was recently retired. A year earlier, he had torn his Achilles tendon. That was the end of his playing career. He was thirty-four. I was eighteen. He was one of my big brothas.

I never asked him why he was there that day. He never asked me why *I* was there that day. We just were. One of those cosmic coincidences.

He came up to me and said something. There wasn't a hint of hype in his voice. It was just a matter-of-fact, kind statement.

"Kevin," he said to me, "you just took on Scottie Pippen. Scottie's the best player in the league. Boy, you could play in the league *right now*."

When those words came out of his mouth, the world stopped turning. Time stopped ticking.

But maybe I was hearing him wrong.

"What'd you say?" I asked.

"Boy," he repeated, this time his eyes getting bigger, "you could play in the league *right now*."

"Damn, for real, Zeke. For real?"

"Hell, yes, for real."

I had to silently say his words to myself.

*Boy, you could play in the league* right now.

Maybe if it had been someone other than Zeke saying those words they would have had less impact. But coming from Zeke, his words took the form of not only a prophecy but a blessing. A benediction.

"Well, what do you think?" he asked. "You ready to go to the league?"

Everything in my brain, body, heart, and soul said, "Yes!"

And after those yeses came . . .

*No.*

I didn't have to fuck with the ACTs and SATs anymore. That shit was driving me crazy. Even though I'd taken them multiple times, I was sure I'd never score high enough. Besides, not attending college wouldn't stop my education. I'm a curious dude. I'm always gonna be learning, always gonna be educating myself. College isn't the only place where learning flourishes. To an open-minded person, learning flourishes anywhere and everywhere.

*No.*

I didn't have to follow a twenty-year-old template.

*No.*

I wasn't obligated to conform to old-school thinking that, after I reexamined that thinking, made no sense.

*No.*

I didn't have to wait. I could run over and see Wolf right now and tell him that, when it came to college, all bets were off.

Wolf was a little skeptical. "You sure?" he asked. "What about North Carolina? What about Michigan? What about your dream of playing college ball?"

Wolf was right. That dream had lived in my heart ever since those games in Billy's driveway in Mauldin when I would pretend to be C-Webb to his Laettner.

"Dreams change," I told Wolf. "This new dream is something I can grab onto. Right now."

Wolf was a talker, but Wolf was also a thinker. I could see him pondering everything I said. I could hear him thinking. And then came the smile. The smile said everything.

"Well," he said, "maybe you're not wrong."

I had to smile too. Wolf was coming round in a hurry.

"I feel like I'm right," I said. "I feel it in my gut."

"If you're ready, big fella, I'm ready. Ain't nobody did this one. Not around here. But if anyone can do it, it's gonna be you. And I'm gonna be with you."

# Isolation

As I was trying to make up my mind about skipping college and entering the draft, I felt a deep sense of isolation. Basketball is full of terms that describe the human condition: "rebound," "assist," "guard," "possession," "transition," "trap." These terms are part of what makes the game a great metaphor for life. In basketball terms, "isolation" is when you've got the ball and the rest of your team gets out of the way to let you challenge your man one-on-one. It's seen in heroic terms. American cowboy mythology. A gunfight duel. Two men facing each other down in a dusty street, tumbleweeds blowing by, only one of them walking away. But I didn't go for that myth. I saw it as more selfish than heroic. I much preferred relying on my

*Bill Willoughby, 2000.*

teammates. And it was the same in my regular life. I didn't like to be isolated. I liked surrounding myself with people. I liked leaning on them for advice. But whose advice could I trust about what was about to be the biggest decision of my life? Before talking to anyone I did some serious research.

Back in the late sixties, Spencer Haywood fought the prohibition that said you couldn't join the NBA before graduating with your college class. Went all the way to the Supreme Court, where Haywood won.

Then in 1974, Moses Malone jumped directly from high school to the American Basketball Association. A year later, in 1975, Darryl "Chocolate Thunder" Dawkins and Bill Willoughby followed suit, going from high school to the NBA. And then that was it for two decades. Nobody tried it again.

I did my due diligence. I read all about Spencer, Darryl, and Bill. I went to the library, worked that microfilm machine, and studied the old magazine stories. I read long interviews with them. I wanted to know how their decision had impacted them. The thing that solidified my thinking, though, was reaching out to Bill Willoughby himself.

Before I tracked down his phone number, I reviewed his story. Willoughby never put up stats like Dawkins and didn't have Chocolate Thunder's gift for gab. Not many did. Dawkins invented modern trash talk with the way he'd name his backboard-shattering dunks. My favorite was "The Turbo Sexophonic Delight." But Bill Willoughby was no scrub, despite what people said. People would use him as an example of why you shouldn't go to the pros straight out of high school. They'd say if he'd gone to college and gotten more polish he'd have been more successful. But these people may have had racist inclinations and were just looking to deprive young Black men of their autonomy. What if it was a white kid who'd skipped college? What if Larry Bird did it? What if he'd bypassed Indiana State and got himself paid? Guarantee they wouldn't be saying the same thing. Guarantee they'd be praising him for making a smart business decision.

True, Bill Willoughby never averaged more than seven points a season, but he played eight seasons, and you ain't no chump if you stick around the league for that long. And real basketball geeks like me know he's one of only a handful of players to ever block a Kareem skyhook. Dude was 6'8" to Kareem's 7'2".

So I decided to call up Bill Willoughby. The man didn't know me from a can of paint. He was thirty-eight and living in Teaneck, New Jersey. At the time, I thought thirty-eight was ancient. Now I realize how young that still is. And only now, in writing this book, am I realizing that he shared the same last name as Miss Willoughby, who had my back at Mauldin. Must be some mysterious synergy between the Garnetts and the Willoughbys. The Willoughbys have been angels in my life.

Bill spoke to me like I was his son. Couldn't have been more patient and considerate. He had my back. He didn't try to talk me out of it, but he wanted me to know it wouldn't be easy.

"When you get in the league," he said, "everything changes. When people look you in the eye, they see dollar signs. No one goes around asking how you're feeling or how you're doing. It's all about how many points you can score. And whether you can get them tickets for the game. For someone who's only eighteen, it isn't going to be easy, Kevin. It's rough. It's lonely. You don't have a wife. You won't have your family. You won't get a lot of playing time. You gotta be extra strong."

"I am strong," I told him.

"Then go for it," he said.

Bill also understood that, aside from the emotional challenges, there were athletic challenges. The hardest part was the basketball. I wasn't that strong or that fast. I had the height of a center, but I'd be playing Scottie Pippen's position—a three. Scottie's a slasher. I'd have to learn how to slash. Use my inner guard. Face the basket. I'd be up against supersmart players with their curls and pop-backs. I'd have to deal with all that.

A year in the Go had taught me toughness. A year in the Go had me facing literally hundreds of different players under street rough-and-ready circumstances. Thank God for my year in the Go.

But the NBA was another world. To enter that world and, as many were saying, to enter it prematurely was bound to be the biggest risk of my life.

# Allen Iverson

At that first Nike camp in Deerfield, I made the All-Star team. But so did someone else, a brotha a year older than me: AI.

That Nike camp was barbaric. AI and I were very similar in how we handled our crew. He ran with a bunch of brothas, I ran with a bunch of brothas. He was fly, I was fly. We respected each other. Never no bullshit between us. Got a thousand percent love for AI.

Our first real bonding happened at the end of camp. The bus was taking us to the airport at 3:30 a.m. so we could make our early flights. Everyone sleepin' 'cept me and AI. We're sitting in the back row. Pitch dark. Two brothas reflecting on what might be ahead. AI is a thoughtful dude. Smart dude. He opens up. His real dream is to go to Hampton University, cause that's where he's from. Hampton is his heart. Plus Hampton has the smartest and most beautiful women of any school. AI is the Associated Press's High School Basketball and Football Player of the Year. But his main thing is to put Hampton hoop on the map. He's gonna be the Hero of Hampton.

Of course history didn't go that way. AI had his trouble with the law, just like me. He got into a brawl, just like me. The criminal injustice system turned his life around. The good part was that when push came to shove, the whole state of Virginia had his back and got him out of jail.

AI wound up at Georgetown and, of course, Philly. Because he was fresh, because he was crazy talented, because he wasn't scared to express his unique style in every area, because he didn't give a shit about the white gaze or the white establishment, he became a genuine icon. AI came in, threw the cornrows up, threw the tees on, rocked eight chains, the latest Rolex. Brotha was all jeweled out. Everyone be looking at him. AI got the crossover from the brothas in DC but gave it a whole different spin. Tim Hardaway had a crossover, but AI had a twist, a head bobble, a smoothness we'd never seen before. AI's crossover was a game changer, a high moment in NBA history. AI even wound up rapping. I love the way the brotha spits. He could rhyme up a storm.

Sitting on the last row on that bus in the middle of the night nearly thirty years ago, hearing him rap about the unknown world we were both about to enter, I sensed his strength. I knew that, like me, he was about to mess up the matrix. In years to come, both AI and I represented things that hadn't been represented before. We represented kids who had worked their asses off. Kids coming from fewer opportunities. Misunderstood

*AI, 2005.*

kids. Kids who needed a second chance. Kids plugged into originality. Kids ready to beat out a new path.

As time went on, AI and I stayed close. As he developed in the NBA, his skill set sharpened to where he became my favorite player to watch.

There are two kinds of guards. First, there's a Terrell Brandon. A go-getter. Very structured. He knew where everybody was supposed to be. Doe fits in that category.

Then you got Sam Cassell and AI. Just give 'em the ball. They get buckets. They know how to get money.

If I had been a guard, I'd have wanted to be like AI. He and I were family. No cross words. No falling out. His mom was my mom. His crew was my crew. AI is a real one. A1 from Day 1.

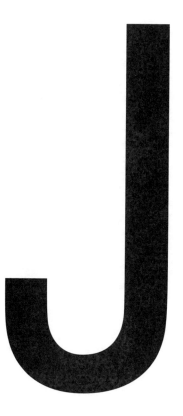

Janet Jackson / Jimmy Jam and Terry Lewis /
LeBron James / Japan / Jay-Z / Jealousy / Johnny Joe /
Magic Johnson / Michael Jordan / June 28, 1995

# Janet Jackson

Much as I appreciated Michael's genius, Janet's my favorite Jackson. She crushed it with *Control*, only to come back stronger with *Rhythm Nation 1814*. She was sultry, sassy, and sweet as sugar. Plus, her dance moves were fire. The fact that her stardom was born out of 'Sota and Flyte Tyme Productions of Jimmy Jam and Terry Lewis made it even better.

What made it absolutely unreal was when she brought her *Velvet Rope* tour to the Target Center, where the T-Wolves hooped. Naturally I got my groove on when she broke into everything from

*Janet Jackson on the* Velvet Rope *world tour, 1998.*

"Nasty" to "Black Cat" to "That's the Way Love Goes." Then things got crazier when, for her sizzlin' hot performance of "Rope Burn," I got called to the stage.

The setup, by now a classic, gave new meaning to the word "provocative."

I sat in a chair with my back to the audience. My hands were tied to the chair. That was a first for me. I'm not really into being tied up.

Janet and her two lady dancers each had a pole they started working.

Janet's pole was in front of me. Janet's body was inches from my eyes. She was wearing a feathery, bloodred boa that floated off her neck, a black bra, and black tights. Her midriff was bare. Her abs were cut. I could smell her perfume.

She went from the pole to a chair across from mine. She worked that chair as she was singing, 'bout tie me up, tie me down, make me moan, whisper fantasies. Then she was out of the chair inching closer to me. Then her two girls were joining her. They were wiping my brow with their feathers, Janet kissing me on the cheek, Janet working her crotch thrusts, Janet backing off, moving in, circling round.

The crowd was crazy. I was even crazier. So if I call myself the world's dopest Janet Jackson fan, you'll now understand why.

# Jimmy Jam and Terry Lewis

*see* **Janet Jackson; Land Cruiser**

# LeBron James

There'll always be talk about monster players who left the league without a ring. Barkley's a good example. Major crime. So many brothas wanted to play with Barkley, but in my opinion, Philly owner Harold Katz was too shortsighted to pay 'em. So Charles goes to Phoenix and then Houston, and in both places the teams can't give him the support he deserves. Same for Patrick Ewing in New York. Reggie Miller in Indiana. Karl Malone and Pistol Pete in Utah. Vince Carter. Chris Webber. Long, magnificent careers, history-making brothas, but no rings.

Let me take you back to 2010, when LB was at real risk of joining that list. Seven seasons with Cleveland and only one finals appearance—a sweep to the Spurs—to show for it. We'd just beat the Cavs in the conference semis for the second time in two years. Didn't just beat 'em—*broke* 'em. That team didn't have the talent to get past us. Wasn't gonna happen. After the game, the TV cameras captured LB in the tunnel stripping off his jersey. I used to joke with Cleveland players and fans that we buried it. The discarded jersey was seen as symbolic—a sign that his days in Cleveland were over. But just before that, after the buzzer sounded and we hugged it out on the court, I had whispered in his ear, "Let this drive you."

LB didn't need my advice. The man is self-driven. But after all my years coming up short in Minnie, I understood what he was going through. I'd been that high school kid who'd gone straight to the league. I'd been that player who loved the small-market team he played for and felt an intense loyalty to the city despite those dreary winters. I'd been that player who was desperate to deliver the long-suffering fans the title they'd dreamed of but never saw. I understood how conflicted he felt.

And so, unlike most everyone else in the world, I wasn't mad at him when he went to Miami to join up with D-Wade and Chris Bosh. The TV talking heads all said he shouldn't have done it the way he did, making the announcement on national TV. Bullshit. Media loved it. It gave them something to argue about for months. As a wrestling fan, I appreciated the sheer spectacle of it. It was great entertainment—and isn't that what all sports are? It was the classic wrestling heel turn—the hero becoming the villain—executed to perfection.

I was amped because now the C's could be the heroes to vanquish the villain. I wanted that matchup between the Heat and the C's so bad. I wanted to show that Miami squad who the real Big Three were.

We did just that the first game of the 2010–11 season. We smacked down Miami 88–80. They only scored thirty points on us in the first half. The TD Garden crowd was lit, chanting "overrated." And we just kept rolling after that. We were in first place in the Eastern Conference at the All-Star break. Ain't nobody could stop us.

Except our front office.

Four days after the All-Star Game, just at the trade deadline, the C's shipped off Kendrick Perkins to OKC. Perk was our heart and soul. He'd been drafted by the C's and been with the team for eight years. In our last three seasons with him as a starter, we'd won the championship and gone to the finals. The only reason it hadn't been three straight finals trips was because I got injured in 2009. Perk was gonna be a free agent after the season and hadn't been able to come to an agreement on a new contract. The C's wanted to get something for him rather than losing him in free agency. We had earned the right to stay together. The trade was idiotic. Why was the front office thinking about *next* season when we had championship potential *this* season? Why jeopardize that? Wasn't the first time a front office would make a dumb-ass move and it wouldn't be the last.

After losing Perk, we were barely over .500 for the rest of the regular season, and we ended up losing in six to LB and the Heat in the Eastern Conference semifinals. But we got our rematch the following year, in the 2012 conference finals.

It'd been an up-and-down regular season. A lockout had pushed the start back a month and cut sixteen games from the schedule. We only finished fourth in the conference, but in the playoffs we found our groove. We won a difficult six-game series against the Hawks in the first round, and an even more difficult seven-game series against a young and scrappy 76ers squad. We carried that mental toughness into the conference finals against the Heat. They won the first two games of the series at home, though we pushed them to overtime in Game 2. We then won the next two games in Boston, including an overtime Game 4. And then me and P went to work in Game 5. I had twenty-six points and eleven rebounds, and P scored

*"Let this drive you": My words to LeBron after the C's beat the Cavs in the 2010 playoffs.*

nineteen—most importantly, a three over LB with less than a minute left. We got the win and headed back to Boston with a chance to close out the series and go back to the finals.

That's when LB, in Game 6, had one of the all-time great performances. From the jump, his demeanor was different. He elevated himself to a sky-high plane. He scored forty-five points on 19-for-26 shooting and fifteen rebounds. And he played forty-five minutes. Granted, our shooting was atrocious. We shot fourteen threes and only made one. But wouldn't have mattered how well we shot that night. LB was unstoppable. As Doc said to reporters after, "I hope now you guys can stop talking about how LeBron doesn't play in big games."

Game 7 in Miami was even bigger, and once again LB put his team on his back, with thirty-one points and twelve rebounds. Doe played a hell of a game. Got himself a triple-double. But it wasn't enough. LB went on to win his first championship—ensuring he wouldn't be added to that list of legendary players without a ring. And he didn't stop there. After getting another ring with Miami, he went back to Cleveland and got Cavs fans their first championship in franchise history. And even then he didn't stop, heading to the Lakers and, at age thirty-five, winning ring number four. Will he get another one before he retires? Maybe two? Nothing he does would surprise me.

Great as Jordan was, Jordan couldn't guard LB. Bean had problems with Bron.

Magic didn't have LB's athleticism. The Miami LeBron was extra crazy. That's when he became the laboratory and got with mad scientist Pat Riley. Six feet nine, 265, a vertical of damn near thirty-eight.

Cat like LB comes along once every century. I want to carve out part of my book just to thank him and let him know it was a pleasure playing against him. He made me better. He made basketball better.

Never will forget him coming to the 2009 All-Star weekend and, in the locker room before the game, giving a beautiful glass trophy to all his teammates on the East: AI, D-Wade, Dwight Howard, Ray Allen, Danny Granger, P, Chris Bosh, Devin Harris, Rashard Lewis, and me. All it said was "Congratulations. Your friend, LeBron James."

A classy move. I've yet to see anybody come close to doing anything like that.

When all is said and done, Bron deserves 20 percent ownership of the Lakers, Cavs, or Heat. In all three places, he changed up the culture and gave the world something it ain't ever seen before.

## Japan

Tokyo is electronic, nutty, neon, full-tilt energy. Minute I stepped off the plane, I was buzzed. When I got there fifteen years ago, I was hypnotized by the crazy grid of a city consumed by the consumption of far-out products we hadn't yet dreamed of: mini phones the size of a finger and tiny speakers blasting out beats big enough to fill an arena. Tokyo was a maze of hyped-out invention and souped-up creativity. I couldn't sleep for days.

Come to learn Osaka was even doper. Come to Osaka and you'll think you're on Mars. Brothas with blond Mohawks coming through there. Muthafuckas wearing diamond-crusted eyeglass frames that make Elton John look tame.

In fashion and music, there's an unspoken bond between Black America and avant-garde Japan. Black America has always been on the cutting edge of looking good. Even in polite circles, fashion is king. Church ladies are famous for their crowns. If you go into God's house, you go in looking sharp. When the hat industry was crushed in the fifties and sixties, brothas kept it alive. Brothas were never gonna give up sporting the stingy brim, the bowler, the slick fedora. The brothas rocked caps like caps were never rocked before. We cocked them to one side, we flipped them around. When hip-hop popped off, all bets were off. In 1996, two kids—one was twelve, the other thirteen—called Kris Kross were rapping while wearing their clothes backwards. Rappers weren't just rapping. They were designing. Here comes Kanye. Here comes Pharrell, who looked to Japan for his inspiration from artists like Hiroshi Fujiwara.

Japan looked at us—brothas creating a style outside the mainstream until the style was so cool that the mainstream was mainlining our fashion dope. We saw the world differently. We bounced, so sneakers had to boost that bounce. We didn't give a flying fuck about tucking in our shirt or pulling up our pants to look proper. We didn't do proper. We wanted

*Coaching a basketball clinic in Tokyo, 2002.*

loose and funky. We didn't want straight-ahead. We wanted off-the-road and out-the-box. The Japanese saw what we were doing and took it to another place. Of course not all the Japanese felt this way. Japan is a highly congested, highly conformist country populated by millions of corporate cats wearing plain-ass black suits. But all that conformity gave rise to a youth movement of artists and clothes designers who said, "Fuck that shit. We going our own way."

I went crazy for brands like A Bathing Ape, the Great China Wall, Y-3, and Red Monkey. I went wild for Japanese denim. I saw how they made that old-school denim with the mill and the wheel. They did like the old '50s, like the old Lee jeans. I became a certified denimhead. I also became a fan of savage stitching and cuffs. In Japan, the manufacturing of denim is an art form. They work that fabric like no one else. When it comes to skinny jeans—and I love me some skinny jeans—the Japanese have perfected the product.

When I was coming up as a kid, I had no sense of "street culture" or "streetwear." I scuffled. We all scuffled. We made do with what we had. Back in the day, a nigga might rip his jeans and feel bad about it. Even ashamed. But then comes along the new nigga who says, "The rip is fine. The rip is even cool." Rip your jeans. Rip tears in the T-shirt. The more rips, the more holes, the more far-out, the better. Far-out is a way of flaunting and even creating style.

So shout-out to the nation of Japan and its brave artists for learning from us even as we learn from them. It's a beautiful cultural exchange. They get us. We get them. They say, *be free.* We say, *go wild.* And the rest of the planet follows in the footsteps of this wild freedom.

## Jay-Z

*see* "**King Kunta**"; **May 19, 2000; The N-Word; Shaquille O'Neal; Flip Saunders; Shoes**

## Jealousy

My personality isn't to be jealous or hate. Ain't in my DNA. I was raised to be happy for the next person. I was raised to be a teammate. Moms's thing was, "It ain't always about you." Not one single time have I been jealous of another player. I've always been a fan of the folks I thought I was supposed to be jealous of. Just as people—family, friends, fans, teachers, coaches—have illuminated me, I try to illuminate others. Jealousy has no part in that equation. Jealousy is built on insecurity. But if you're secure in yourself, if you're comfortable in your skin, you're free to be a giver, not a taker. You're free to be a lover, not a hater.

## Johnny Joe

The famous Celtics equipment manager, Johnny Joe Connor, is one of my favorite people in life. Johnny Joe's a legend. Irish dude, St. John chain around his neck, medium height, in great shape for his age. Loves Notre Dame. Looks a little like Ray Donovan's uncle. Got that bop-bop-bop bada-bing bada-boom style of North

*Johnny Joe Connor.*

End talking. A supreme charmer who the ladies love, JJ is only devoted to his wife.

JJ is part of the commission, the guys who ran our lives and ran them smoothly. Vlad Shulman is a therapist who works in the equipment room with trainer Ed Lacerte. Jeff Twiss is the PR man who's been there since Bill Russell days. Phil Lynch is security. Everyone in the commission made us feel secure.

When I first got to Beantown, Johnny said to me, "Hey, Ticket, what number you want?"

I immediately thought, *If we gonna win this thing, man, it's gonna take five brothas to get it done.*

"I'm rolling with 5, JJ."

## Magic Johnson

*see* **DMX; Escort; LeBron James; Michael Jordan; "King Kunta"; Ben Wilson**

## Michael Jordan

February 27, 1996. T-Wolves playing the Bulls at the United Center. It's my first time back in Chicago since becoming a pro. I was pumped, but, hell, I'm always pumped. Especially pumped that day, cause all my Chicago people were there. Farragut was in the house.

My pump was a little crazier than usual cause I didn't have no sleep. Soon as I landed in Chicago, I found out my friend Ronnie Air Fields had been in a bad car accident. He swerved to avoid

something in the road and slammed into a guardrail. Broke a bone in his neck. He could move his hands and feet. That was the good news. The bad news was that he wasn't sure when he'd be able to play again. This was heartbreaking. It was only three weeks before the state play-offs, and he'd been having a fantastic season, averaging over thirty-two points and twelve rebounds a game. He was one of the top high school prospects, along with Kobean, who was considering going

*My first professional game against Jordan, February 1996.*

up with him all night and was amazed to see that his spirits were so high, but by the time I got to the United Center, I was a basket case.

Like I always did, I translated all that emotion into the game. Get chills just thinking about it. All those Bulls games I'd watched on TV, and now I was there on the court hearing PA announcer Ray Clay say my name in the starting lineup. Then the lights going out. Then the spotlights flashing around. Then that slow-building Alan Parsons Project instrumental kicking in and Clay's voice going all guttural as he launched into his famous line, "Annnnd noooow the starting lineup for yoooour Chi-*ca*-go Bulls." I was tripping. But I was focused. The whole team was. We were down by only three at the half. This game was our championship. We were 16–37 with no chance of making the playoffs. The Bulls were 49–6 and undefeated at home—on their way to setting a record for regular season wins that would stand for twenty years. But if we could win this game, it'd feel like the season was a success no matter how bad our final record.

We stayed close throughout the third period. With under two minutes left in the quarter, we were only down two, 74–72. Up until then, Jordan had been ice-cold, just five-for-fifteen. Meanwhile, J.R. Rider—the cat they call "Easy Rider"—was red-hot, with sixteen points. J.R. was a bad boy. Back in 93–94, he made the NBA's All-Rookie team. He also crushed the Slam Dunk Contest with a slick move he called the "East Bay Funk Dunk."

Turned out J.R. was one of the realest dawgs in the league. He wound up giving me big brotha jewels of sound advice.

straight to the NBA, just like I had the year before. Now all that was uncertain.

When I got to the hospital, I saw that Ronnie had one of those halos around his head to support his neck. I hated to see my boy like this. Shook me up. I stayed

During this game at United, MJ was having a hard time guarding J.R. So I started pushing J.R. even harder.

"That muthafucka can't guard you!" I screamed to my teammate. "Keep killin' him! He don't know what to do with you!"

I was yelling so loud, Jordan couldn't help but hear me.

Being more experienced than me, Easy knew that trash-talkin' MJ was tantamount to suicide.

"Young kid don't know the rules," he told Jordan, trying to chill the situation.

But there was no chillin' me. I didn't give a fuck. "Stay on his ass!" I screamed to Easy. "He can't handle you."

That's when Jordan hit me with the death stare. Death stare felt like it went on forever. His eyes were locked. His eyes were fire. His eyes were saying, "Watch me now."

After that stare, about all I could do *was* watch. With under a minute left in the third, MJ scored six straight. Then in the fourth he went to work as only Jordan could. Inside the paint. Behind the arc. Midrange jumper. Everything falling in. Smooth as silk. After every basket, looking at J.R. and then back at me. Crushing us like a trash compactor crushing Coke cans.

J.R. and I each had twenty points. Didn't matter. We got pulled from the game with a little over two minutes remaining and the Bulls up fifteen. They'd go on to win by twenty-one. The two of us collapsed on the bench, totally gassed from MJ working us. He'd finish the game with thirty-five points.

"My bad, dawg," I said to J.R., struggling to catch my breath. "I'm sorry, man."

"I told you to shut yo ass up," he said, gasping for air.

Mike comes by us next possession. Breathing nice and easy. Barely breaking a sweat.

"Okay, young fella," he says. "Y'all good? Y'all done?"

The lesson couldn't be clearer. Mike is one dude you never wanna trash-talk. And I never did again. From that moment on, I knew that Jordan was the best offensive player on the planet. He was the top of the food chain.

That story illustrates MJ's competitive side. But what doesn't get talked about enough is his generous side.

In 1997, Shaq made the All-Star team for the Lakers but couldn't play due to injury. So I was selected to replace him. It was only my second season. I was the youngest player to make the All-Star team since Magic in 1980.

The game was in Cleveland. Our Western squad got smoked by the East. MJ put up the first triple-double in NBA All-Star history. At halftime, I saw him in the hallway changing shoes. He had on the Air Jordan XII Playoffs. When he took off the pair he was wearing, I stopped and said, "Let me get those joints."

He threw 'em at me.

"You can have 'em," he said, "but I ain't signing 'em."

I didn't argue. I just thanked him, grabbed those babies, hurried to the locker room, put 'em in my bag and zipped 'em up. They had this yellow curve on the side that I loved. I made a place of honor for them on my shelf. I could look at them for longer than I'm willing to admit. Twenty-four years later I'm still looking at them.

# June 28, 1995

When it came time to announce my decision that I was going straight from Farragut to the draft, I wanted to hold the press conference in a place where I felt comfortable. Didn't want no hotel conference room. Home Run Inn Pizza suited my style. Joint was packed, reporters crowded up front trying to get in their questions, homies in the back clownin' and cheerin'. Fired up the ovens, ate a slice, and told the world I'm heading straight to the league.

The end-of-June draft was a little more than a month away. College scouts all knew who I was, but not a lot of NBA teams did. So my agents organized a workout in a Chicago gym. A bunch of execs showed up. Cats like NBA legends

*Announcing my decision to enter the NBA Draft at Home Run Inn Pizza, May 1995.*

Kevin McHale, the T-Wolves vice president of basketball operations; and Pat Riley, who'd just been named head coach and president of the Heat. I was nervous as fuck. Damn near hyperventilating. I had Kiwane Garris, a little guard from the West Side, pushing me the ball, and also John Hammond, an assistant with the Pistons who later became general manager of the Bucks and Magic. Hammond saw how I was wigging out and had me shoot free throws to calm down. That's when I heard Riley.

"Come on, what the hell is this? I gotta watch some high school kid? Why am I here?"

*Okay*, I thought. *You don't know why you're here?*

That's all I needed.

I raced up the court, dribbling between my legs and behind my back before raising up just past the free-throw line to throw down the most ferocious dunk of my life.

Not a word from the execs.

"They wanna see how high you can jump," said Hammond. "So I'll throw it up on the glass; dunk and pass it back to me."

We did it, not once, not twice, but five times in a row. Each time Hammond threw it higher, each dunk became more emphatic. At the fifth dunk, I roared out a sound that went on for fifteen seconds.

"YAAAAAAAAAAAAAAAAAAAA AAAAAAAY!"

After my scream, I looked up at Riley and said, "Now do you know why you're here?"

Riley's disposition did a 180. Slowly he started to clap.

"Nice workout, young fella," he said. "Very nice workout."

That day McHale was with T-Wolves general manager Flip Saunders. I later heard that they'd come to the workout only as a decoy. They had the fifth pick in the draft, and their plan was to rave about me in the hopes one of the teams ahead of them would be persuaded to pick me and allow a player Kevin and Flip really wanted to fall to them. But then after the workout, they were both convinced they were going to pick me. Flip said it was the best individual workout he'd ever seen.

I didn't know that at the time. All I knew was to mind my manners.

"Pleasure to meet you, Mr. McHale," I said, extending my hand. "Pleasure to meet you, Mr. Saunders."

By the end of that week, I had an invitation to go to the draft. That pretty much meant I'd be picked. My stock was growing, but there were other hoops I had to jump through. Still in Chicago, I had to get a pre-draft physical down at the Hilton Hotel. That meant running on the treadmill, lifting weights, and a few other drills. I was nervous and excited. This was still another life-changing chapter. Soon as I arrived, I was looking at Joe Smith, Corliss Williamson, and Scotty Thurman. I was looking at everyone I loved watching on their college teams.

"Whassup, Scotty," I said. "Man, you were great at Arkansas. You and Corliss both."

He saw I was a fan, and he was super cool. Not all the brothas were that cool. Some gave me a hard time cause I never went to college. Some made me feel like an outsider. Some said, "You missed your education, bro. You missed out on a lot."

I felt like there was joking—almost hazing—at my expense.

When I could barely lift 146 pounds, they said, "You ain't strong enough to play in the league."

Weightlifting was never part of my program. I weighed no more than 175. I was light. I was long. Seemed like everyone up in that bitch was bigger, thicker, stronger, more confident. I was in culture shock.

Scotty read my mind and came over. "Man, they laughing at you cause they know you're right. They feel threatened. You don't need to prove nothing."

But I felt like I did. I felt like I had this extra no-college burden on my back. At the same time, I had a bag of street experience I could dip into. Hell, I'd lived a year in the Go. Played on every court from one end of the city to the other, took on every monster hooper, paid the deepest dues you could pay. Fuck it. If this college fraternity of draft prospects didn't see me as fit, now I had even more reason to prove them wrong.

Time to head to Toronto for draft day. But before I could get on the plane, more hassles. I was still on that parole that had been transferred a year earlier from Mauldin to Chicago. Parole board started tripping and saying I couldn't leave the USA. I had to get documents to prove I was going only for the draft and would be coming right back. Until that shit got straightened out, I was holding my breath.

Finally, the plane lifts off from O'Hare and lands in Toronto ninety minutes later. Step off the plane and get driven into the city, where everything looks clean and beautiful. I've never been out of the country before. I think I'm in Europe.

But I'm in Toronto because it's the first draft for the two Canadian expansion teams, the Raptors and the Grizzlies. I'd turned nineteen just over a month before. It's me, Moms, my girlfriend, and my boys Bug, Nod, and Kareem. Got my two agents there as well. Get to my hotel room and my phone's blowing up. People wanting to party. I ain't about to party. I just wanna be alone. I can't take any more stimulation. Lemme see if I can go to sleep without my mind running through a million thoughts. Wanna slow down. Wanna be steady. I'm going to be picked. Of course I'm gonna be picked. A week before, the *Chicago Tribune* had reported that a dozen NBA GMs did a mock draft and had me going number five to the T-Wolves. I try not to pay attention to what the media is saying but everyone around me is chattering. I hear people talking about it. To go that high would be wild. Still, there's always that voice in your head, the voice of the Devil, the voice of Mr. Doubt. "You done made a bad mistake," says Mr. Doubt. "You about to be made a fool of. You done fucked up. Why didn't you listen? Why didn't you go to college? Your dream was to go to college." Before Mr. Doubt drives me crazy, I answer him, I say, "This *is* my dream. My dream is the draft. So shut the fuck up." Dueling voices in my head keep me up half the night.

Dawn breaks. The day is here. June 28, 1995. I shower. I shave. I shine my shoes. Put on a slate-gray double-breasted suit custom made at Rochester Big & Tall over on Michigan Avenue. It's a long way from when Moms would slap me in the head and tell me to pick out some outfit from the thrift shop basket. It's a lot different than those mothball-smelling Goodwill suits I used to wear to Kingdom Hall. When the tailor at Rochester had approached me and said the suit would be custom, I didn't even know what custom meant. I didn't about getting measured versus rolling up the sleeves to disguise the misfit. Wow, the sleeves of this shirt actually go all the way to my wrists. Wow, this cotton is soft against my neck, these trousers actually hit the top of my shoes.

My girl fixes my Saks Fifth Avenue silk tie with a dope triangular design. I'm rocking a circular gold earring. Ready to roll over to the Skydome when the phone rings.

"Kevin, it's Wolf. You standing up?"

"Yeah."

"Well, sit down. Got good news."

"How can you have good news when the draft ain't even started?"

"Ain't about the draft. But it's about something you gonna love."

"What? What you saying, Wolf?"

"Your last ACT and SAT scores came back. You did it, son. You improved something like twenty percent. You passed. Any college will take you now."

Don't know what to think. I'm glad, I'm proud, I'm even thrilled. I'd been fooling with those tests for so fuckin' long, and finally, after all this time, I've met the challenge. I'm college material.

At the same time, why is this news coming to me seconds before I walk out the door to the draft? What's the universe trying to tell me? Just because my ACT and SAT scores are now acceptable, am I supposed to change my mind and suddenly change directions? That sure as hell would make news.

I'm already on the cover of *Sports Illustrated* with a headline that says, "Ready or Not . . . Three weeks ago Kevin Garnett went to his high school prom. Next week he'll be a top pick in the NBA draft." Wouldn't it be something to overturn that prediction and back out? That would stop all the talk—which exists to this day—claiming the only reason I was skipping college was cause I couldn't get into college. Now I know I can get into college.

With all this rattling through my brain, I look at myself in the mirror and tell Wolf, "Fuck it. It's too late. Fuck college. I'm going to the college of hard knocks. Going to the NBA—that's where I'm going. See you downstairs in ten."

My girlfriend looks at me and asks if I'm okay.

"I'm fine," I say. "I passed my tests. But there are bigger tests coming up."

Inside the Skydome there's the stage where Commissioner David Stern will do the announcing, the tables for all us potential draftees and our people, the brand-new court for the Raptors, and thousands of fans filling the arena. I'm feeling like I'm in a fish bowl. Feeling all this energy. Sistas waving at me. Aunties. Cousins. Bumping into some dudes I know like Rashard Griffith, who was Mr. Basketball in Illinois a couple years before me and was coming out of the University of Wisconsin. Rasheed Wallace and Jerry Stackhouse, who I played against at the Nike camps and who'd just led North Carolina to the Final Four. I'm getting dapped, getting some hugs, but also getting some of that same attitude I got during the physical from other hoopers who'd put in their college time and weren't crazy about someone who hadn't.

Don't matter none. I'm at the table with my people. Bug is there. I'm remembering when Bug and I would watch the draft on TV. Now we're here. We in the TV show. My stomach's rumbling. My mouth's a little dry. I take a sip of water. Breathe. Look at the big board in the back of the stage naming the teams and showing a blank where their picks will be listed. Here's Commissioner Stern, who goes through his welcoming monologue using his big vocabulary of marvelous charm words to set the ambiance.

Talking about these future athletes. These future gods. Stern salivating over the future. Stern doesn't stop talking. These opening remarks may only go on for a few minutes, but those minutes feel like hours. Hurry up. Let's get this bitch started. Stern's still blabbering.

Finally he gets to it.

"With the first pick of the 1995 NBA draft, the Golden State Warriors select Joe Smith from the University of Maryland."

I'm happy for Joe. I'm hearing this news as a fan. Joe's a future superstar. Everybody had him going number one.

"With the second pick of the 1995 NBA draft, the Los Angeles Clippers select Antonio McDyess from the University of Alabama."

McDyess was the baddest big in the SEC. Great pick. Great player.

"With the third pick in the 1995 NBA draft, the Philadelphia 76ers select Jerry Stackhouse from the University of North Carolina."

I also know Stack from AAU ball. Humble but fiery guard. Well respected in high school. Followed his college career. Good for Stack.

About now, my legs start trembling and my hands start sweating. Players getting picked and I'm still sitting there. Don't got no coolness to me. Everyone can see I'm jumpy. Got no experience at this thing.

Pick four belongs to the Washington Bullets. Washington would be cool. I could get down with Washington. They finished dead last in the Eastern Conference last season, but they got Chris Webber. Would be a straight-up dream to call myself his teammate. Would be almost like getting to go to Michigan *and* play in the NBA. I was also curious to get an up-close look at Gheorghe Muresan, the 7'7" center from Romania. Figured going up against him in practice would sharpen my post game.

But that's also why I guessed they wouldn't pick me. They already had Muresan at center, and his backup, Jim McIlvaine, had just finished his rookie year. They didn't need another young five. Not that I considered myself a center. I worried being seen as a center wouldn't let me reach my full potential. In fact, I always insisted that my height be listed as 6'11", because once you're listed at seven feet and over, people look at your game differently. That one inch makes a huge difference.

"With the fourth pick of the 1995 NBA draft, the Washington Bullets select Rasheed Wallace from the University of North Carolina."

Sheed's just a couple of tables away. Sheed's mom is screaming. The whole table is up and hollering. Sheed's getting his just rewards. All the cameras on Sheed. I love Sheed. I'm happy for Sheed.

Then, suddenly, all the cameras are heading toward our table. Heading toward me.

"What's going on?" I ask my agent.

"Showtime," he says.

What does he know that I don't?

"With the fifth pick of the 1995 NBA draft, the Minnesota Timberwolves select . . ."

Everything turns silent except for the sound of my name. Everything stops. I don't know how to act. Don't know what to say. It's surreal.

I stand up and give Moms a big hug as Ernie Johnson tells a national TV audience, "Why is he going to the

*Hugging Moms after hearing my name called at the 1995 NBA Draft.*

*Congratulated by NBA commissioner David Stern at the 1995 NBA Draft.*

NBA now? His test scores were not high enough. He did not want to do the junior college route." I love Ernie. I worked closely with him when I was at TNT. He's a good man. He did not know about my ACT and SAT scores. But what he said was straight-up wrong—would've been even without my earlier phone call with Wolf—and him saying it on national TV . . . man, that cemented a narrative I'd have to deal with for years to come.

But in the moment, all I know is I've made the top five. I'm handed a T-Wolves cap. I put it on, make my way to the stage. Stern offers congrats, shakes my hand.

"Pleasure to meet you, Mr. Stern. This is the dream."

"Let's see what you do with it," he says. Pointing to the photographer, he adds, "Look this way."

My eyes are watering. Chrysa Chin, a PR lady who will be a positive force for practically every player who comes through the NBA, shuffles me off to do interviews. I try to sound halfway coherent. At one point, I cock my cap to the side. "Straighten your hat out," Chin says. "We're not doing that." I do it anyway. My cap is cocked.

After all the press stuff, Upper Deck, the trading card company, hands me a check for $1 million. I gotta count all those zeroes four times before I believe it. Never had seen a check like this. I'm used to getting money in a brown paper bag. Now I'm being told this bread will be directly deposited. That's a new term. Everything is new today. I'm new.

We go to dinner and come back early cause I'm flying out in the morning to New York to do *Live with Regis and Kathie Lee*. I'm looking through a PR kit. My first. Looking over my schedule. Nonstop interviews. Nonstop attention. My girlfriend is in the bathroom getting ready for bed while I'm sitting in a chair, thinking how a year ago I was living in a brotha's dark basement in Mauldin, reading the lessons that Miss Willoughby brought me while worrying about landing in jail. Now I'm here in the Shangri-La Hotel in Toronto thanking Jehovah God and praying for the opportunity to create change.

I look out the window and see a twinkling star. And just like that, life starts.

Kareem / Martin Luther King Jr. /
"King Kunta" / Kingdom Hall / Kobe

# Kareem

*see* **Dunk; Isolation; "King Kunta";
The National Anthem**

# Martin Luther King Jr.

*see* **Fists; Zero Tolerance**

# "King Kunta"

Dope song by Kendrick Lamar. You gotta love it. But what makes it extra cool is that if you listen carefully, you'll hear the killer groove of James Brown's "The Payback," the same groove used in "Can't You See" by Total featuring Biggie. JB cut "The Payback" in the '70s, Biggie in the '90s, and Kendrick in 2015. That's over three decades of mashed-up Black music.

So when people diss hip-hop for being too radical or dirty or for discarding the past, I say hip-hop is a fresh look at the past pulled into the present and aimed toward the future.

If, at age twenty in 1996, I'm listening to Jay-Z and Foxy Brown's "Ain't No Nigga," I'm hearing them rewiring the same song sung by the Four Tops—"Ain't No Woman (Like the One I Got)"— from the '70s. That's the kind of song

Moms and them would be blasting on the radio while we were mopping the floors and washing dishes. Jay-Z is pushing me forward while bringing me back to my childhood. It's beautiful.

So many other examples: In 1988, Eazy-E bites the bass line from the Temptations' "Ball of Confusion" from 1970 in "Eazy-Duz-It." My uncle Pearl loved him some Temptations. Hearing Eazy, I'm remembering how much I love my uncle Pearl.

Kanye and Jay-Z put Otis Redding's "Try A Little Tenderness" at the heart of their song "Otis" in 2011. Otis dropped his joint in 1966, a time when my grandma Mil was loving on it.

My main man DMX is leaning on Bill Withers's "Ain't No Sunshine" when he spits about his own "No Sunshine."

Lil Wayne is paying homage to his R&B soul mama Betty Wright by rapping as she's singing, calling it "Playing With Fire."

The generations are all hooked up in hip-hop just like they're hooked up in hoop.

Kareem is sampling Wilt. "Round Mound of Rebound" Charles Barkley sampling Wes Unseld. Larry Bird biting off Rick Barry. Anthony Davis building on Jerry Lucas. Dirk Nowitzki looking like a modern Arvydas Sabonis. Follow the generations from Oscar Robertson to Magic to Jason Kidd. Alonzo Mourning looking back at Bill Russell. Everyone ingesting everything Earl the Pearl spun out on the court. I'm looking at Chris Webber who's looking back at Derrick Coleman.

All the generations becoming one generation.

An accumulation.

A continuation.

A process where old excellence breeds new excellence, a different excellence, where the sounds you hear on the radio and the sights you see on the court are linked over more lifetimes than you can count. The link is rooted in respect. The link is based on love.

# Kingdom Hall

*see* **Arrival; The Book of Job; Cosmetology; Homework; June 28, 1995; Questions**

# Kobe

I never imagined he'd die before me.

In writing about Bean, I'm feeling so many things at once. I'm still having trouble wrapping my head around what happened. Disbelief. It was too sudden. Too awful. Too painful to process. But once I face the awful fact, I eventually get to pride—pride at what Kobean accomplished and then gratitude that he was in my life and that we became brothas.

We first met in Philly, the Spectrum, my rookie season. I liked the Spectrum because the lighting was dark and dramatic. I had a decent game, came off the floor, and when I walked into the locker room, there he was, sitting on my stool.

"Whassup, KG," he said. "I'm Kobe."

"Whassup," I shot back. "But why is yo ass in my seat? Get the fuck outta my seat."

He jumped up right quick and we had a little chuckle. He was super animated, boisterous as a little boy. He was lit. I could see the spit on his words coming off his voice. He came at me straight-ahead.

We were teenagers. He was seventeen. I was nineteen. I was already in. He was a year away from getting in. He was fixing to do what I'd done—go straight from high school to the draft—so right away we related. Never had met nobody with so many questions. One tumbling out after another.

"Is it really as aggressive as it looks out there?"

"Hell, yes, it's aggressive."

"Is it rough being a rook?"

"Rough as fuck."

"How do you mean?"

"It's about paying dues. About standing up to vets who see you as a threat. About getting your ass kicked. About standing your ground."

"You got a crew? You got your people?"

"I got my people, but I'm a to-myself kinda dude. I can feel you're more a people person."

He proved me right. Kobean was my kid brotha. He was the extrovert. I was the introvert. His dad was a hooper who helped take him through the maze. Later,

*Goofing with Kobean at the 2004 NBA All-Star Game.*

when we tightened up, he'd be telling me stories about the Italian league. He'd start spittin' in Italian. That was some funny shit. But on those endless All-Star locker room talks and lunches, after the media sessions were over, we'd be sitting in the hallway, two hoopers just chopping it up. That's when Bean would tell me about the challenges of fitting in as an American kid after all his years in Europe.

Not just as an American kid, but a Black kid. He went through his own culture shock before he shocked the world. Me and Bean were molded differently, but in some ways I saw him as the 2.0 version of me. He did his due diligence.

He could have approached all kinds of dudes to get the download on the league. And I know he did. But the idea that he came to me early makes me happy.

In many ways, the press did him like they did me. Media started hounding him when he was still at Lower Merion High School in Philly. Followed him to his prom when his date was Brandy. Let him know that his life would never be as private as he would have liked. As all of us would have liked.

I watched him get drafted. Watched him during those early years when it wasn't easy. He took a beating. Everyone does. The more talent, the worse the beating. Some of his own players were making fun of him, saying shit like, "Okay, Showtime." I remember him telling me how he felt like they were laughing *at* him rather than *with* him. Took him a while to trust his teammates. But he was able to do it, he was able to get with D-Fish and T-Lue and Brian Shaw. They were his real niggas.

I'm remembering his first All-Star Game. It was also Timmy Duncan's first. It was my second, 1998. Madison Square Garden. First All-Star with Kob and Jordan. The press was playing up how, at nineteen, Bean was the youngest All-Star ever. The press was getting to him. Sooner or later, the press gets to all of us. The press was saying that Jordan was already polished to perfection and we'd see just how much polish Kob had going for him.

Larry Bird was coaching the East and figured Bean would be overboisterous. He was saying shit like, "Let Kobe shoot. He gonna shoot himself outta this game." Bird was toying with him. Everyone was messin' with him. The buildup was putting heavy anxiety on his head.

But because we were always copasetic, I could read his vibe, I could say, "Forget that nervous shit, Kob. We here now, boy. We *here!*" I gave him a double-dap on his chest with my fists and screamed right in his face. *"We starters! We the future!"*

I told him I'd be looking for him, and then some five or six minutes into the first quarter I saw him heading into the paint. That's when I launched the Lob from God. I put on the proper touch so that bitch just stayed up there big as the midnight moon, hanging for a split second until Bean grabbed the muthafucka two-handed and dunked the shit out of it. Place went nuts.

"Told you," I said.

"Woof," he said. And he slipped right into the mix.

Our All-Star team was tough—Bean, me, Shaq, Gary Payton, Karl Malone. At one point, Karl got pissed cause of a messed-up pick and roll. A lot of the vets got peeved. But that was part of the fun. Young dudes coming in. Old dudes storming back. Not just East versus West, but generation versus generation, a bruisin' battle of the ages.

The East won the game. MJ got MVP for his twenty-three points, six rebounds, and eight assists. But Kob did himself proud. Led us with eighteen points. He played his heart out and I never did see him nervous again.

So many beautiful moments between us. So many snapshots in my mind. Warm feelings. Family feelings.

All-Star weekend in Dallas, Saturday night dunk contest, me sitting in the front row with my two-year-old daughter, Bean and Vanessa sitting right next to me, Vanessa making a big fuss over my baby—"She's so adorable! She's so gorgeous! You're so blessed, Kevin"—Kob and I taking the turn from single dudes to married men.

*The "Lob from God" at the 1998 NBA All-Star Game at Madison Square Garden.*

Now I'm thinking about the good things, the funny times, even the times when we got crossways.

Just after Bean was drafted, I started spending summers in LA to shoot Nike commercials. Kob wanted me to practice at Loyola Marymount, but I never liked that floor. It had concrete underneath. For me, UCLA was the spot. UCLA had all the street players. That's where the run was at. Everyone had their boys, wasn't no foolin' around in there. Say some slick shit and it could go down in a hurry. I liked that environment.

Bean never would come to UCLA. He'd be saying, "KG, you need to play in Venice."

I'd played in Venice, but that was earlier in my life. Now I saw Venice in a different light.

"Why?" asked Bean. "Venice Beach got some good-ass games."

"Playing on concrete ain't the smartest thing. Playing on concrete will fuck up your legs."

Playing in Venice was where Bean broke his wrist. But a broken wrist didn't stop him. Nothing did.

During regular-season games, we were consistent with each other. We banged, we fought, we trashed. I picked him when I had to pick him. Blocked him when I could block him. He'd be saying, "You can't guard me." I'd be saying, "The fuck I can't."

Two thoroughbreds out there, two fierce competitors seeing how far we could take it. Never was a game, no matter how fierce, where we didn't dap each other after.

Only time I can recall real frustration was the summer of 2007, when I was fixing to bust a move. I'd come to the end of the road with the T-Wolves. It was between three teams—Suns, Celtics, and Lakers—and I wanted to get Kob's take on whether he thought his Lakers were right for me. I called him. No answer. Called a second time. No answer. Checked my phone to make sure I had the right number: Bean Bryant. Go over the digits carefully. Yes, sir, that's the number. Let me try this again. Fifth time. Sixth.

Before calling the fourteenth time, I asked my wife, "Should I try him again?" "Yes," she said. "It's your future." I even asked T-Lue, who was close to both of us, to get him to holler at me, but Bean never did. After my twentieth time, I figured enough was enough. Only later did I learn that he was in China for a long while. But that didn't mean he wasn't getting messages.

The planet kept spinning. That summer the Celtics traded for Ray Allen and suddenly things came into focus. T-Lue was telling me, "Ticket, this is it." Chauncey was saying the same. "Ain't gonna be a better opportunity. You gotta jump over to Beantown, baby." That summer, Gary Payton renewed his marriage vows in LA. I wanted to show support for GP. Antoine Walker was there as well. Antoine was coming off his Heat championship. He got him a ring. Antoine and I got to talking. He was echoing Shot and T-Lue.

"Boston is what's up, big fella. You gotta make that move. You gotta get that ring."

I could feel Antoine. He was being genuine. He had my best interests at heart. Brotha gave me some of the best advice of my life.

I made the decision. Made it with confidence. Made it with determination. I put away the fantasy of being Bean's teammate. Wasn't all that easy, but I did what I had to do.

And after I did it, after the season was underway, there we were, November 23, facing off against one another at Staples, me a Celtic, Bean a Laker, with someone at the free-throw line. I avoided lining up next to him cause I didn't wanna hear his punk-ass excuse for not calling me back. Then he switched so he could be next to me. Then, again, I moved away. Finally, the ref had to say, "You guys get somewhere and stop!"

When he approached me, my first words were, "Man, you never called me back."

"Never got the message."

"Bullshit."

"What number you call?"

"The right number. The one T-Lue gave me."

"You know how it goes, KG. We change numbers like we change drawers."

"I'm believing you got the message."

"Messages get lost."

"Not when a message is sent twenty fuckin' times."

"Look, man, I had China. I had the new Nike line poppin' off. I had more shit happening than ever before. I was moving in eight different directions."

"I understand all that, but you sure as shit wasn't moving in my direction."

We kept beefin' for a minute or two. It got caught on camera, and folks made more of it than was really there. I had me some hurt feelings. Finally, Bean apologized, and that was good enough for me.

Between Kob and me, bad feelings always faded away. That's because Bean was basically a beautiful human being. He had a dry-ass style of humor he got from Jordan. Matter of fact, Kob was consciously following the Jordan script. That was no different than any hooper of our generation. Bean moved to Orange County knowing that Jordan was living less than an hour away. He even walked like Jordan. He used to tape his pinky like Jordan. Then he started to believe he was better than Jordan. If you're as great as Bean was, you gotta get yourself to believe that—or else you ain't getting any better. Can't no one intimidate you.

At the same time, Kob was always supportive of me. In 2000, he got his first title by beating the Pacers 4–2. Back then, we had the Sky Page device with those pins and shit. I sent him a message that said "Congratulations." He hit me back with "Oh man, it's been a crazy whirlwind." Then, when he started winning rings, he called and said, "Don't worry, dawg, you gonna get there."

I was like, "Man, get the fuck outta here. I don't need that big brotha shit. Now I'm the *little* brotha?"

"The script has done flipped," he said.

"Well, it's gonna get flipped all over again. So watch yo ass."

I watched him go through what he went through. When it looked like Humpty Dumpty was falling off the wall, he put Humpty Dumpty back together again. And he came out of it stronger, smarter, humbler. He turned the thing around. Bean 3.0 was the best Bean of all.

Love and respect. That's what I felt when he hit eighty-one points January 22, 2006, against the Raptors. I saw that

*Showing love to Kobean prior to a Celtics–Lakers game, Christmas Day 2008.*

as his conviction and culmination. He manifested his rhythm. He hit 'em and continued to hit 'em. Sixty wasn't enough. Seventy wasn't enough. Even eighty wasn't enough. Eighty-one was the number. Damn near couldn't believe it. Thought I was watching a video game. And it was against one of my greater friends, Sam Mitchell, who was coaching the Raptors. I even got mad because I was rooting for Kob to outscore Wilt, who dropped in 100 back in 1962.

And then came the 2010 championship, when Bean beat us with a broken index finger on his shooting hand. That was real beast mode.

We told ourselves in that Game 7 that we were gonna stop Kob. That was our strategy. But Kob found a way to win anyway. While he was struggling, he was quick to see who wasn't. Metta Sandiford-Artest, still called Ron back then, had a hot hand. He scored twenty. The last three were the most important.

We played that critical possession perfectly. Fourth quarter. Minute left on the clock. Lakers up three. Bean has the ball on the wing. Ray is playing him straight-up. Everybody in the building knows he wants to take that shot. Fuck no, we ain't gonna let him. Rasheed comes over to double and Kob drives right. But Ray cuts him off, doesn't let him in the lane. So Bean goes up in the air and gets off a tough pass to Metta behind the arc. P has already rotated over and gets a hand in his face, makes a nice contest. We do everything we're supposed to do. Ball just goes in.

There were a lot of tears in the locker room after the game. A lot of hugs. More than ten years later, that loss is still hard to accept. That C's team was too good to only get one ring. But Bean's brilliant pass and Metta's three did us in.

Kobe's final season, where every city showered him with love, led to some of the most sentimental moments in the history of hoop. The world came out to cheer him, embrace him, and say, "We love you for more than your play. We love you for your character, your intelligence, your dignity, your devotion to carrying on what Jordan had started—taking this game around the world, fighting through the muck and media to where you wind up standing taller than Mount Everest."

In his last game, of course he'd score sixty. No-brainer.

If I have any guilt, it's that I didn't take our friendship to another level. After we retired, I could have reached out more. I wish I had. But Kobe had gone down to Orange County and I was up in LA. We were leading two different lives and moving in different directions.

When I got the news that Kob and his precious daughter and all those other good folk had gone on to Glory, the first person I called was Paul Pierce. He'd be hurting the way I was hurting. I had to talk to P. But I couldn't talk. All I could do was cry. Well, it's okay to cry like a baby. When I think how Kob's time was cut short, I gotta cry. No other reaction is real. This grief ain't going away. But somehow I gotta move from grief to belief. I gotta go to spirit. Spirit is real. Spirit is something we can feel. The spiritual truth is that I, along with the rest of the world, will be feeling Bean's spirit for the rest of our days.

Land Cruiser / Lawyers / Leadership /
Eldrick Leamon / Learning / Bruce Lee / Lil Wayne /
Loyalty / Tyronn Lue / Lynching

# Land Cruiser

When you land in a new spot, you need guides. Kevin McHale, a native-born Minnesotan who'd been promoted to the T-Wolves general manager, introduced me to the team trainer, Clayton Wilson, an old-school cat who was all about drinking beer, walking around in his jockstrap, scratching his balls, and looking to party.

Clayton says, "Take these shorts. We were saving them for Damon Stoudamire, but they'll fit you fine."

Damon "Mighty Mouse" Stoudamire was 5'10". The shorts wouldn't even cover my nuts.

Took me a while to catch on to Clayton's sense of humor. I also didn't realize that Clayton was Kirby Puckett's right-hand man. Kirby was the powerhouse hitter who had led the Minnesota Twins to two World Series victories. Prince might've been king of Minnie, but Kirby was the mayor. No one knew Minnie better than Kirby. He gave me my first and best download. He knew the Twin Cities landscape like the back of his hand. Showed me Plymouth, Lake Calhoun, North Side, South Side. Here's where the Somalians live. Here's where the Ethiopians live. Both those populations are growing. Cool people all over.

Minnie is the first city where I saw Black and white folk dating, holding hands, having kids who were curly-haired, beautiful, strong. I'm digging it, breathing it all in. It's quaint but funky. In St. Paul, an R&B/gospel choir called Sounds of Blackness is singing songs with titles like "Optimistic" and "Spirit," lifting hearts and making a joyful noise.

In Chicago, I never ventured out much. I was locked inside the city. You got no money, so you're basically a slave to the L. Your radius is relatively small. Minnie was the opposite. I moved to a huge penthouse in an apartment complex that faced Ridgedale Center, a suburban mall. It was a perfect place to start off. I wanted to stay where I could jump on the freeway and have a straight shot to practice.

I had dope teammates. Sam Mitchell, JR Rider, Doug West, and Terry Porter. They were all guides. I needed these cats to show me the real hood. That meant the North Side. Harold's Chicken. The part of Minnie that seemed to be mimicking Chicago. I liked that mimicking.

But I also liked the burbs because they were quiet. I hired Moms's sister Aunt Betty to manage my home. I knew good home cooking would do me a world of good. So would being surrounded by family.

The only hassle was snow. I had me some cars—my first—but they had rims and low pro tires that couldn't cut through the snow. Bought a Land Cruiser cause Biggie talked about it in "Machine Gun Funk"—the jeep with the Mach 10 by the seats. Wasn't thinking about no Range Rover or Tahoe or Suburban. No sir, had to have me a ride just like Big's.

One night, learning to drive in the snow, Bug and I were doing donuts in an empty parking lot. When we got tired of doing 360s, we went in a store to buy some snacks. Store's empty except for two guys: Jimmy Jam and Terry Lewis. Had never met 'em before. Of course I knew and loved their music. Knew that they, Morris Day, and Prince had put together the Time. The Time had Jesse Johnson, the guitarist who gave me goose bumps, probably the baddest gunslinger since Jimi Hendrix. Jimmy and Terry had also cut the S.O.S Band, not to mention "Saturday Love" by Cherrelle and Alexander O'Neal, a jam that had me half-crazy every time I heard it. When it came to R&B, Jam and Lewis were Minnie royalty.

"Hey, KG," said Jimmy, "you got practice in the morning, don't you? Does Flip know you're out so late?"

I had to laugh, pay my respects to the music these brothas made, but also had to push and say, "What are y'all doin' here? It's way past old people's bedtime."

"We're not too old to have you guys over the house," said Jam.

"Now?"

"Why not?"

House was on a mansion on the lake. Looked like Yves Saint Laurent did the interior design. It was a fortress. It was immaculate. Something out of a magazine. Jam was the first brotha I knew to have a screening room with a hundred-inch TV in the wall. Indoor pool.

| Favorite Football Players |
|---|
| 1 Lawrence Taylor |
| 2 Walter Payton |
| 3 Randy Moss |
| 4 Randall Cunningham |
| 5 Mike Singletary |

Elevator in the crib. Three generators. Six-car garage. Ferrari.

Turned out that Kirby Puckett lived in Edina, just outside the city, where Jam and Lewis had their Flyte Tyme studio. I could drop by the studio any time I wanna. Watch Mariah Carey cutting a track. Watch Mint Condition and a reunited New Edition. Minnie's music culture is blasting all over the world, and, lucky me, I'm in the control booth with the cats making it happen.

I'm chillin' at South Beach, a dope downtown nightclub. I'm with my boys, Bug and them. We run into all kinds of brothas. Brothas going to the University of Minnesota, brothas from South Dakota, brothas from a junior college in Kansas or Nebraska. I'm hearing about their lives on campus. Wanna know what I'm missing out on.

I'd go as far as to call it Mellow Minnie. Take the football brothas. Football brothas are aggressive. Cats like John Randle, one of the best Vikings to ever suit up. In a couple of years wide receiver Randy Moss—we call him Mossy—comes along.

These dudes are tearing up the NFL. At the same time, they're treating me like a long-lost friend. Much respect all around.

All I gotta do is show up at the Target Center in downtown Minnie and get the team going. I was determined. I was built for the grind. I was going for a championship.

Easier said than done.

## Lawyers

The first thing you learn about the league is that the league is two-thirds counsel. Those lawyers are looking through contracts, looking at language to change, looking for diversions, looking for alternatives. Looking for ways to gain an advantage, to come up with a strategy. The NBA is about fine print as much as it is about basketball.

## Leadership

My mom always told me, "If you're in the room and you're looking for the leader of that room and you can't find him, that's because you're it."

Facts.

## Eldrick Leamon

First brotha I knew who started putting cuts in his eyebrows—that was Eldrick. Big man. Six feet four, over 200 pounds. Some of the kids called him "Uncle El,"

cause he looked older than his age. In Greenville, when Southside High won the state championship in 1992, Eldrick was just a sophomore. My cousin Shammond Williams, a junior, played on that same team. Eldrick was the first young brotha I knew who had real bread. He worked the streets. For a while, we were on the same AAU team. That was the first time in Carolina I traveled to other gyms in other cities. Eldrick was sharper than me. He'd point out the differences of how brothas from all-Black schools played.

*Eldrick Leamon, 1994.*

"Check out their swag," he'd say.

Brothas from predominantly white schools had a different swag, maybe a little more low-key.

Eldrick saw the subtleties. He also had a big heart. Mr. Generosity. When his business was good, he'd go around the hood helping folks with their rent; he gave out everything from food to sneakers. Took care of his people. He was a real one.

Then came the summer of 1994.

Phone rang. It was one of my boys.

"Eldrick's dead."

I didn't wanna hear what I heard.

"Say what?" I said.

"Eldrick Leamon. He's dead."

Big breath. Big sigh. Heart beating out my chest. I took it in. Stayed silent a second or two.

"Street shit?" I asked.

"Nothing like that. He got killed in Myrtle Beach. He was riding one of his motorbikes when someone ran a light."

Every summer in Myrtle Beach they had Black Beach Weekend. Black college kids would show up. Eldrick loved roaring into those carnival parties on his Kawasaki. He was the first cat to come through the neighborhood with those rides, switching up from mopeds to bikes. We loved looking at those joints; we loved the loud-ass sounds they made. We loved Eldrick for bringing the noise.

Those were the thoughts racing round my mind as I took in the news. Only a couple of weeks earlier, Uncle El had graduated high school. He was eighteen. When I think back now, I remember that Eldrick's teammate Merl Code had a big career at Clemson. His other homie Mike Menniefield wound up at St. John's.

Now Eldrick's future became his past. His past was all we had of him. His past stayed with me, not only cause he was a boss hooper, but because his heart was big. His past sat next to me when I got to the league and signed with the T-Wolves. I made it my duty to remember him. Before pregame introductions at the Target Center, I made sure that the seat to my left was empty. That was Eldrick's seat. I wanted him with me at every game. I wanted his past to be my present. I wanted him present with me. And he was. And he is. And always will be.

# Learning

Two Bible quotes about seasons stick in my mind:

Genesis 8:22: "As long as the earth endures, seedtime and harvest, cold and heat, summer and winter, day and night will never cease."

Ecclesiastes 3:1: "There is a time for everything, and a season for every activity under the heavens; a time to be born and a time to die; a time to plant and a time to uproot; a time to kill and a time to heal; a time to tear down and a time to build; a time to weep and a time to laugh; a time to mourn and a time to dance."

Like everyone, my life has been marked by seasons. The season of my Carolina childhood had pain mixed with joy. The season of my time in Chicago was super intense. I'd never felt anything as cold as that city's season of winter, but even more, Chicago seasoned *me*, a country kid.

Now here comes Minnie, a season that lasted twelve seasons. There were seasons within seasons—seasons of hope, seasons of heartbreak, seasons of triumph, and seasons of fierce frustration.

My first NBA season wasn't easy. Bug was my roommate, which was cool, because we spent a lot of time playing CDs and Sega. I didn't drink or smoke—and that helped keep my mood from roller-coasting. The two-times-a-day practices under Coach Bill Blair were brutal, but when I got to the league, I expected brutal. In the actual games, Blair subbed me in for forwards Tom Gugliotta and Christian Laettner. I thought back to when I was a kid playing with Billy who pretended to be Laettner. *Man, if Billy could see me now!* I wasn't a starter right away and didn't expect to be. The T-Wolves got off to a sluggish start. We were six and fourteen. So just before Christmas, Kevin McHale canned Blair and made Flip Saunders, his teammate from the University of Minnesota and general manager of the team, the new coach. Flip and I were always on the same page. Respect both ways. Flip knew the game and saw my potential. He raised my basketball IQ.

I had lots to learn, which I realized the first time I played against Chris Webber. C-Webb was one of the players I molded my game after. Brotha wasn't laying up. He was dunking on your ass. He had these huge hands. Huge heart.

*With (right to left) Kevin McHale, Flip Saunders, and Timberwolves owner Glen Taylor, October 1995.*

Well, that first game against him, he did his trademark jump hook. Now I knew Webb's game. I knew the jump hook was coming. That was his favorite move to get him started. Little baby hook in the middle—back you down, two dribbles, right over left shoulder. I'd seen it before, but never in an actual game playing against him. My reaction was to stand there and watch it in amazement. Minutes later, when I got to the bench Sam Mitchell set me straight.

"I know that's your boy, KG, I know he's your favorite, but you can't be no fan out here. You gotta compete. This ain't no fan shit. You gotta bust his ass."

Then Sam gave me a little slap. Sam woke me up.

Next game against C-Webb, I goaltended his first shot and launched the ball into the second row.

"Get that fuckin' shit outta here!" I screamed.

"Oh, now we talkin' like that," said Webb.

"Hell, yes!"

Chris answered me calmly. "Hey, young fella, why don't we just keep it about hoop?"

He was right, and, taking the cue, I chilled. Webb was a beast, and I looked forward to every time I went up against him, but he also had a coolness that helped me build character.

When it came to character building, Sam Mitchell became the main man. It

*First day of practice, October 1995.*

didn't start out that way. In our first practice, before the season even started, Sam
and Doug West were doing some dirty
shit to me. I didn't take to it. I also didn't
like being referred to as "Rook." Sure, I
was a rookie, but the term felt demeaning.

Doug and I got into it. And that wasn't
my only brawl. I found myself fighting
my own teammates more than I ever
expected. I was getting beat up pretty
good.

That's why I withdrew from them
socially. Stayed to myself. Only hung
out with Bug.

First road trip comes along and I'm
in my hotel room. Phone rings. Sam
Mitchell.

"Let's talk."

I hang up on his ass.

*Knock knock.* Someone's at the door.

I cracked it open with the chain still
attached.

Sam Mitchell.

"What you want?" I asked.

"Wanna talk," he said.

"About what?"

"Just open the door, dawg."

I did. Sam came in and sat in the easy
chair across from the bed where I'd been
trying to nap. He broke it down.

"Look, man, you taking shit too personal. We're just seeing what you're made
of. That's all it is. We in the trenches
together and we gotta make sure you got
what it takes. We out there against the
best in the world. Jordan. Hakeem. Barkley. Karl. Got no time to fuck around."

Sam went on to teach about bonding
versus being focused on myself. It was
about giving up my own shit for the bet-
terment of the team. More Sam talked,
more I liked him. He was a Georgia

*Sam Mitchell, 1999.*

brotha who related to me as a Carolina
brotha. We came from the same mud.
But now he presented himself to me as
a grown-ass man. He had kids. He had
businesses, assets. He wore sharp suits.
He cared about his appearance. He was
also a fighter, rough and tough, a junkyard
dog, a scrapper, one of them old-school
dudes who had something to say about
new-school dudes making a bunch of
money. He understood what I needed.
He saw that I was actually crying out for a
mentor. We had a connection and wound
up talking three hours that night. I give
Sam props for patiently working through
my salty attitude.

Another teammate who helped me let
my guard down was Malik Sealy. Malik
came to Minnesota from Detroit in 1998.

I know Sam taught me not to be fan, but around Malik I couldn't help it. The reason I wore the number twenty-one was because that was the number Malik wore at St. John's. Now here I was sharing a huddle with him.

Malik came from strong roots. His dad had been one of Malcolm X's bodyguards. Malik was named after El-Hajj Malik El-Shabazz, Malcolm's full name. He was sophisticated and quiet. Took it all in. Less is more.

More I was around Malik, more I liked him. We even looked alike. His big eyes reminded me of mine. He had the low-cut fade. Unlike me, he wasn't standoffish. Though I wasn't about to make the first move toward a friendship, he did. He called my room and said, "Man, there's a dope little restaurant downstairs. Let's grab something to eat."

"I'm cool," was all I said.

"Well, I'll be there if you wanna come. You feel me?"

I went and was happy to see that Sam was with him. Sam was the one who got him to call me. Sam, Malik, and I became a trio. Those two brothas brought me into a comfort zone. Malik had something I lacked: patience. He taught me to slow down. Not to interrupt when someone was talking. Listen for the right pause in a conversation before butting in. Malik's smoothness rubbed off on me.

Initiation into the world of the NBA ain't easy. Sam and Malik walked me through the process. They didn't have to. They could have let me continue my standoffish ways. But they broke me down and got me to realize that, through kindness and care, we all need each other.

In an interview, Sam said it best.

"They talk about me helping Kevin, but I was the older brother [or] uncle. Malik was the best thing for Kevin. He had someone his own age to talk to. He really taught Kevin to enjoy being Kevin. Kevin used to kid that being in his shoes was a chore. When Malik came along, all of a sudden it was fun to be Kevin Garnett. He made it not a chore."

## Bruce Lee

*see* **Chauncey B-B-B-B-Billups; The Great Kabuki**

## Lil Wayne

*see* **Glen Davis; "King Kunta"; The N-Word; One-and-Done**

## Loyalty

Loyalty is based on love. If you're loved—if you give and get love—you stick around. If not, you split.

Basketball teams can be like a family. Some fams are harmonious, some dysfunctional. If you come from a dysfunctional fam, you want out soon as possible. If you find a loving family, like I did in both 'Sota and Boston, you stick around.

But a deeper truth is that loyalty that wasn't misplaced—loyalty in brothas like my boy Bug and my coach Wolf—turned out to be lifesaving. Even when

I think on how lack of loyalty fucked me up—how my friends turned on me in Carolina and had me nearly in jail—I see that positively. I can safely say I see practically everything that happened to me positively. If I hadn't had to escape Carolina, I would have missed Chicago. The Go forced me to grow a second skin. The Go toughened me to where I could face the NBA. Even Moms's decision to keep me from playing in Cali with Paul Pierce my senior year—a decision that didn't make me happy—forced me back to Wolf who, more than anyone, had my best interests at heart. Don't know what kind of experience I would have had at Inglewood High, but Farragut Career Academy was the boot camp I needed.

No regrets. Just major gratitude for the forces that shaped me as a man-child looking to stay steady in the world and make my way through the maze.

## Tyronn Lue

Loooooooooooooooooooooooooooooooo oooo . . . aka Hef.

Hef as in Hefner.

Women love him cause he's suave. Women love smooth-skinned, short guards who can box.

First time we met was through trainer Joe Abunassar, famous for his Impact Basketball program. Joe had more energy than anyone I'd ever met. He was a JV Indiana Hoosier grad who'd been a manager under Bob Knight and came up with a whole new structure of wellness that included nutrition and body-composition analysis as well as marathon running.

Cross-country had always been one of my strengths, so I locked into Joe's thinking right away. Joe was like Wolf in that he had me working against the guards, had me playing against the threes and twos to better my ability as a big.

One summer after I'd been in the league three years or so, I'm training with Joe, who's also recruited Antoine Walker into his program. Antoine and I have a history of going after each other, so having him in the mix is fun. We're playing super hard when I notice this little guard who's hooping like a house on fire.

"Who's that?" I ask

"That's Ty Lue. He's from Nebraska."

Chaunce, who's always there, calls Ty Lue over to meet me.

He's all excited, super gassed. "Ticket! You my man! Meet my cousin Doodles, we're big fans. We love you, bro. We can't believe we're actually here with you."

T-Lue and Shot were tight cause they'd played against each other in Nebraska. (Jump up a couple of decades when Ty is named head coach of the Clippers and his first hire is Chaunce as his lead assistant.) That summer, the bonding between Ty and me was instant. Like we'd already been friends forever. He was a different kind of brotha. Cool dude. Wild, but not out-of-control wild. Had him a short fuse. Also quick as fuck. Fighting spirit. Razor sharp. Super smart. Always had slick shit to say. Always positive. Once he entered my life, he stayed in my life. No matter where our careers took us, nothing came between us.

There are lots of T-Lue/Ticket stories. Here's my favorite:

On a Saturday night, we sitting around my crib, chilling out in front of the TV.

*Tyronn Lue goes up for a shot, 2002.*

When it comes to TV shows, I don't get all that worked up. I'm laid-back and just taking it in. But this one show, for some reason, has got me going. I love the concept. It's P. Diddy's *Making the Band*. Brothas come in trying to knock out a band that's ruling the roost. I like this new band. They got a bop that should get 'em over. Trouble is, they ain't asserting themselves. They gotta come on strong. I'm relating to them because I see if they do push hard, they'll make it.

I'm actually talking to the musicians. My competitive juices are boiling over.

"They can't hear you, Ticket," says T. "You know that, don't you?"

T is reasonable. I ain't. I keep hollering.

"Do it! Get up in that other band's ass and blow 'em outta there."

I'm seeing myself on the court playing hoop. Grabbing a rebound. Dunking. These dawgs gotta dunk!

"Easy, Ticket," says T. "It's a silly reality show."

"Ain't nothing silly about this shit! These brothas gotta get it together. They gotta come together."

But they don't. They don't do what I tell them to do. They squabble among themselves. They don't act like a team. Don't make the moves they gotta make. Something snaps in me. I'm thinking they're a basketball team and how pissed I'd be if one of my teams acted how they're acting. I scream at 'em even louder.

"Ticket," T tells me. "You're going nuts over nothing. Calm your silly ass down."

But by then, I'm gone. I'm so enraged at the TV band that I take my fist and punch a hole clean through the wall. Plaster all over the place. All over some crazy TV show.

"Ticket!" screams T, who's laughing hysterically. "You crazy!"

# Lynching

In Carolina I saw how the idea of lynching got flipped around to be used against me. That was so crazy that it made me go back and learn something about the original narrative. Historical facts get forgotten cause we're so caught up in what's happening today.

In 1932, Franklin Delano Roosevelt was elected president and became the hero of liberals for decades to come. I get it. He started the New Deal and helped beat back the Depression. In 1934, his wife, Eleanor, worked with the NAACP on legislation to outlaw lynching. Imagine that shit—there were no laws against lynching! Mrs. R and the NAACP got a couple of senators to sponsor the bill, but Mrs. R's old man wouldn't endorse it. The president of the United States of America was too worried about his racist white voters to come out against publicly murdering Black men. You still see these photographs of Black men being hung in town squares with white folk looking on, some smiling, some cheering. This is the sickening legacy of American history. Eighty-nine years later, the legacy lives on. Lynching may change forms—it's a chokehold, a strangulation, a shot in the back, a blow to the head—but cold-blooded murder is cold-blooded murder.

I've had people say to me, "Black folk always be complaining. Black folk can't get over the past. But you, of all people, got no right to complain. America's been good to you. You got famous. You got rich."

Facts. But the bigger fact is that the owners of the teams employing me got even richer. Another fact: My accomplishment was possible because of others who busted down the doors. Jackie Robinson busted out by joining the Dodgers in 1947. Three years later, Earl Lloyd

broke the color line in the NBA. I already mentioned Spencer Haywood who had to go to the Supreme Court to get the green light to jump from high school to the NBA.

These were brave brothas who never backed down. These are the pioneer warriors who deserve the credit. When the white world said no, they said, "Fuck you."

So, the way I look at it, America didn't give us nothing. We took it. We took it cause we got so good they couldn't deny it. We not only turned these sports into art forms, we kept changing and improving the art form until the fans, no matter how racist, had to give it up to us. So when someone says, "Be grateful to America," I say, "America, be grateful to us." We entertained your ass, we thrilled your ass, we innovated, and we invented. Whether on baseball fields, football fields, basketball courts, tennis courts, Broadway stages, movie screens, science labs, concert halls, nightclubs; whether in novels or poetry or raps or business—we changed up the game at a brutal cost. Whatever you pay, no matter how big it is, we've paid more as a people who've suffered vicious abuse.

Bottom line: you owe us a lot more than we owe you.

Just saying.

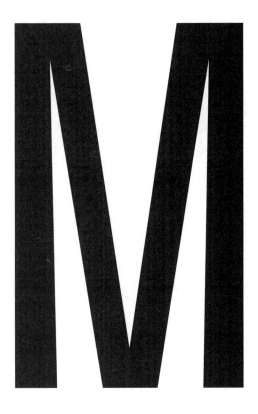

Karl Malone / Gucci Mane / May 19, 2000 /
Kevin McHale / Sam Mitchell / Alonzo Mourning / MV3

# Karl Malone

see **Charles Barkley; LeBron James; Kobe; Flip Saunders; Tough Guys; Rasheed Wallace**

# Gucci Mane

see **Headphones**

# May 19, 2000

My birthday celebrations were low-key. On May 19, 2000, when I turned twenty-four, it was enough to have dinner with some of my closest friends: Reggie Goldsmith, the Greenville star hooper who had moved to Minnie to help me out, and Malik Sealy. 1999–2000 had been my best year yet. I averaged nearly twenty-three points and twelve rebounds per game, made the All-NBA first team for the first time, and helped the T-Wolves to the playoffs for the fourth year in a row. Along with Sam Mitchell, Malik was my anchor.

It was a rainy, miserable night, but soon as the three of us arrived at Monte Carlo, my favorite restaurant in Minnie, it was all good. We talked the night away. Malik could always calm my hype and make me feel like the world was right. Sam Mitchell came by at some point, warming up the vibe even more. My two big brothas sitting side by side. My consiglieres. We talked the night away. Malik talking about Baseline, a recording studio he'd set up with Jay-Z. He'd been an actor in films like *Eddie* with Whoopi Goldberg and mentioned other movies he'd like to make. Also talked about the summer free agency and all the combinations that might come down. For his part, Sam talked about his future plans to coach. He'd also started playing golf and telling us how it'd help us relax. We made cracks about Big Sam rocking goofy golf outfits. Just niggas having fun.

Around 2 a.m. someone suggested we go over to Déjà Vu, a strip club, to see what was happening. I got pulled onstage, and the girls gathered round to sing me "Happy Birthday." Joint wasn't jammed. Just half-filled. Bangin' music. Dancing. Joking. Nothing heavy.

Now it's 4 a.m. Time to head out. No one's drunk. No one's fucked up. We go outside and wait for our cars. Dude pulls mine around. We all hug up. Sam talks about us playing golf tomorrow, but tomorrow's already here and I ain't committing. I get my final happy birthdays from my brothas and I'm on my way to

*Celebrating with Malik after he hit a three at the buzzer to beat the Pacers on January 17, 2000.*

drop Gold off in Minnetonka and then I'm off to my house by the lake.

Twenty-four years of age. Sounds okay. Life's okay. I feel really grateful that Malik has gone to such lengths to embrace me. Brothas like him and Sam are rare. Older cats who care about guys coming up under them. Closer than family. Closer than blood.

Highway's deserted. Driving's a pleasure. Reggie gets out at his crib and I get home in a hurry. Fall in bed, turn on *SportsCenter* and, thinking happy thoughts, fall asleep.

The world knows the end of the story. While driving home that night, a drunk driver going the wrong way hits Malik's car head-on. At age thirty, Malik is gone.

It's hard to speak about the shock, the loss, the hole in my soul.

Everyone was looking to me, everyone wanting to know how I was gonna process.

I didn't. I didn't deal with it—not emotionally at least. I went through the motions. The memorial. The funeral. Taking in the fact that he was buried in Hartsdale, New York, next to Malcolm X, the man he admired so deeply.

But did I break down and cry the way I wanted to? Was I able to sob like Aunt Betty was sobbing when she told me the news? Did I scream up to God? *Why let this happen to a good man like Malik?* Did I go crazy with grief?

No. And the reason I didn't was cause I was scared of losing it. So rather than lose it, I used it. I used the grief to push me, motivate me, make me play harder in the spirit of a friend I loved so much. I knew how much he meant to me when he was alive, but the meaning became that much clearer—and that much more painful—when he passed. My grief had no bottom.

Besides turning the hurt to hustle on the court, my only other outlet was getting in my Porsche and driving from Minnie halfway to Chicago, top down, cranking up the music, the music blastin' up to the heavens.

Wanting to be free from pain, using the power of the Porsche to accelerate me out of one zone to another. The roar of the engine. The sight of twinkling stars. The white light of the moon. Crank up DMX. Rhyme it up. Wrap up all the hurt, turn it into song, get the feelings to flow from bad to good, don't let the feelings destroy me, distract me, do anything to keep this German sports car from running off the road, keep me in my lane, keep me from exploding, let me live my life with this loss.

Looking back, I probably should have gone for help. Mental health often requires counseling. I needed counseling. I'm hoping people reading this who suffer big loss and pain ain't too proud to get help. Get professional support. Protect the mind and spirit.

I remember back to all those times when I was scared of making friends with a teammate because they might be traded, I never once considered the possibility that they might be killed. Wasn't even a thought. Now it was everyday reality. Now I wished I had told Malik how much he meant to me. Now I realized that we can't take anything for granted. Tomorrow ain't promised. Tell the folks we love that we love them. Tell them now. Tell them every day.

Shot signed with Minnie that next season, and sometimes I think God sent Shot to be with me just so I wouldn't go

*Holding up Malik's son Remi at the Malik Sealy Gym of Dreams at Gethsemane Episcopal Church in Minneapolis, 2001.*

insane after the loss of Malik. Just the strength of Shot's character helped me survive the emotional crisis.

Time may be a healer, but this hurt has outlasted time. The Wolves retired Malik's #2 jersey—and that was good. I wrote "2Malik" inside the tongue of the Adidas Garnett 3 shoes—and that was also good. When in 2013 I was traded from Boston to Brooklyn, I rolled with Malik's #2 on my jersey. When I came back to Minnie for my last dance with the T-Wolves in 2014, I wore a #2 sweatband.

These gestures came from the heart. Remembering Malik, along with Kobean and Eldrick Leamon, in this book is another gesture. As I write, I see their faces. I hear their laughter. I feel their warmth. Their spirits live inside me, but the absence of their flesh and blood still burns my soul to cinders. The tragedy of their deaths has not diminished. The pain is permanent.

## Kevin McHale

"Look what Robert Horry can do, KG," Kevin McHale would always say to me. "He's shooting threes. He's slashing. Look at Shawn Kemp. Look at his game. Look at Scottie Pippen, maybe the best at what he does. Now it's your turn. Your turn to do it all. Bigs have problems on pick-and-roll defense. You need to overcome that problem. Watch Hakeem set a pick. Watch Larry Johnson set a pick. Watch Charles Oakley. These are your teachers."

Kevin turned into one of my mentors and maestros. He was the Yoda to my young Luke Skywalker. I have a feeling that brothas like Rasheed Wallace, Antonio McDyess, Corliss Williamson, and Joe Smith would have given an arm and a leg to switch positions with me to get coached by McHale. Kevin gave me all the one-on-one time I needed. He was always about "Be a four that can handle the ball. Be a four that can pass the ball. Master the simple stuff: show the rock, come over the top, turn around and jump, now do it off the glass, pump fake, be creative, be in the moment, never settle for what you think you can do. Master what you think you *can't* do."

McHale was also a master of moves. He had this slippery eel thing. He had the dipsy-doo. He had the gotcha. He might have been the best power forward because of his ability on the block. Different moves for different defenses. He had a solution for everything. He polished me in a way no one could have. He taught me a skill set that he alone knew how to demonstrate. The absolutely perfect coach, who came along at the absolutely perfect moment.

"It's all about creativity," he said. "Creating space. Creating innovation. Creating confidence."

Kevin taught me that satisfaction is the enemy of progress. If you're satisfied with your game, you ain't growing your game. Turn frustration into fearlessness. Don't let your mistakes fuck you up. Be grateful for your mistakes because they're the key to improvements. Victory is beautiful, but you learn more from your losses. And in Minnie, I'd have plenty of those.

By the end of the 2003 season, we'd made the playoffs seven straight years—and been knocked out in the first round every time. I also no longer had my support system. Malik was dead. Sam Mitchell retired in 2002—same year Shot went to Detroit. With the squad we had, we were never gonna be able to compete. And so, in the summer of '03, McHale made some moves just as impressive as the slippery eel and dipsy-doo.

## Sam Mitchell

*see* **Kobe; Land Cruiser; Learning; May 19, 2000; Kevin McHale; Shaquille O'Neal; Flip Saunders; Tough Guys**

## Alonzo Mourning

*see* **Derrick Coleman; Dunk; "King Kunta"; Shoes; John Thompson**

## MV3

First trade Kevin McHale made ahead of the 2003 season was with the Bucks for Sam Cassell. Then he acquired Latrell Sprewell from the Knicks in a four-team trade. The media called us "MV3." Some journalists also referred to us as "The Big Three"—that was the first time I'd ever heard that term used. *Sports Illustrated* put us on the cover, with Sam quoted as saying, "They've been taking baby steps around here for years. It's time for a leap."

I loved Sam's attitude. At this time, before being traded to a number of teams,

he'd won two championships with Houston, playing a big part in their run and hitting key threes. He was also the master of the midrange. His background was strong. He was taught by no-nonsense old-school brothas in Baltimore and was brimming with confidence. But he also possessed an underlying patience and calmness that kicked in at just the right moments.

The dynamic between me, Sam, and Spree was fire. By the beginning of March, we were 40–16—the third best record in the entire league. Sam and I were both averaging more than twenty points a game, and Spree—in his twelfth season—was playing as well as he had in years, averaging nearly twenty points a game himself. The narrative in the media was that Spree was a "difficult" player, but not so. He was a great teammate—one of my all-time favorites—willing to do whatever he could to help us win. Intense to the max. Spree brought the same high energy all forty-eight minutes. And if anyone on the team's energy or focus flagged, Sam stayed on 'em and made sure they picked it up. If Spree was the most intense player I ever hooped with, Sam was the most vocal. He talked so fast you could barely understand him. He was like the dude who used to do those Micro Machines commercials. He was always chirping at teammates—always pushing us. He knew what it took to win it all. It was like he told *Sports Illustrated*: "You take Spree's emotion, my emotions, Big Ticket's emotions, and stuff all that together? It's the atom bomb. . . . There's talk that me and Spree are getting old. Yeah? Well, we're kicking these young guys' asses."

*With Spree and Sam, 2004.*

One last thing about Spree that not everyone knows: he was a real live nerd. A techie genius. A cat who could take a computer apart and put it back together in thirty minutes. He has his own computer with an alien face—some next-level shit—that he'd built himself.

Spree, Sam, and I went to work. We finished the season 58–24—the best record in all my years there and the first time the T-Wolves ever had the best record in the Western Conference. Having Sam and Spree take the pressure off me allowed me to push my game to new heights. Shout-out to all my other teammates—Gary Trent, Trenton Hassell, Troy Hudson.

That year I became the first player to win four NBA Player of the Month awards in one season. I led the league in rebounds and total points—the first time that had been done in twenty-nine years. I broke eleven T-Wolves single-season franchise records. And I won the regular season MVP. Not bad for a country boy from Carolina. More than that, though, I'd never loved playing on a team more than this one.

Commissioner Stern presented me with the trophy at half-court at the Target Center before the start of the Western Conference semifinals against the Kings. We'd beat the Nuggets in five games in the first round. Finally advancing in the playoffs felt sweet. So did hoisting up that MVP trophy. It was crazy to shake the commissioner's hand just like I had on draft night nine years earlier. Crazy to think about all that had happened in my life since.

I didn't savor it for too long. As I held the trophy up with one hand, I waved my teammates over with the other. The MVP didn't mean shit compared to winning a championship. In order to do that, we would need to get past the Kings. It would be an epic showdown between myself and my idol C-Webb.

*Receiving the MVP Award trophy, May 2004.*

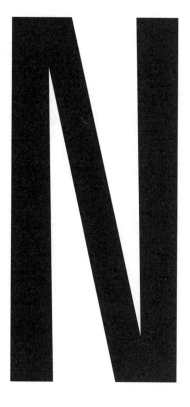

Nas / The National Anthem / Negotiating / Nicknames /
Nike / The Notorious B.I.G. / The N-Word

# Nas

*see* **The Go;** *Illmatic*

## The National Anthem

Going back in time, my rookie year had been unbelievably chaotic. I was running this way and that. Working my ass off. Making money like I had never made before. But also seeing something that, although it didn't make a huge impression on me at the time, makes a huge impression on me now.

Shout-out to Mahmoud Abdul-Rauf.

I knew him as Chris Jackson when he played for the LSU Tigers. He had these cool-ass shoes and his own swag. Not as flashy as Pistol Pete, who everybody compared him to. More a quiet assassin. Master of the transition three. Was doing that twenty years before Steph Curry. There's the famous story about how his high school coach had players shoot free throws at practice until they missed. One day my man stepped to the line and hit 283 straight and delayed practice for forty-five minutes. I saw him as one of the dopest players anywhere. Averaged thirty points his freshman year.

I followed his career into the NBA when he was drafted by Denver in 1990. He had a crazy free-throw percentage of .956. What impressed me even more was that he had Tourette syndrome and still found a way to be great. Made me less embarrassed about my dyslexia and learning challenges. The more I learned about him, the more I realized how much we had in common. Southern kid who grew up in the ghetto. Never knew his pops. He was one of the cats who showed me it was possible to overcome.

The same year he joined the league he became a Muslim, and a couple of years later he changed his name to Mahmoud Abdul-Rauf. Along with Dikembe Mutombo, he helped turn the Denver Nuggets into a competitor. They made NBA history in the 1993–94 season when they bounced Seattle from the playoffs—the first time an eight seed knocked out a one seed. And in the 1995–96 season, they were one of the few teams to beat the 72-win Bulls—Mahmoud pouring in thirty-two that night.

It was that same season when he decided not to stand for the national anthem. He wasn't the first person in hoop to protest that way. Kareem had done it back when he was at UCLA, leading to Coach John Wooden keeping the entire team in the locker room until the anthem was over.

The thing is, nobody cared about Mahmoud's protest at first. Nobody even

*Mahmoud Abdul-Rauf stands in prayer during the singing of the national anthem, March 1996.*

noticed it. He certainly didn't make a big deal about it. When the anthem was playing, he either stayed in the locker room or stretched on the sidelines. It wasn't until a reporter noticed and asked him about it. Yet another example of the media trying to stir up shit. And that's just what they did.

The flag, he said, is "a symbol of oppression, of tyranny. This country has a long history of that. I don't think you can argue the facts. You can't be for God and for oppression."

The league said they'd suspend him if he didn't stand.

"You do what you have to do," he told the league.

So they did. They suspended him. He missed one game and was fined more than $30,000. He was prepared to leave the game for good, but decided he could use his platform as an NBA player to bring attention to oppression. He came back, and from then on he stood for the anthem with his palms turned up and his head bowed in prayer. It was a powerful statement, but of course the media criticized him for it. Said he was compromising by coming back. And then after they made him a pariah, they moved on to the next story.

Mahmoud wanted to move on, but he couldn't. He led the Nuggets in scoring and assists, but that summer they traded him to Sacramento for a second-round draft pick and the injury-prone vet Šarūnas Marčiulionis, who only played seventeen games for Denver the following season before retiring. Mahmoud played two years in Sacramento. His minutes were steadily reduced. By the second season, at just twenty-eight and in what should've been his prime, he was no longer a starter. After his time in Sacramento was up, he only got one offer from an NBA team, and it was so insultingly low he left to play in Turkey. He quit when the team wasn't issuing paychecks and stayed out of the game for two years. In 2001, he signed a veterans' minimum contract with the Grizzlies but didn't play much. That same year, the brand-new house he built in his Louisiana hometown was burned down. It'd already been vandalized a couple times before, the garage torn down, "KKK" spray-painted in big letters. Mahmoud wasn't surprised. Before he moved in, he'd predicted the hate crime. "This is just an indication of how far we've got to go in terms of human relations in this country," he said.

It took another twenty years before the issue of protesting the national anthem came up again when Colin Kaepernick took a knee. And then another four years after that for the world to see that Colin—and Mahoud two decades before him—was right.

The brave stance taken by Mahmoud Abdul-Rauf should not be forgotten. I was nineteen when it all came down. I wish my political consciousness had been higher. I wish it didn't take the world another twenty-five years to understand that athletes' right to protest social wrongs is absolute. Mahmoud paid a big price. His protest curtailed his career. Cost him at least five or six years in the

NBA when he could have come off the bench and knocked down a quick fifteen or twenty. He was that good. After his season with the Grizzlies, he played wherever he could—Russia, Italy, Greece, Saudi Arabia, Japan—earning a fraction of what his talent merited.

"I want to live and die with a free conscience and a free soul when it's all said and done," Mahmoud told *The Undefeated* in an interview a few years back. "That's the journey I'm on."

Now we are—finally—listening to you, Brother Mahmoud, and thanking you for seeing what we didn't see. Thanking you for informing our hearts and inspiring our souls. It took us too long to catch up with your courage and conviction, but better late than never.

# Negotiating

We are all on a journey. When we're in the middle of it, it's hard to see exactly where we are. But it helps me to remember that the journey has twists and turns, highs and lows, and that junctures where we feel lost are, in fact, where we need to be.

My professional journey starts early. I'm just outta high school. I'm gullible. I'm naïve. I believe in the tooth fairy. I think that this world I'm walking into is some kind of dream. A perfect dream. I put the league on a pedestal.

I get to the NBA thinking that everyone up in here is divin' on the floor and giving 100 percent. Ain't true. Some brothas be working their asses off, but some ain't. Then I see I've been bamboozled. League ain't about hoop. League is about money and merchandising and marketing. I've seen street hustling back in Carolina and Chicago, but who the fuck knew about big-time institutional hustling? As an institution, the NBA never stops hustling. The year I was drafted—1995—was the first time the NBA instituted a rookie cap. Before that, a rookie could negotiate as a free agent. I couldn't. A year earlier Glenn Robinson signed a $68 million ten-year deal as the number one pick. The OGs pushed back. The vets knew that young cats like Big Dog getting big bread hurt their ability to squeeze more money out of the owners. They liked the salary cap and, of course, the owners loved it. Owners loved locking up rooks for cheap.

In the draft when I was the number-five pick, Joe Smith was number one. Golden State signed him for $8.53 million and ten years. My deal was $5.4 mill and three years. My rookie year, I earned $1.6 mill.

Next year, '96, was big in free agency. Shaq jumped to LA, Barkley to Houston. That was when I got deep into the world of agents speaking for me. I didn't like that. I didn't want no one speaking for me. I had to be hands-on with my business. Everything had to come directly from me, my words, my emotions. Then when it came time for my contract extension in '97, I had to be extra cool. Never had been privy to money of this magnitude. I'm reading and studying and learning high finance fast as I can. I'm having a million meetings talking about insurance and estate planning and deferred money. All information I was never privy to as a kid. I'm rushing to catch up, rushing to educate myself.

First rule I learn in Negotiations 101: Don't take the first offer.

The first offer is $103.5 mill for six years. I have to gulp. I have to remind myself of that first rule. I have to turn it down. I do.

Sometimes I sit in my agent's office when he's on speaker talking to T-Wolves management. They don't know I'm listening. I'm hearing how blatant they are in discussing me. I'm hearing how they're trying to undervalue me. I take it personally until I remember the second rule in Negotiations 101: Don't take anything personal. It's business.

Rule three kicks in. Rule three maybe is the most important one. Rule three can be summarized in one word: Chill. Be patient. Don't act eager or anxious. Let the T-Wolves take all the time they want. Don't hang around waiting for a counteroffer. Fly off to Jamaica. Enjoy the island. Check out the blue sea, the sunny sky. Watch the gulls flying over the water. Snorkel. Scuba dive. Feast on jerk chicken. Sip on piña coladas. Smell the ganja. Check out the pink-orange-gold-purple sunsets. Be in the bliss.

But then get to the pool and look at the *USA Today* someone just hands me. Big story saying Kevin Garnett just turned down a $122 million offer from the T-Wolves.

What the fuck!

I get on the phone with my agent, who tries to calm me down by saying this is just how negotiations go. I'm not sure. I'm not happy about being left out of the loop. I fly back to Minnie in a hot hurry. I fire my agent and use his assistant to take over the negotiations. We settle on $126 million.

Then comes the night when the documents are all written up. I'm at Flyte Tyme studios listening to rough mixes of *The Velvet Rope*, Janet Jackson's new record. I'm loving it.

"You can go down to the Target Center and sign the contracts," says my man.

"Now?"

"Well, they took their time in putting this deal together, so you take your time. Come down whenever you feel like it."

"Good, cause first I wanna listen to the rest of the new Janet joint."

Contract gets signed but the celebration doesn't last long. Press ain't happy. Press points out that $126 mill is only $30 mill less than what Glen Taylor paid for the whole fuckin' franchise three years earlier. Should I feel guilty about that? Hell, no. I had nothing to do with Taylor's purchase of the T-Wolves. Press also points out this is the richest contract in sports history, surpassing Shaq's $120 mill, seven-year Lakers deal. Other owners are pissed—so pissed that it all leads to the 1998 lockout and the establishment of max contracts.

Suddenly Glen Taylor ain't so witty with me anymore. Kevin McHale looks at me differently. So does Flip. What used to be casual and chill turns icy. More professional. Now it's all business. Cats start hating on me. I gotta look at the book of business and the book of basketball. I see that the book of business *is* the book of basketball. The league falls off its pedestal. In spite—or rather *because*—of my successful negotiation tactics, I'm getting hit from all sides. Moments like these, I thank Chicago and everything it taught me about the murderous reality of hard knocks.

After my big payday, stories start in about how I'm gonna lose my head. Opposite happens. I keep polishing myself with financial knowledge. Keep studying the art of investment. Keep staying the course as a conscientious student of monetary matters.

I also learned about negotiating from lockouts. I went through four of them. The first one is 1995 when I'm a rookie. I'm quiet, attentive, watching it all come down. I'm sitting there and watching David Stern talking slowly and patiently. Classic David Stern. I can see he's an autocrat. When it comes to negotiations, he's a beast. Talks in belittling terms. Talks about hierarchies. A master at smoke and mirrors. Uses a highly educated, tricked-out vocab. He's fucking with us mentally.

But at the same time, Jordan is there. Jordan is very present. Jordan is very educated on the business of basketball. I'm studying Jordan. I'm pulling out nuances from Jordan's approach. Just like on the court, Jordan is looking for the angles to play. I find out MJ is the only brotha allowed to buy naming rights back from the league cause of his impact on the game. Props to Jordan.

But I got a question. How you explain to us what happens with that fine money we pay out? Stern doesn't like the question. Says it doesn't apply to this discussion. Please don't bring that up now. Okay, that's what's up. But the question don't go away.

Meanwhile, I'm researching. I'm soaking up info like a sponge. The internet is out. AOL. I jump on and jump in. Learning, learning, learning. Now I'm glad they put a bull's-eye on my back. Without that bull's-eye, I wouldn't be driven to learn my shit.

Second lockout comes the next year and lasts only a few hours.

But the third lockout is a long one, 191 days from July 1, 1998 to January 6, 1999. It's largely over collective bargaining. I'm showing up in a suit. I'm dressed in black. I'm ready to rock. I got shit to say. I'm assertive. I'm asking tough questions, and if the answers are bullshit, I say so.

The owners are on the stage, looking down at us. I don't like that. I call them out on that. I make my point. I never sit down. Stand up the whole time. Jab when I need to jab. Hold my ground.

The fourth lockout postponed the start of the 2011 season by 161 days. Billy Hunter is exec director of the Players Association. Stern's the commissioner. Little by little, more players are coming to our meetings. At first, it's mainly mid-level guys, but soon I'm seeing LeBron and Kevin Durant. Things are heating up. We're at a deadlock. What I didn't know, though, was that Stern is strategizing to where he's looking to Kobean to resolve the thing. With his huge salary, Bean is understandably interested in getting back out there. With his big influence on everyone—owners and players alike—Bean is part of these exclusive meetings. By Christmas the shit gets settled, but I'm not happy. A lot of us are feeling excluded from the decision-making.

I saw it as Bean telling Billy, "I'm all you need." Bean and I had different views. It wasn't all pleasant. Our brotherhood was strained, but our brotherhood survived.

The summer of 2020 reminded me of what had happened nine years earlier.

This time the league was trying to figure out whether they were going into the Orlando bubble to finish the season during the COVID-19 pandemic. Patrick Beverley tweeted, "Hoopers, say what y'all want. If King James said he hooping, we all hooping, not personal, only BUSINESS."

Players like Jordan, Bean, and LB have tremendous leverage. At various times in NBA history, it's undeniable that, whether you like it or not, they've been bigger than the league.

# Nicknames

There have been a lot of athletes nicknamed "The Kid"—shout-out to Ken Griffey Jr. They called me "*Da* Kid." Can't remember who was the first to call me that, but Nike ran with it—did a whole commercial around it. The thing about anyone nicknamed "Kid" is that eventually you grow up and there's always another "Kid" coming up behind you. So then I became "The Big Ticket," for the number of tickets I sold. I'm not sure who was the first to call me that—it was one of the T-Wolves play-by-play guys, Trent Tucker or Kevin Harlan.

Harlan was the one who always used to say "With no regard for human life!" when I threw down an especially ferocious dunk. I loved that line—it was exactly how I felt on the court. Loved how fired up Harlan would get doing the play-by-play. There would be times when I'd be running up the court and catch him out of the corner of my eye jumping up out of his chair and yelling, spit flying everywhere. He reminded me a lot of the famous wrestling announcer Jim Ross. And whether it was "Da Kid" or "The Big Ticket," having a nickname made me feel like I was one of those wrestler heroes of my youth.

# Nike

*see* **Charles Barkley; Dunk; Father Figures; Fists; The Go; Hollywood; Allen Iverson; June 28, 1995; Kobe; Nicknames; Shoes**

*Big, 1995.*

# The Notorious B.I.G.

February 1997. My first All-Star Game in Cleveland. I was on the street, coming into the hotel, when Biggie and Puffy were getting out of a limo. Biggie was wrapped up in a fur coat so long it was dragging in the snow. Puff spotted me and said, "Big, come over here, man. You gotta meet Kevin Garnett."

I said to myself, *Oh shit, I'm about to meet the royalty of rap. A dude who's been in my ear since someone slipped me that demo tape called* Microphone Murderer.

He spoke to me like he had asthma. Deep voice. Deep breaths. Long pauses before every word. "Hey, man . . . wanna . . . wanna come up and smoke with us?"

"Wish I could, but I got some business."

"We'll . . . catch you later . . . big fella."

He had his arms around two fine chicks who were actually standing under his giant fur coat. They were shorter than him but looked like they were carrying him. At the same time, I could feel Biggie's power. He was a commander, a true-life gangsta, with a face no one would ever forget.

**Favorite Rappers**

1 Biggie
2 Nas
3 Jadakiss
4 Eric B. & Rakim
5 Snoop
6 Jay-Z

Biggie and them went their way and I went mine. First homie I ran into, I said, "Man, I just met Big."

"When? Where is he?"

"Gone up to his suite. But he was on the street, real as rain. You should've seen the chicks. Should've seen the fur coat dragging in the snow. A Russian czar. Puffy was there too. They stylin' like billionaires. Asked me to get high with 'em."

"Why didn't you?"

"Maybe I was intimidated."

"You?"

"Everyone gets intimidated. Sam Mitchell taught me not to be intimidated by anyone on the court. But this is off the court. This is Biggie Smalls. I'm looking at real-life Big. It's a lot to take in. And besides, I don't got shit to say except 'Wow, you're a hero. You're my hero.' So I gave them their space and let them be."

Never in my wildest imagination could I have foreseen that a month later the genius rapper would be dead.

# The N-Word

"Nigga" is a righteous word. "Nigger" is a wrong word. "Nigga" is born out of the shared blood, sweat, and tears spilled by brothas and sisters. "Nigger" is about hate. "Nigga" is about love. "Nigger" is separation. "Nigga" is togetherness. A huge world separates someone who says "You my nigga" from someone who says "You're a nigger."

"Nigger" is an ethnophaulism, a word used strictly to insult an ethnic group. For generations of Black men and women before me, that word was like a knife through their hearts. I understand why they never want to hear it again, in any form.

But times change, words change, meanings change. The genius of a new generation of niggas was to take the worst word we could be called, reinflect it, reinvent it, and give it soul.

Back in time, whites talked about a "good Negro." Today I'm talking about a bad nigga. LeBron James is a bad nigga; in hoop history, along with MJ, maybe the baddest. Travis Scott, with his inventive mind, is a bad nigga. When it comes to words, flip the script. If a cat can sing, like Maxwell or Anthony Hamilton, he's ill. If a book is written beautifully, like the *The Autobiography of Malcolm X*, that's dope, even if Malcolm gave up dealing dope when he saw the light.

There are bougie niggas, many educated and even brilliant politicians and professors, who not only don't want to be called niggas, they want the word obliterated. I know where they're coming from. They're not hearing "nigga"; they're hearing "nigger." They're feeling the pain of the past when whites looked down at us as a lower form of humanity, or not even human at all. Enslaved people were called niggers. Our grandparents and parents fought for dignity. Negro meant dignity. They insisted upon it. God bless them for doing that. But God bless us for being able to switch up the game.

I listen to my own language and I hear a combination of country and concrete, Carolina and Chicago, backwoods and big city. That's my evolution. I got the southern-fried lingo thing from my childhood and I got the ultra-urban rap from the hard-edged ghetto.

I like thinking and learning about the origin of language. For instance, I know that "jazz," our music that came out of the whorehouses of New Orleans, was a synonym for fucking. Man might tell a woman, "I want to jazz you." I also heard an interview with an early inventor of jazz. Cat said he didn't like using the word "jazz." Said it was too vulgar. He was looking for a more respectful term. But hell, today "jazz" is a beautiful word. We think of Miles Davis or Herbie Hancock.

The arguments against the term "nigga" continue but, as far as I'm concerned, they don't matter. That train has already left the station. You ain't gonna get tens of millions of niggas not to say "nigga." I understand that the argument is about self-respect. And I agree. But if I call you "my nigga," it's because I *do* respect you. If I call you bad, it's because I believe you're good. If you're ill, you're sure-enough well.

Another thing: I call many white cats by that name. Flea, the crazy bass player

for the Red Hot Chili Peppers, is a real nigga. So is Eminem.

Hip-hop proved that words without melody can make music. Words are like notes. The jazz musician needs his or her blue notes. The rapper needs his or her dope words. "Nigga." "Thug." "Gangsta." "Bitch." "Ho." Depending on the context, these are notes that can be made to sound beautiful. These are words that, in the hands of poets like Kendrick Lamar, make stories come alive. Make them real. Keep them real. How you gonna tell someone like Jay-Z or Drake or Lil Wayne or J. Cole to write more respectfully? How you gonna get them to censor their vocab? Their voices *are* their vocab, and it's their voices that let us know what they're spittin' is righteous. If the voice has to be cleaned up, the voice loses its authenticity.

To sum up, I don't call myself an African American. I call myself a **N I G G A**. And all real niggas know what that means.

Barack Obama / OGs / Official Block Family /
Hakeem Olajuwon / One-and-Done / Shaquille O'Neal / Onyx

# Barack Obama

There are times when I think about my year in Chicago and wonder if I ever crossed paths with Obama. Did he ever come see me play at Farragut? Did he ever watch the Midnight League? When he was out doing his community organizing, did he ever knock on my door?

The only thing that would've made the Celtics championship sweeter is if we'd gotten to visit the White House when he was president. Don't get me wrong, it was an honor to visit the place and meet Bush. But Obama was the first basketball president. His love for the game is real. This is the cat who, when he arrived at 1600 Pennsylvania Avenue, turned part of the tennis court into a basketball court.

I never got to play in any of those famous games he organized. Probably for the best. Would've been hard for me to keep my beast contained, and the last thing the leader of the free world

*President Obama gets up some shots on the White House court between meetings, 2010.*

needs is a black eye from a KG elbow. I remember when there was a big news story about a dude in one of those games who accidentally busted the president's lip and gave him twelve stitches. I could see something like that happening if we'd been down on the block. Then again, you know what Obama did to that guy afterward? He sent him a framed photo of the incident. That's the kind of man he is. He understands hoop is like politics. Rough shit.

My only misgiving about Obama is this: I wish at least one time he'd gone all-out nigga. Just as police brutality has never stopped at any point in our history, it continued during his time in office. I understand the need for presidential dignity, but enough is enough. I would have loved to see the fury of a Black man voiced for all the world to hear.

No matter, the man is still a hero. Nothing made me happier when, while campaigning for Biden in a Flint, Michigan, gym, he casually hit a corner three and, swagging out, said, "That's what I do."

Mr. President, if you're ever in LA and want to play some one-on-one, hit me up. We can do it at Snoop's crib. Like you, the Dogg's got game.

# OGs

Knowledge. No one knew the option was there. No one knew the league had all

*Me and Bill Russell after winning the 2008 finals.*

these little, minute intangibles. Only the knowledgeable knew that. Only the ones searching and looking. This is when you gotta tap into the network of the NBA. This is why you talk to OGs. This is why OGs are in your locker room. This is how you get better. You do better by being around better.

Rooks need to understand the importance of OGs. And understand that sometimes when the league deems a player too old to sign, that ain't the real reason. Another phrase they like to use is "injury-prone." Ain't always the truth. Sometimes the truth is they don't want the OGs around the rooks. Because they know the OGs will school 'em in the more treacherous and devious ways of the league. Sometimes when they take OGs out of the locker room, it's because of the information being passed along. They don't want us to exchange it. Because that's how we protect ourselves.

When the league puts a bunch of puppies in the locker room that don't know shit and only listen to each other, then guess what? It makes it simple for the league to get things passed. That's why you always gotta show respect for the OGs—not just in the NBA but in any business. Don't just assume they're old and out of touch. Don't just dismiss them with an "Okay, boomer." Download everything you can from the OGs. They can help you help yourself.

# Official Block Family

*see* **Crews**

# Hakeem Olajuwon

*see* **Charles Barkley; Dunk; Learning; Kevin McHale**

# One-and-Done

Going on a side trip. Need to take that side trip cause all this talk about skipping college and heading straight to the league has me thinking ahead to 2005 when Commissioner David Stern pushed through a rule that said an NBA player has to be nineteen and out of high school for at least a year. They called it the One-and-Done because a slew of hoopers, in order to qualify, attended college for a couple of semesters before dropping out and hitting the draft.

The system changed in '95 when I went from Farragut to the T-Wolves. In the following ten years, others did the same. Kobe. Sweet Lou Williams. Dwight Howard. Tracy McGrady. Bron. Huge talents who had huge impact on the game.

So why did the NBA change it up in '05?

It has to do with the institutional power of the NBA and the power of the National Collegiate Athletic Association. It has to do with a combination of leverage and lack of knowledge in our community. And racism. Young athletes often don't know their options. They need to.

Coach Stan Van Gundy said it right. He made the comparison between hoop and other sports. He pointed out that no one is complaining when a kid goes from high school to minor league baseball or minor league hockey. That's because most of those players are white, and, even more, big money isn't involved.

The NCAA is all about big money—big money earned by mainly Black kids. And mainly Black kids coming from working-class or impoverished backgrounds.

Why should such a kid have to give a year of his physical treasure that could be ruined with a knee or ankle injury?

There's a scene in a documentary about Michigan's Fab Five when Jalen Rose and Chris Webber are walking past a department store window where they see C-Webb's jersey on display. Neither can afford to buy it! It's bad enough for a school to use your drawing power as a player to build up their attendance and lend prestige to the institution. But it's even more outrageous when they're cranking out merch that carries your number and your name—and you ain't making a dime.

When the NCAA asked Condoleezza Rice, President George W. Bush's secretary of state, to look into it, she said One-and-Done "played a significant role in corrupting and destabilizing college basketball . . . and restricting the freedom of choice of players." In this instance, she turned out to be a righteous sista.

The argument from the other side says that the players need a year to mature. In some cases, maybe. In other cases, bullshit. The game has advanced to where younger brothas are picking up skills earlier and earlier. College coaches are there to mature the players, not only from a sports perspective but also from a social and mental perspective. But if they use their power to control the player, that's just plain wrong. Sports is on the back of these players who make millions for the colleges. These players deserve to be benefitting in major ways in all aspects of their lives. Makes me furious to see them used as cash cows.

I'm all for education. If a young hooper wants a college education, great. Beautiful. Let him go to college for however long he wants. But then there are the kids like me, kids who, even in high school, are already playing on a league level. And you can always go to college after you're done playing if you really want to. That's what Bill Willoughby did. When I called him to ask his advice about turning pro, he was in his freshman year at Farleigh Dickinson University. Eventually graduated when he was forty-four. Jordan and Shaq too—they went back to college to finish their degrees. Props to Juwan Howard. He took independent study courses during his rookie year with the Washington Bullets and graduated that spring.

Then there's Vince Carter. In 2001, he walked in his cap and gown to receive his diploma from UNC, then jumped on the Raptors owner's private plane and flew to Philly, where his Raptors were playing the 76ers in Game 7 of the Eastern Conference finals. Vince missed a last-second shot that would've tied the game. Of course, the snarky media couldn't resist criticizing him for going to the graduation ceremony.

Bottom line: The two sports where Blacks dominate—basketball and football—have a fucked-up hookup with the NCAA. The NBA won't let you in until you're out of high school for a year; the NFL makes you go to college for at least three years.

Little Stevie Wonder became a pro at eleven.

Aretha Franklin became a pro at eighteen.

Lil Wayne became a pro at fourteen.

Talent is talent. Genius is genius. America is about money, and even though hoop is different than the arts, I know damn well that hoop is an art form. Hoopers are artists.

To handcuff the prodigy artist from making money is criminal. And when the handcuffing is done by primarily white institutions, and when the artists being handcuffed are mainly Black . . . well, I can't do better than go back and quote Marvin Gaye, who sang, "Makes me wanna holler and throw up both my hands."

## Shaquille O'Neal

He's four years older than me. When he hits the league, he looks like a god. Over seven feet. In total control. The court belongs to him. The game belongs to

*Practicing at Mauldin High in my Shaq jersey, 1994.*

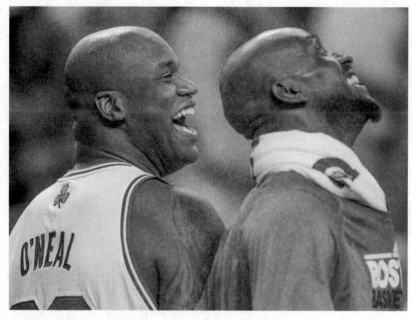

*Sharing some laughs with Shaq, 2010.*

him. He came in with a new superpower we ain't seen before. I copied his script. He became a household word, a brand. Never got in trouble. Brilliant in business. On the court, he always looked the same to me, always looked 7'12". I was always grateful he wasn't an angry man. If he had been a super goon, none of us would have had a chance. I thank him for being a great person and role model. Him and Jordan both.

I first met Shaq on the set of the 1994 film *Blue Chips.* I had an uncredited part playing in one of the games they filmed. Didn't get to spend much time with Shaq or his teammate and costar Penny

Hardaway, but seeing him up close, I was like, "Damn, how the fuck is anybody supposed to guard this dude?"

Then comes the day when I actually have to try. For all my ain't-no-one-gonna-intimidate-me attitude, I got to check myself. Gotta remember what Sam Mitchell taught me. I gotta find my bad self, but the kid inside me who watched Shaq dominate as an Orlando Magic, breaking backboards with his dunks, was now about to face this giant on the floor of the Forum in his LA Laker uniform.

Gulp.

Then, seconds before the game, here comes the Big Diesel, the Big Aristotle, all 325 pounds of the NBA's undisputed Superman. As he approaches, I'm wondering, *What's he gonna say? How's he gonna unnerve me?* It won't take much.

He looks me straight in my eyes and, like he's known me my whole life, smiles and asks, "What's up, brotha? How you doin'? Your mama good? Everybody good? I see you doing good. I see you here to stay."

And with that, he gives me a quick handshake, not a dap, just an old-school handshake. I'm flattered and thrilled and, once the game starts, I realize that, in his own sweet way, Shaq found a way to unnerve me.

Every time I got to play him was magical. No trash-talking, either from him or me. He just gave me looks. He communicated so much with his eyes— surprise, disdain, admiration. Shaq was in Cleveland when we were making our run with Boston. I felt like this was a chance for me to get a little redemption on all the times him and Bean beat up on the T-Wolves. Doc told me one of those nights when we were playing the Cavs, "I need you to guard Shaq for a couple minutes." Perk, who usually took him, was getting a breather. Guarding Shaq is like holding up the side of a house. After those two minutes, I couldn't raise my arms to give anyone a high five. I'm not exaggerating. My arms were that tired. If you had slapped me, I couldn't put my hands up to defend myself.

That following season—his last— he came to the C's. Seeing him in the green-and-white after so many years in the purple-and-gold took a minute to get used to. I knew he was a great teammate

from the All-Star Games we'd played together, and it was the same in Boston. He brought such a good vibe to the team. Had the team not traded Perk to OKC, I have a feeling Shaq might've gotten himself a fifth ring.

Shaq found a way to do most everything he's wanted to do: acting, broadcasting, DJing, even rapping. Hoops fans got on him for rapping. Not me. I supported him. Love talking music with him. My fav Shaq joint was, "You Can't Stop the Reign," where he was with Biggie and a sample of "You Can't Stop the Rain" by the British R&B group Loose Ends. It was a crazy mash-up of different genres and talents. Shaq put his shit on top of all that with respect and grit. Fact is, that whole album, where he had everyone from Jay-Z to Mobb Deep to Rakim to Bobby Brown, was bad.

# Onyx

DMX was by far the biggest influence on my style and swag as a player, but the Queens hip-hop group Onyx also had a big impact on me. They were in your face—rap's version of punk rock. Their big 1993 hit "Slam" was an ode to slam dancing, but I also heard it as an ode to dunking. I'd listen to that joint and feel like they were telling me to tear off the rim.

They also made the bald head look cool. In their song "Atak of Da Bal-Hedz," they rapped about the wisdom of getting a razor and making hair disappear. There was a lot of truth to that. I had hair my rookie season, a tight little fade, but I realized I was spending too much time on it. I was being way too vain—and being a rookie in the NBA, it was hard enough staying humble. So I shaved my head and kept that look the rest of my career.

Which brings me to the hoodie. A lot of people ask me how I manage to keep my hoodie on the back half of my head without it sliding off. Some people have even said I use tape. No, it's all about the shave. When you shave against the grain, it gives your scalp a little sandpaper quality. It's like grip tape on a skateboard. The fabric of the hoodie clings to that.

# P

Pain / Candace Parker / Partnership / Gary Payton /
Peanut Butter and Jelly / Rosie Perez / Perfection /
Kendrick Perkins / Paul Pierce / Scottie Pippen / Players First /
Prejudice / Prince / Promenade / Kirby Puckett

# Pain

Twenty-one seasons. Four of those I played all eighty-two games. Four other seasons I missed just one or two games. That's 1,462 games total. Number seven all-time. And that doesn't count playoffs: 143 more games. Plus fifteen All-Star Games. Plus eight Olympic games. Ten seasons I averaged more than thirty-eight minutes. Seven playoff runs I averaged more than forty minutes. I'm not saying this to boast. I'm saying it to emphasize how much strain I put on my body. How much physical punishment all players endure.

Doesn't take much to twist an ankle, break a finger, tear a tendon. There's a long list of dramatic injuries that sadly short-circuited careers. Thinking of Grant Hill. Thinking of Penny Hardaway, Derrick Rose, Andrew Bynum. Brothas who suffered bad breaks. My heart is with them.

Sometimes you get lucky and avoid injuries for long periods. Sometimes you don't. I got unlucky in February 2009. The Celts were 44–11 and looking good to get back to the finals and defend our championship. Then in the second quarter of a game against Utah, I went up for a lob and came down weird, tweaking my right knee. I missed the next thirteen games. I tried to come back for a few only to aggravate the injury. That meant I was out the rest of the season. The team

still put together a hell of a year, going 62–20. But we lost to Orlando in the conference semis. I know I'd have made a difference. Also feel sure we would've gotten back to the finals for a rematch with the Lakers. Counting the next season, that would've been three straight years of Celtics-Lakers finals. Would've been historic. And in those 2010 finals, we

*Leaving the court after a leg injury against the Pistons, 2010.*

got unlucky again. Perk went down with a knee injury in Game 6 and couldn't play Game 7. If we had Perk, do I think we win that game and the title? Absolutely. But I'm not gonna make excuses or blame our losing on that.

After the 2009 season, I had knee surgery. Removed a bone spur the size of my thumb. Came back feeling good but not pain-free. There's no such thing in the NBA. You can heal from an injury, but pain ain't going away. After you deal with fear, even after you shut down fear and play like a demon, you're still dealing with pain.

When I came into the league, if you had ten or twelve years as an active player, that was good. You'd be grateful. Hoop wasn't seen as a sport of agility and longevity. Then modern medicine entered the picture. Drink more water. Stretch. Lift weights. But don't lift too much. Plyometrics are just as good. Resistance bands. Balance balls. Swimming. Spinning. Parachute sprints. Altitude training. Anti-gravity treadmills. Advanced ultrasound. Cold tubs. Pneumatic recovery units. Low-level laser therapy. Sleep. Get as much sleep as you can. Eight hours minimum. And naps. Drink even more water. Carb-loading. Low-carb. No carb. Sugar-free. Gluten-free. Paleo. Keto. Vegan. Raw. Nutrition. Balance. Flexibility. Endurance.

*Taking a hard foul then doing some push-ups in a playoff game against the Heat, 2012.*

I grabbed that wisdom early. Even in high school, when kids would just grab the ball and start shooting, I'd be stretching for twenty minutes before I did anything. When I sprained my ankle a couple of times, I learned about ankle rotations, an exercise to make those muscles strong. I did them religiously. But none of that stopped the onslaught of pain. Eating right, exercising right, doing all the things the experts prescribe—none of that prevents pain.

Take my feet. I always had issues with big blisters on the balls of my feet. During the off-season, when I wasn't hooping hard, my feet went through a transformation. They'd swell up and I'd ice them. That made my soles tender. I'd have to put Vaseline in my socks.

Then came a summer day when Shot challenged me to play with him and his boys. I forgot my socks but figured, fuck it. I played anyway. We hit it hard. Halfway through the game, I took off my shoes and my feet were bathed in blood.

"Holy shit!" said Shot. "We gotta get you to a hospital."

"Ain't nothing new," I said. "Blisters. Blood. Business as usual."

"You gonna fuck up your feet, KG."

"They already fucked up. Let's keep hooping."

Once I saw that basketball was gonna be my life—and my livelihood—I devised a way to deal with emotional and physical pain. I went back to the worst pain I'd ever felt. Was nine or ten when I was making a sandwich for my baby sister. Wasn't paying attention to what I was doing and, as a result, sliced my finger. Nearly sliced it off. Pain was unbearable. Another time, I got into a fight with a kid who busted open my head. Then, a little later, I got into trouble at school. My mom went off on me and got physical. More pain. At thirteen, I was hooping up at Crosby Circle. The court was slick from a recent rain. When I went up to a dunk on a kid, I slipped and fell on my head. Un-fuckin'-believable pain.

Those were the pain points I kept in mind when I became a pro. Nothing was gonna be worse than those incidents. If I could endure what I had endured as a kid, I could endure it as an adult. I started seeing pain as an itch. Itches are annoying, but if you try hard enough you can keep from scratching. Don't scratch for ten seconds. Then don't scratch for another ten seconds. Then for thirty seconds. And soon you've forgotten about the itch.

I get hit in the chest or even 'bowed in the neck. Pain is immediate. Pain is sharp. Pain cries for a reaction. You wanna scream, retaliate, or fall to the floor. But—at least for a second—you can go out-of-body. You can look at what happened outside of space and time and say, "Oh, all I gotta do now is calm down."

Pain caused by nightly wear and tear is one thing. Pain caused by your opponents is another. Zach Randolph tells a story about how when he was at Portland he and I were trash-talking. He got fed up with my bullshit and fouled the fuck outta me. That's when I took him by surprise. Rather than strike back, I fell to the floor and did five straight push-ups. That's some beautiful mindfuck shit right there. Z-Bo didn't know what to make of that. Getting clocked and responding by dropping to the ground and doing push-ups? Ain't nobody trying to fuck with you after seeing that. They know you must be crazy.

Wish I could say that's how I always handled being provoked. But when I'm on the court, I'm not a turn-the-other-check kinda guy. All you gotta do is go to YouTube to see me pop off when I think I've been mugged. Sometimes I'm popping off to the pain I'm feeling; other times I'm popping off cause I think a cat is bending the rules too fuckin' far. My reputation as a fighter is something I earned and nothing I'm ashamed of.

Either way, this pain business don't go away. I found that if the out-of-body method didn't work, I had other choices. Let's say that in going for a rebound I mess up my knee. Knee hurts like hell. I can talk to the pain; I can talk to the knee; I can say, "Knee, fuck you. Stop crying. Stop whimpering. Stop telling me some sob story. Get over it. You're just a knee. I got a million other body parts that are working just fine. So just straighten out and let me get on with my business."

If that doesn't work, I try breathing. Just breathe the pain in and breathe the pain out. Don't scream. Don't stress. Don't think. Just inhale and exhale. Find the right rhythm for your breathing and give it a go.

And if the breathing don't work, there are always pills. If I took Vioxx, I couldn't take anything else. Without Vioxx, though, I could down two Advil or Tylenol or Indocin. On average, I'd probably take five pills before each game.

All these ways of dealing with pain have a deeper purpose: Don't turn hurt to hate. Think I better say that again: *Don't turn hurt to hate.* It requires repetition cause it's probably the only way I kept from hating.

I had lots of reasons to hate. We all do. We all been wronged. Personally, we all got legit grief. We all been fucked over—and that goes even for those who don't know they've been fucked over. You can say hate is justified. You can argue intelligently that hate is a genuine reaction to cruel and unfair treatment. So you wanna hate back, or hurt back, or retaliate in some vicious way.

What I've learned, though—and this goes back to the Book of Job—is that if you wanna get to the Promised Land, hate ain't the ticket. It's that simple. One way or the other, we gotta follow the lead of the mighty O'Jays when they tell us to get on the "Love Train." That's the only train taking us to where we wanna go.

# Candace Parker

*see* **WNBA**

# Partnership

I'm not about to be owned by somebody because I'm given a stash of cash. I believe in partnership, not ownership. To consider a player property is a direct throwback to slavery. For me, that concept is out of bounds. It's an idea I'll never accept.

# Gary Payton

Gary was someone I wanted to be on and off the court.

When G was in the room, I sat back and soaked it all up.

Watching him on the floor, here's what I'm seeing:

G talking to his coach.

G talking to his players.

Now a fan's got something to say to G, and G's got something to say to the fan.

Now G is mouthing off to the ref.

Now G is mouthing off to the nigga guarding him.

Now G is slashing and scoring.

Gary Payton is a machine, a master of multi-conversations and multitasking. He's where I got my yelling from. I flat out copied him. G was the champion trash-talker. He didn't use it with anger the way a lot of guys do. There wasn't an aggression to his trash talk like there was with guys like Charles Barkley or me. G was more of a politician. There was a nuance to his talking, depending on the scenario. He could get in a dude's face with gangsta shit or he could put his hand on a dude's shoulder and talk to him all calm and rational. He could manipulate everybody to get what he wanted—without them knowing they were being played. He learned the art early. Growing up on the playgrounds of East Oakland, G always played against OGs. He wanted to make a name for himself, and just like me in Chicago, he'd go from block to block taking on the baddest hoopers. That whole time he'd be talking trash to make sure they knew who he was, remembered his name. At first a lot of guys wanted to fight him, so he quickly learned how to adjust and adapt his approach.

If you went to a party with G, he'd be doing the same thing. He'd be talking to the bartender, the bouncer, his boys, the girls. "Where the drinks at? Shots over

*GP and me, 2004.*

here. Who that crew with? Get them out of here." That's just who G was.

In a game, he'd come down and yell out your play. "We trappin'! We trappin'!" Well, when you in the post and you hear that, you don't know where the trap is coming from. G cashed in on that confusion. He had all sorts of strategy that I implemented. I owe so much to G and the cats of his generation. I used their slick tricks on the generation that came after me, knowing they wouldn't know what the fuck I was doing.

There was also another side to Gary. As competitive as he was, he was also generous with his basketball knowledge. At the

2000 All-Star Game in Oakland—the one where Vince Carter put on his epic Slam Dunk Contest performance—GP pulled Kobean and me aside after practice and gave us a thirty-minute tutorial on how he played defense. Again, this was after practice for the All-Star Game. The weekend that we were supposed to be chillin'. Not GP. He was schooling us. GP had been Defensive Player of the Year in '96 and had been NBA All-Defense First Team for six straight years, so this was like getting a private lesson in painting from Picasso or in singing from Luther Vandross. He showed us his secret tricks, like how to reach for the ball without getting called for a reach-in foul. He said when you try and rip someone, you should go through their chest. Most people just swipe at the ball with their hand. The way G taught it, you take a step forward and shoot your hand straight into their body cavity, almost as if you were about to snatch out their heart. That way they can't cross the ball up. The only way to avoid it is to dribble with your back to the defender, which impedes your court vision. So even if you aren't stripping the ball, you're diminishing your opponent's game.

Next time I saw Kobean play on TV after the All-Star Game, he was using those tricks Gary taught us. There wasn't no texting back then, and I didn't see Bean for a while after the All-Star Game. First time I did, I said, "You used that shit GP showed us."

"You saw it?" he said.

"Hell, yeah, I saw it."

By the end of that year, Bean had made NBA All-Defense First Team for the first time. And of course G did too—his seventh in a row.

# Peanut Butter and Jelly

I've dined in five-star restaurants. I like five-star restaurants. Don't matter if I can't pronounce the food on the menu. I'm game. I could be in Paris or Rome, Berlin or Bangkok, Sydney or Honolulu. New culinary adventures are fun. I'm willing to go on the trip and eat a few morsels I've never eaten before.

I'm not a connoisseur of fine food, but I did develop an appreciation of some exotic shit like Japanese Wagyu beef and shark fin soup. At the end of the day, though—and especially before a game—I gotta go back to basics: peanut butter and jelly on white bread.

Going back to basics means going back to childhood. And going back to childhood means going back to comfort. Going back to when food was simple and basketball was simply fun. Maybe that's why before the game peanut butter and jelly was a must. Became a ritual, and rituals are important. Rituals anchor your ass. Rituals help your world make sense. You can count on them.

In Minnie the team staff knew about my PB&J obsession and accommodated me. The sandwich was always there. But when I got to Boston and mentioned how it was part of my regimen, no response. No one cared. Well, muthafuckas, I care. I cared so much I got the ball boys to start making the sandwiches. They did 'em good, so good, in fact, that before I knew it half the team was devouring PB&J before every game. Maybe that was the magic ingredient that helped us eat up the league and win the title. Don't underestimate the power of peanut butter and jelly.

# Rosie Perez

*see* **Questions**

# Perfection

I already mentioned about how much I love the movie *For Love of the Game*, where Kevin Costner tries to throw a perfect game in his last start. But there's no such thing as perfect. Even in a perfect game, how many balls hit the catcher's glove at the exact place the pitcher intended?

The idea of perfection was something I struggled with for much of my life. At one AAU tournament in 1993, I had twenty-four points, twenty-one rebounds, ten blocks, and six dunks. Yet when I came off the court, I was pissed cause I missed an easy block. I was aiming for perfection. Perfection isn't possible. Aiming for perfection will make you crazy. I was crazy. Took me a lifetime to learn that perfection is one thing and *perfecting* is another. Perfection is a goal. Perfecting is a process.

In my personal life, that's been an even harder lesson to learn. I still struggle with perfectionism every single day. I work on myself. I wanna be better. Everyone should wanna be better. Self-improvement is a duty. But when we make mistakes and start beating ourselves up for not being perfect, it's time to remember that perfection is an illusion.

# Kendrick Perkins

Perk and I had rough beginnings. He's a bruiser from Texas, blocking shots like he's swatting flies. First young kid out of the new generation to talk shit. He got to Boston when I was still in 'Sota. First time we played, he went right after me.

"Muthafucka," he said, "you ain't that good. I seen the film."

"Well, nigga," I said, "this ain't no film. Besides, who the fuck you think you are?"

"A nigga who's gonna kick your skinny ass—that's who I am."

That was Perk's mentality. I responded hard. First couple of years we got into fights, got kicked out of games. Neither one of us were about to back down. The shit was brutal.

Then I got traded to Boston, where I was about to play under the banner of greatness. One of the first things I did was take Doc aside and say, "I don't really know this kid Perk, but every time we play, we wind up beating the shit out of each other. I don't need for everyone to love me, but this brotha plain-out hates my guts."

"KG," said Doc, "you got it all wrong. Perk loves you. You're his favorite player. He couldn't be happier that you're here."

"You sure you got that right?"

"Positive."

That same day Perk called me.

"Ticket," he said, "whassup, fool? You don't know how glad I am that you're here. Been dreaming of playing with you my whole life, dawg. Now this dream is sure 'nuf coming true. With you on board, we fixing to win it all. Can I tell you how I really feel?"

*Perk and me, 2008.*

"You already have."

"I love you, bro. We 'bout to make history."

Perk turned out to be right. He also turned out to be one of the most soulful cats in life.

In 2011, we were on the road when Perk came to my room and said, "Ticket, I been traded. They're sending me to OKC for Jeff Green." Perk had no advance notice. Neither did I. There were tears in his eyes. There were tears in mine. Crying without shame. Crying because the brotherhood between us was no bullshit.

"Ain't nothing gonna change this brotherhood," said Perk.

And nothing has.

If Perk's riding with you, he's in it for the long haul.

Bagley. I felt like I had a duty to them. I felt like I had joined their brotherhood. It felt sacred.

Of course, the 2008 championship was the culmination of it all, but it was also a testament to the attitude I had adopted when I first arrived. Respecting the storied tradition of the Celtics was one thing, but even more critical was my relationship to Paul Pierce. Before I arrived, some people were saying our egos would clash. But those people didn't know my history with P, and they didn't know me.

They also didn't know that the first person I called after the trade was established was P. Not only did I consider him my brotha, he was also one of the most poised players in hoop history. He kept that poise under wraps until it was time to

# Paul Pierce

Get to the Garden and you feel something entirely different. The team is an institution unlike any I'd ever seen. In Minnie, I had the luxury of soaking up Kevin McHale's knowledge. But the T-Wolves were a relatively new team. After the Lakers left Minnesota in 1960, there was no NBA team there until 1989. That newness had its own vitality. I thrived in that vitality. But Boston had this old-school flavor I found fascinating.

I came early to the games just to put my hands on my jersey. I'd look at the G. I'd look at the A. I'd check out the stitching on the two T's. I'd study the 5 on the back. In my locker, they listed all the players who wore 5 before me. John "Big Ace" Thompson. Bill Walton. John

*Me and P during a playoff game against the Cavs, 2010.*

explode. Then watch out. Only other cat with that kind of poise was Sam Cassell.

Before calling P, I thought back to a game the previous season when the T-Wolves were playing Boston. Both our teams were suffering through miserable seasons. P told me that was the night he screamed at Celtics owner Wyc Grousbeck, "If you serious about winning a championship, then you need to get that guy." P pointed to me. During that same game, he said, "KG, what's gonna happen, brotha? Either you coming here or I'm going to Minneapolis."

P saw it all coming, so when I finally called him, I had to give him respect.

"Look," I said, "I know this is your team. I know I'm late in coming to the party, and I also know you're the man. So don't go worrying about me looking to stand in no spotlight. I got no problem standing in your shadow."

"You too big of a man to stand in anyone's shadow."

"You know what I mean."

"I know who you are, Ticket. You here to win. Nothing else matters."

"Facts."

When I think on all the many wonderful memories of my time with P on the Celtics, the one that jumps out, even before winning the title, is our first game together at the Garden. November 2, 2007, against the Washington Wizards. We won 103–83. P had twenty-eight points. I had twenty-two points and twenty rebounds. Though I gotta be honest, my first shot attempt as a Celtic was a total brick. As Doc told reporters after the game, "He was so hyped tonight that the first shot almost broke the backboard."

*Me and P on the mountaintop, 2008.*

With two and a half minutes left, Doc subbed us out. Even though it was a blowout, nearly the entire crowd had stuck around. It had been a long time since Celtics fans had something to cheer for. Just like they had at the start of the game, they gave a huge standing ovation. They knew how special this team was and wanted to appreciate every moment.

As P and I headed to the bench, I threw my arm around him. More than fifteen years after the McDonald's All-American Game, we were once again teammates. We were ready to show Boston and the world what we could do. We both raised our fingers to the cheering crowd. They hadn't seen anything yet.

# Scottie Pippen

*see* **Hollywood; Invitation; Isiah; Kevin McHale**

# Players First

Doc Rivers, Paul, Ray, and I helped build a structure in Boston. We built a culture around a players-first mentality.

We ran the locker room. It was our own little sanctuary.

Someone—don't care who it might be—would try to invade our space.

*Touching the shamrock on the way out to the court.*

One of us—usually me—was quick to say, "Get the fuck outta here. Why you even in here? Where's security at? Get him outta here."

If we got any pushback, I'd let 'em have it. "This ain't the old shit, this ain't last year. This how we doin' things now."

We went to dinner together, movies together, interviews together.

Doc was instrumental in instilling that steel-curtain mentality. The strength of that curtain protected us from any outside negative energy. Positive energy is self-generating, and it was that players-first positive energy that got us over.

# Prejudice

At the end of the 2013 season, Jason Collins came out as gay. It was a big deal because he became the first openly gay person to play in the big leagues of hoop, baseball, football, or hockey. Later he rolled with #98 cause that was the year Matthew Shepard was tortured and murdered for being gay. Collins's #98 jersey became a bestseller at the NBA shops. Jason signed and auctioned off his game-worn jerseys and gave the proceeds to the Matthew Shepard Foundation.

That did my heart good. I'd play with Jason on the Brooklyn Nets later in my career. He was a dope teammate. His sexuality was never an issue. He was one of us. As a kid, I inherited a lot of the prejudices of my generation. As a young athlete, I never called out gay guys or tried to shame them. To be truthful, I wasn't even aware of them. But as I grew up and the gay movement became public,

I underwent a transformation. I looked into myself and saw that I had some deep-down prejudice. I didn't like that prejudice. I don't like any prejudice. So, I had to confront myself. What was that prejudice about? Like most prejudices, it's fear of the unknown. Whites don't really know Blacks. Whites fear Blacks. Because fear is such an uncomfortable feeling, it transforms into hate. It's easier to deal with hate than fear. Same with straights and gays. Straights fear gays because they're scared of even the slightest gay feeling they themselves might exhibit. So again, fear turns to hate.

Shout-out to cats like Jason Collins who had the courage to call out that fear and hatred and, in the face of it all, stand tall.

*Jason Collins, 2013.*

# Prince

We had downhome parties—both at Moms's and my aunt's—where the music was cranked up. Peabo Bryson. Curtis Mayfield. Aretha. Stevie. Clouds of reefer, Crown Royal, barbecue and biscuits, everyone sitting around the card table and gamblin' round 'bout midnight. Meanwhile, we kids were out in the yard, jumping around till all hours of the morning.

Moms had her records: Sam Cooke, Gladys Knight, Sam & Dave—all the good stuff. While me and my sisters cleaned the house, she blasted that music loud and laughed when I started dancing with the broom. She saw that I had me some moves. It was only when Prince came along that she gave me a hard time. I grew up on Prince. Loved him before I understood him. It was the grooves, not the stories, that got to me. "Darling Nikki" was my favorite. Had it on heavy rotation. The words went over my head. Prince was talkin' 'bout masturbating to a magazine, but I wasn't listening to lyrics; I was dancing.

Moms would break off my dance, turn off the box, and ask, "What you know about Nikki?"

"I like the song."

"Stop singing this song."

"Why?"

"You don't need to know why. You just need to know not to play it."

Naturally that made me like "Darling Nikki" even more.

First met Prince early in my T-Wolves career. I'm in his club the Quest. It's 2 a.m. There's a back room, big enough for no more than eight or nine niggas. I asked to go back there.

There he is. Sparkly suit. Bad fedora. Platform gators.

He nods at me.

"Wanna talk?"

You know I wanna talk to Prince.

His bodyguard, Big Chick, a white mountain of a man who sometimes carries Prince on his shoulders, is on guard, making sure no one bothers us. Prince wants to talk hoop. He knows hoop. He played hoop at North Community High. He's got a lot to ask, got a lot to say. But the thing he says that I like the most is, "Yo, we're going to Paisley Park. Follow me."

My heart starts racing. Jump in my ride and follow the caravan. Had to be at least ten cars. Another dream coming to life.

Paisley is a combination of a giant museum/gym/dance floor/office complex/auditorium. We're up in that joint when Prince disappears for nearly an hour. We're down in the section configured as a concert space. Big stage, big space, no chairs. Everyone's standing. Everyone's anticipating. Everyone's cheering when the band comes out with Prince right behind 'em. He's changed outfits. Now he's all in black leather, glitter gold, and thigh-high silver boots. It's like he's ready to perform at the Super Bowl even though there ain't more than fifty or sixty of us waiting. We don't gotta wait long.

*Boom!* The funk is on. He plays old joints like "Kiss" and "Let's Go Crazy" and more recent stuff like "Cream," but he also plays new shit that none of us have heard. He ain't mailing it in; he's

playing like his life is on the line. Guitar screaming, singing in his soaring falsetto, falling into splits, switching up from one grinding groove to another. Prince don't play for an hour, or even two hours, but three, four hours of nonstop jamming. We more exhausted than him. We never seen or heard nothing like this.

Muthafucka still ain't tired.

"Lemme change and we'll go for breakfast," he says.

An hour later we walk outta Paisley into a blazing sun. It's 10 a.m.! Mailmen making their deliveries. A new day has started, and I'm high as a kite on his magic music that's still all up in my system.

Go to an out-of-the-way ham-and-eggs joint. Prince, three other brothas, and me. Prince don't eat no meat. Just tomatoes and a little lettuce. I get me some flapjacks and bacon. He teases me. He questions me. He wants to talk more hoop. Cool. We'll talk about whatever he wants. He gives me his download on Minnie—how the hoods are changing up, why he likes staying far outta town.

"I like being on the outside looking in," he says. "Distance gives you a different perspective."

I relate, thinking of myself as a little kid in Nicholtown, looking over the trees to see the cars in the distance.

Prince pushes the subject from geography and goes into the concept of chakras. Ain't ever heard that term before. I'm fascinated. He's talking yoga, talking visualizations, manifestations of mind over matter, breathing exercises. Knowledgeable cat. Deep resonant voice. Talks in waves. You could practically see the waves before your eyes. Just as when he sings he draws you into every note, when he talks he draws you into every word. Every word is the right word. Shit gets heavier when he realizes I grew up Jehovah's Witness. It'd be a few years before he officially converted, but he was already getting immersed in the faith. Witness brothas got a certain way of talking to each other. We talking in truth. We talking scripture. I'm not there to argue. What matters is that I understand where he's coming from. He found something he needed to find. I get it. He gets me. In my eyes, in my past experience, he can see part of himself. We a funny couple. I'm nearly two feet taller than him. But he's my big brotha, bigger than me. I'm intense, but he's more intense, in a spellbinding way. He's proof that stature has nothing to do with height. In some ways, Prince was the tallest cat I've ever met. He towered over everyone.

I don't have to tell him that his records that turned me into a stone fan were those joints about eating pussy and jacking off. I realize he's grown and matured and don't need to put his shit out there the way he used to. He went out and captured a world market. He wasn't afraid of letting his hair down. Literally. He didn't mind putting rollers in his hair. Didn't mind looking less masculine. Had those soft features that stood out. Highlighted those features. Made metrosexuality cool, confident. Ladies loved him. Cats copied him. He established his identity the way he wanted. Fuck the culture. He changed up the culture. He was always on his shit.

Those spur-of-the-moment, 4 a.m. Paisley performances were dope, but even doper was an outdoor show he put on in downtown Minnie in front of the famous club from *Purple Rain*—First Avenue. I was lucky enough to be sitting on the stage. I looked over and saw an ocean of people that went all the way down to the Target Center. Seemed like the whole population of Minneapolis was standing shoulder to shoulder to see this cat do his thing.

Prince came up from the street to the stage. Speakers everywhere. Crowd buzzing louder than a billion bees. In one of his fitted Martian outfits, Prince

*Prince courtside, 2002.*

walked to the mic and let the buzz keep buzzing for what seemed like an eternity, until he raised his hand to stop the buzz. Then, dead silence. You-could-hear-a-pin-drop silence. He looked out at his city, looked out at those thousands of faces staring at him. He breathed. He sighed. He let the silence linger until I was feeling I couldn't take no more. And then he brought the mic to his mouth and sang the words, "I knew a girl named Nikki . . ." and brotha, the whole world jumped. The jolt was seismic. Minnie went nuts. He rocked us out of our minds. Prince loved to write, he loved to record, but there wasn't nothing he loved more than to play live and drain his fans dry. When the show was over—and the show seemed to last forever—he'd done everything he set out to do. He wasted us. He fucked us up. He gave us more fun, more pure pleasure, more of himself, more of the holy ghost soul sauce than we could digest.

Years after I'd established myself in Minnie, I remember one writer calling Prince the Commander in Chief of Culture and me the Commander in Chief of Cool. Naturally, I was flattered to be in the same sentence with him. Everyone likes being called cool, but I didn't feel worthy of the title. Prince commanded both titles. He was King of Culture and also King of Cool. That part of his culture and cool that rubbed off on me was a gift, a privilege of getting to know a man who was unknowable. His mystique was magic. If you figure out the mystery behind the magic, the magic dies. And in that respect, as far as I'm concerned, Prince is still alive.

# Promenade

In 2013, I was playing for the Brooklyn Nets. I was excited to be living in Manhattan's West Village. It was an easy choice. I'd always wanted to live in New York. When I came to the city over the years, I had explored certain neighborhoods. I liked the West Village because it was quaint and quiet and looked like something out of a storybook. The skyscrapers in Midtown were cool, and I know folks like living on the ninetieth floor, but I wanted me a town house six stories tall with lots of room for the family.

I'm chill. Into the arty feel of the hood. Walking my kids over to the Hudson, watching the boats, checking out the galleries and restaurants, living a kind of urban life I'd never lived before. Everything right there on the block or just around the corner.

Everything is cool except for one thing: I didn't realize the depth of Knicks culture inside the city. Even though I'm no longer with Boston, fans come up to me and say, "Fuck you, Celtics." Or "Fuck you, Brooklyn." When it first happens, doesn't bother me much. But it keeps on happening, even when I'm with my kids. Now, I'm not the brotha who's gonna pop some ignorant fool and get busted for assault, but I'm tempted.

The summer training camp is on the Jersey side. Practices are grueling, but I keep giving it all I got. And then, for reasons I can't explain, I find myself experiencing a magical moment on a magical night:

*Getting congratulations from Jay-Z for a Brooklyn Nets playoff win, 2014.*

After dinner with my teammates in Hoboken, I walk along the promenade beside the Hudson. I'm alone. Crystal clear sky sparkling with stars. The water is calm. A few seagulls dip and dive into the dark water. The sound of a foghorn. The sight of a tugboat. Across the river the skyline of mighty Manhattan is blazing. Skyscrapers shining like diamonds. The distant lights of cars riding up and down the West Side Highway. I keep walking, keep looking. Come across a soccer field. Find a bench. Sit and stare across that river. Watch the ripple of moonlight on the water. Look up at a jet winding its way toward LaGuardia or Kennedy. Remember that picture-perfect scene back in Nicholtown, where I looked over the trees to see the cars. Thinking how beautiful it feels—how comforting, how satisfying—to sit in stillness. Thinking that being in the middle of the mix is fun, but sometimes looking at the mix from far away is more fun. Imagining what's happening up and down the length of Manhattan. Taxis honking. Restaurants bustling. Hustling uptown; hustling downtown; Tribeca trillionaires turning funky old lofts into palaces; hookers; society chicks; fat-cat Wall Street money-bags in limos; homeless living in parks; strung-out junkies; bright-eyed college kids; babies being born in one wing of a hospital; folks dying in the other wing; stars twinkling up in the sky; me breathing in; me breathing out. Moments when you stop and do nothing but look. Turn off your mind and gaze across the river. Beyond the beyond, out there in space, planets be spinning, universes inside universes, endless space, endless time, Jehovah God the source, the strength, the creator. Creativity, life-giving creativity, never stopping, now and forever.

# Kirby Puckett

*see* **Land Cruiser**

Questions

# Questions

What words start with the letter "Q"? That's some championship Scrabble shit. Hmmmm, let's see . . .

There's "quince"—the fruit that Rosie Perez uses as a *Jeopardy!* response in *White Men Can't Jump*. But only thing significant about "quince" is that it makes me think of fine-ass Rosie Perez. I'm grateful to the quince for that, but it don't deserve to have its own letter in my book.

There's *Q\*bert*, that old-school arcade game I played as a kid. Had this cute little orange dude with googly eyes and a tube nose who always cussed, which I thought was hilarious and now that I think about it maybe subconsciously had a little to do with why I've always cussed so much. But that was hardly my favorite game, and I'll get into all that when we get to the letter "V."

Of course, there's Q-Tip and Questlove—shout-out to both those cats. Love everything you do.

When it comes down to it, though, I only got this one word for the letter "Q." And it's a big one—one of the most important words in this whole book.

Questions.

Questions are the key to learning.

If you're a youngster reading this, I urge you to ask questions to your elders.

If you're an elder reading this, I urge you to encourage your kids to ask questions.

Anyone reading this should know that I'm all about questions.

I don't have the answers, but I do have the questions—questions that have been rattling around my mind since I was a kid. As an adult, I've realized questioning is good. I grew up in Kingdom Hall, and in many ways that did me good. But Kingdom Hall was more interested in providing answers than encouraging questions.

I got nothing bad to say about any religion. Whatever good people derive from their beliefs, God bless them. At the same time, if I'm gonna be honest, I gotta express those questions that keep popping up in my brain.

The Bible is a beautiful book. Might be the most beautiful book ever written. I don't know. I haven't read all that many books. But one question about the Bible has nagged me for years:

Why didn't Jesus write?

The only thing the Bible says he wrote remains unknown. It's in the story of the woman who committed adultery and was brought before the Lord. The lawmen said that according to Moses she should be stoned. Jesus said, "He who is without sin, let him throw the first stone." No one threw nothing, and then Jesus wrote something in the sand before sending her on her way, saying, "Neither do I condemn you. Go and sin no more."

Love the story but still wonder what he wrote. I also wonder this: If Jesus wanted to be understood—as opposed to being interpreted—why didn't he just write down exactly everything he thought and felt and commanded? Why leave it to his followers to write down the stories? Why not write down the stories himself? He was Jehovah God, and Jehovah God can do whatever Jehovah God wants. I'm guessing Jehovah God wanted us to keep asking questions.

Here's another question. This one's about evil.

Why didn't Jehovah God zap evil? Why did he let cats like Hitler do the shit they did? You could say that God set up a battle for us to find good in the face of evil. But then you could also ask why is that battle endless? Go back through history and bring it up to today and you'll see the battle is still raging. Can't the battle ever stop? Can't God put an end to wars that cause more pain than any of us can imagine?

Babies die of cancer. Why?

Cities wiped out by tsunamis. Why?

Disease destroys millions worldwide. Why?

Technology pops up, and technology looks like a force for good, and then the bad guys take over tech and use it to broadcast hate. Why?

Why can't people stop hating and killing each other in the name of religion?

Why can't peace prevail forever?

Why can't Jehovah God hurry on back—now, today, this very minute—and turn our human misery to joy?

By writing out these questions, I ain't saying I don't believe. I do believe in the ultimate creator and the ultimate force. I always will believe. But being a believer, being a thinking human being doesn't mean that, with all those beliefs, questions still don't haunt me. They do.

The thing that keeps me believing is faith. And to me, faith says, "Your questions are reasonable and right. You can have all the questions you want. But if you're faithful, if you live a loving life, you'll express a spirit of love that'll wash over others. You can do that even while your questions continue. You can do that even when your questions remain unanswered."

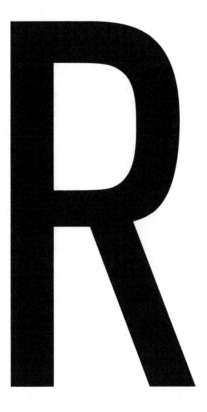

Referees / Retirement / Pat Riley / Dennis Rodman /
Rajon Rondo / Routine / Rubber Band / Bill Russell

# Referees

*see* **Rasheed Wallace**

# Retirement

Not for me. Don't like the word. Especially don't like the "tired" association with the word.

Fans ask, "What about hoop? You miss it?"

I answer, "No." I didn't always like myself when I was playing. I was a different person. I transformed. I wasn't Kevin. I was playin' ball, I wanted to be all over the place, and I wanted you to remember me. I wanted you to remember this experience with me out here. And that's how I played. I played all out. Practiced all out. And I always wanted to say, "When I'm done with this, I'm never going to think about ball again. Because I'm gonna leave it all out here."

I don't miss nuthin' about the game. I don't pick a ball up, I don't fuck around. You would think that I would actually go and play sometimes. My body hurts tremendously after I play. To the point where I'm out of commission for two days. I've had to find a new regimen that, while still ultra-disciplined, fits my post-playing condition.

Now, when I get up in the morning, I'll go jog and walk the beach. When I get back home, I get forty-five minutes in with weights. Then I sit in the infrared. And then I go swimming for thirty minutes before starting my day at eleven o'clock. A lot of my business is later in the day, so I take those hours in the morning for myself.

No, I gave hoop all I had. And then some. I don't go around moping that I ain't playing no more. I watch NBA games on TV with pleasure, not regret. I don't fantasize about being out there. I'm happy where I am. I'm still hyperactive in more ways than ever. For me, hyperactive and happy go together.

# Pat Riley

*see* **LeBron James; June 28, 1995**

# Dennis Rodman

Say what you want about Worm—one of the illest rebounders and most flamboyant brothas ever to play sports—but the thing I cherish most is his stamina. I saw it firsthand.

*Dennis Rodman, 1998.*

T-Wolves and Bulls just finished a blood-stained battle at the Target Center. Rugged, mean, mano a mano. Went into overtime. Overtime rougher than regulation. Finally, we squeezed it out. Might have been the first time Minnie ever beat Chicago. We acting like we world champs. Confetti and shit.

After the game, I go to our weight room, not to work out but to decompress. I'm sitting there when who struts in but Rodman, wearing these big-ass combat boots that come up to his knees. He's wearing sweats and combat boots! It's him and his trainer. He looks at me right quick and says, "Good game, young fella. Love your energy." Then he climbs on the treadmill and runs like he just robbed a bank with the law hot on his ass, all the while talking shit to me.

"Tomorrow playing this kid in Jersey. They say he's the best rebounder. Fuck that shit. I'm gonna pull down forty-five rebounds. Watch me."

I do. He ain't slowing down. He's drenched in sweat.

I'm thinking, "Man, it's time to go home!"

But no, my man is turning up the speed. He's anticipating the next challenge and putting in extra work to meet that challenge. He's crazy. He's telling me all about his early injuries and how strength training bulked up his body and boosted his stamina. Running in combat boots, talking a mile a minute, and not nearly out of breath.

I'm thinking, "That's the kind of crazy I need to be."

# Rajon Rondo

When Danny Ainge, head of operations for the Celtics, flew me to Boston to meet with him before he brought me to the team, he showed me a vision. As he was laying it out for me, he disappeared, and I could actually see it in front of me, like a hallucination or a hologram. That's Danny Ainge's greatness. He knows how to lure people in. And I didn't even realize it. That's how good he is at that shit. Makes you think it was all your idea.

"Whassup with the little African guard you guys got?" I asked him.

In preparation for the meeting, I'd been watching some C's game tape. And one play that stood out was against the Knicks in MSG. This little rookie guard scored the ball, stole the inbound pass, and then scored again with the and-one. I loved his energy. But because of my dyslexic ass, I didn't know how the hell to pronounce his name. I thought he was African or some shit.

Danny looked at me strange.

"African?"

*Damn,* I thought. *Danny's gonna make me try and pronounce his name.*

"Yeah," I said. "Raj-oon."

"Oh, you're talking about Rajon. You're talking about Rondo. He's from Kentucky."

"Yeah," I said. "Rondo. You got keep him, yo. I'll come to Boston but you gotta keep him."

Danny hesitated for a second. They were gonna include Doe in the package for me.

"Nah," I said. "We can't do it then."

So Rondo stayed in Beantown. I call him Doe. I also call him my little brother. When P, Ray, and I landed in Boston, they tagged us the Big Three. But Doe was just as much a part of the winning equation as any of us.

Doe and I got along from the get-go. Maybe that's cause I saw him as a younger version of me—and cause he saw me as an older version of him. He's just a little over six feet and ten years my junior, but his intensity level matches mine. Sometimes, like me, he'd do left-field shit. His quirks were crazy, but so were mine. His thinking was out of the box, but so was mine. We ran parallel.

Like the night we were in the Go playing the Bulls. It was a Friday. Cold as hell and snowing like a muthafucka. Fans were throwing snowballs at our team bus. Chicago was feeling themselves. They had this young player, Derrick Rose, who everybody was tripping out over. They came out with a ton of energy and got us down early. We looked bad. Turning the ball over constantly. Not at all focused. One possession, Doe brings the ball up the court and calls the play. But rather than just throwing the pass to initiate it, he starts freestyling with the dribble, behind the back and through the legs, then sails the pass out of bounds. Nobody says anything. Next time up the court, he does the exact same thing. Calls the exact same play, puts the exact same drip on it, and once again throws it out of bounds. Now, we're all pissed, me especially.

"C'mon, Doe!" I shout. "What you doing? Just deliver the pass. Don't have to be all complicated."

He says some shit back to me. I say some shit back to him. A couple more possessions go by, and finally Doc calls a time-out.

"What, you think you can just show up and win?" he says in the huddle. He's hot. "You think this team is intimidated cause y'all are the mighty Celtics?"

One of the ball kids hands me a cup of water. I go to pass it over to Doe so the ball kid won't have to reach over us. Doe just ignores me. Pretends he doesn't see that water and that he's all focused on the huddle and what Doc is saying. Well, now I'm really pissed. I kill that water in one gulp, then crush the paper cup against the side of my head. Doe then stands up and reaches around me to get his own water and sips it all gentleman-like, to show he's unfazed by me. But the water goes down the wrong pipe. He starts coughing but tries to stop, turning his back so no one will see. Cause now he's embarrassed. I look over

*Me and Doe during the fourth quarter of Game 7 against the 76ers in the 2012 playoffs.*

at him, and I'm like, "Nah, boy. Choke. Choke."

I push all the other guys back.

"Watch out, Perk. Give him some room. Choke! Kill yourself! Die! Die!"

As I'm yelling this, the huddle is still going on. Everybody is looking at us like we're crazy.

"Now, when somebody says pass the ball," I shout, "you pass the ball!"

He finally stops coughing and catches his breath, tears streaming from his eyes. He was really choking.

"Everybody put it in," Doc says.

We put our hands in and break the huddle. And we run the Bulls out of the building after that.

That was the kind of relationship I had with Doe. We fed off each other. If anyone is more stubborn than me, it's Doe. If anyone is more stubborn than Doe, it's me. He had a similar relationship with Doc. Man, they'd get into it. Sometimes they looked about ready to put hands on each other. But it came from a place of love and respect, because they both wanted to win so badly.

When it comes to big games, some cats can crumble. Doe is the opposite. He thrives on big games. I never worried—not once—about him showing up for a big game.

If something's bothering Doe, he and I could talk it through for hours. We liked breaking the shit down. Getting deep. Turning over a problem and looking at it from every angle. We liked analyzing.

Doe is a thinker. One of the smartest hoopers. Off-the-chart basketball IQ. He'll make a great coach. I never would because I lack patience. I don't do well with people with massive potential who won't push through to make it happen. If you don't got the right work ethic, it's hard for me to hang. On the other hand, Doe has patience to motivate anyone.

# Routine

One of the things I had to learn as a young player was to take routine seriously. When you come into the league, you have a shooting time, weight room time, mealtime—a whole schedule you have to follow. It was hard for me at first, especially with my ADD. But after a while, I got into it.

Starting around my third year in the league, I locked in my routine. I was having leg problems and a friend suggested running the beach. Great suggestion. Love the beach. Especially love running the beach in Malibu during the summer.

4 a.m. Alarm goes off.

4:20 a.m. I'm dressed and out the door.

4:30 a.m. I park the car at the beach and run two miles down and two miles back. All soft sand. Feeling especially driven because I know the East Coast players are already up and working where it's 7:30. Gotta keep up with those dawgs.

During the second two-mile segment, I'd do skip jumps. They help me on double taps on rebounds. They help me with timing. I do fifty skip jumps, then rest. Another fifty, another rest. Do this for the entire second-mile segment. Next, defensive slides. Then switch off between walking and jogging.

Singing is key. Beyoncé's trainer taught me how singing expands the lungs. So I'm singing out loud, "Pick left, pick right."

I'm singing, "You need love, love, love." I'm singing whatever pops into my head, singing to the deserted beach, the empty sky turning gray to blue, singing to the faint morning light, singing to make sure that sun rises outta the water and shines on my head.

Then off to the gym and the hoop workout. Warm up for ten minutes. Start J's from seven feet out. Go around, seven spots, make ten free throws, come back around. Back it up to inside the three, college three. Shoot fifteen, seven spots. Come back around again. Free throws. More threes. In between, work on zig-zags. Defensive zigzags. Get to half court. Go back down. Shoot on the other rim. Then ten post-steps, both blocks. Then hop. The free-throw box. Face up moves, one dribble getting to the rim. Elbow work. Glass work. Go around the world. Five spots. Back to free throws.

Weights are next. Can't neglect weights. Don't neglect weights. Arm day. Leg day. Presses. Curls. Five days straight. Two decades straight.

As an active player, I'm craving the routine. If anything fucks with it, I'm out of whack for the rest of the day.

But something's always gonna fuck with it. In life, there is so much noise coming at us every day and there are so many unexpected things that happen. In the NBA, they do their best to keep you in a bubble and make sure you're pro-tected from distractions. But real life doesn't work like that. Man, that's all real life is: distractions. Routine helps you deal with that. It gives you a stable foundation you can rely on no matter how haywire things get. It can be very small things. Like breathing. Establishing a

> **Favorite Places for Playing Ball in the Summertime**
>
> 1 LA
> 2 Vegas
> 3 Chicago
> 4 Atlanta at Peachtree
> 5 NYC

few minutes each day when you just sit and breathe. You don't even have to call it meditation. Doesn't have to be that deep. It could be anything. Even making the bed first thing when you get up in the morning. Just a little ritual to provide structure to the messy chaos of being human.

Without routine, I'm a mess. With it, I'm good to go.

# Rubber Band

When I first got to the league, I would take a Magic Marker and write on my shoes: "Mauldin," "Basswood Drive," and "Springfield Park." I wanted to remind myself of where I came from. I never wanted to forget that. I also kept up my ritual of wearing a rubber band on my left hand.

I started doing that when I was thir-teen or fourteen. I got the idea from

*Dawn Staley, 1991.*

Dawn Staley, one of my early idols. Dawn was this sharp, short energetic point guard who played for the University of Virginia. Loved watching her. She wore a rubber band that she'd pop when she missed an assignment or turned the ball over. I saw it as good discipline and a way to be accountable for yourself.

So, if I forgot a homework assignment, I'd pop the band. If I didn't do a chore Moms asked me to do, pop the band. Same in sports. Miss a pass, mess up an easy layup, pop that band. Wasn't punishment, but a way to remind myself to do better next time.

Shout-out to Dawn for showing me the way. Dawn went on to a great pro career and won the WNBA championship with the Charlotte Sting in 2001. After I made it into the league, I was thrilled to meet her at an All-Star Game. I was in such awe of her talent that I was super bashful to even say hello. But because Sheryl Swoopes, another great hooper, did the introduction, it went smoothly and Dawn actually gave me a hug. I've met too many famous people to mention, but that hug stays with me as a highlight.

# Bill Russell

*see* **Johnny Joe; "King Kunta"; OGs; John Thompson; Zero Fucks**

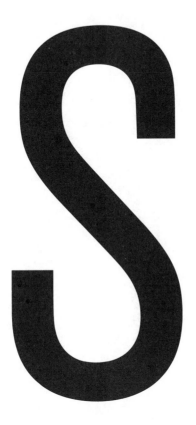

Arvydas Sabonis / Craig Sager / Adam Sandler /
Flip Saunders / Screens / Malik Sealy / Shadowing / Shoes /
Showdown / Silence / Skateboarding / Snoop Dogg /
*Sports Illustrated* / Latrell Sprewell / Springfield, Massachusetts /
Dawn Staley / Suits / Sheryl Swoopes

# Arvydas Sabonis

*see* **Euros; "King Kunta"; Zero Fucks**

# Craig Sager

Shout-out to Craig.

Rest in peace, dear brotha.

I gotta say how I miss you. Gotta testify to how all of us miss you. Gotta say it cause it's important to distinguish the jive-ass journalists from the cats that merit respect.

The media can turn anyone into a madman. The media is a machine, a heartless monster that'll eat your momma for breakfast, your baby momma for lunch, and your kids for dinner. Media wants to build you up to tear you down. Media ain't got no scruples. Media runs on ratings. And you get ratings by getting dirt. Facts don't count. If it'll attract readers or viewers, make the shit up. If it'll bring attention to your interview, provoke the hooper so he'll say something he shouldn't say. Go for the throat. Disrespect his privacy. Do whatever you gotta do to create controversy.

But that wasn't you, Craig. You stood out and carved your own niche. You knew the game and kept your questions about the game. You pressed the right buttons. You pushed the right issues.

First time you interviewed me was at the draft, right after I'd shaken the commissioner's hand and walked off the stage in my T-Wolves ballcap as the number-five pick. I was still buzzing and not even sure what words were coming out of my mouth, but you seemed to sense that. There was something gentle and reassuring in your manner that put me at ease. You didn't treat me like I was just a stat sheet, the way other reporters did. You treated me like I was a nineteen-year-old kid who was both ecstatic and scared shitless. You asked me what my interests were outside of basketball, and when I talked, you listened.

You had pride in your work but never took yourself all that seriously. You could tell a joke and take a joke. And of course you were fresh. Your freshness, though, had its own flavor. The brothas loved that.

Your crazy-ass clothes were your own inventions. Your plaid sport coats were fighting with your pinstriped slacks and your purple polka-dotted socks were hating on your cream-colored gaiters. I was always clowning those suits. I remember one night in Boston during my first year with the Celtics, after we put a straight-up ass-whooping on the Knicks, 104–59, and you interviewed me post-game.

*"You take this outfit home and you burn it": Giving fashion advice to Craig Sager, 2008.*

"Straight-up," I said, "you can't just grab something from the 1970s and try to bring it back. Retro is a look."

"Well, you're trying to bring back the glory of the Celtics," you said.

"But you see it's working. And that," I said, pointing to your suit, "is not."

My favorite interview with you—hell, they were all favs, but this one especially—was when I was coming out the locker room after the 2008 All-Star Game in New Orleans. I was heading to my ride. You caught me and asked if you could just have a few seconds. You were wearing this ugly-ass pinkish-red plaid suit with matching handkerchief and red shoes and a red pinstripe shirt. The camera was right there and already rolling. I went right into it.

"Look here," I said, "I know we going off the air but I need ten to fifteen seconds

to say something to you . . . I am stressing to you . . ."

I took one of that whack-ass suit's lapels between my fingers. It was fine-quality material. Italian craftsmanship. Your shit was an eyesore, but it wasn't cheap. Didn't matter. I had to let you have it.

"Look, Craig, I know you don't double back with outfits. I've never seen you in an outfit twice. You take this outfit home and you burn it—"

I grabbed the lapel even more forcefully.

"I don't care if it's Versace—"

"Isaia," you said.

"Don't matter," I said. "You take this and burn it till it ain't nothing but cinders."

"There's not any part I can keep?"

"Nope. Nuthin'. So when you get done with this, you should be butt-ass naked." You'd been handling the interview like the pro you were up until then. You knew I was on a roll. You knew we had something special cooking, some real TV gold. You knew to play it straight and not interrupt. But "butt-ass naked" got you. You couldn't help letting out a chuckle. "And the shoes too," I said. "Burn 'em. Don't ask no questions. Just burn 'em. And the red socks, which people can't see at home. Take all this. Handkerchief. Lime thong. Burn it. Okay? Gasoline. Kerosene. Either one."

You cracked up, Craig. You laughed your ass off. And later I learned that you actually had a burning ceremony.

All this is to say that your spirit still burns bright. The media culture is a cesspool. But somehow you came outta that culture clean as the board of health.

The love you gave us, and the love we gave back, ain't going away.

# Adam Sandler

*see Uncut Gems*

# Flip Saunders

Kevin McHale fired Flip in February of '05. At the time we were 12–20. Personally, I didn't see the sense in it. Flip was a great coach. Six years earlier, it was Flip's strategic moves that helped us turn the team around in two consecutive fifty-victory seasons.

The frustrating years that followed were rough, but I didn't put the blame on Flip. Yet apparently Kevin thought he could do a better job, because he made himself head coach. The vibe was super strange because, like Bug and me, Kevin and Flip were best friends. I looked at all this from afar. Kevin never had a single conversation with me about what was going down. Bad enough that Sam Mitchell was gone, but then the T-Wolves low-balled Latrell Sprewell on his contract and, just like that, Spree was gone. I saw that as a big mistake. Sam Cassell was another one of my closest brothas. Sam, who didn't want Flip fired any more than I did, wasn't offered an extension on his contract. Bottom line: We missed the playoffs for the first time in nine years. And soon I was gone to Beantown.

Eventually I'd get the chance to be reunited with Flip. He was the one who brought me to 'Sota the first time. And he would be the one who brought me back the last time.

In 2013–14, the Celtics made a deal that sent me to Brooklyn. The year before the Nets had moved from Jersey to the new Barclays Center, a state-of-the-art arena. I liked that Jay-Z was one of the owners and I loved that Paul Pierce was part of the deal that kept us together as teammates. Jason Kidd, a superstar in his own right, would be our coach, and Brook Lopez, the center, had been averaging close to twenty points and over ten rebounds a game. Lopez was a great post player but had injury problems. No matter, prospects were good. P, Jason, and I had won championships not that long ago—so we were in the spirit of that.

But Jason was looking for the Boston Big Ticket and the Boston Paul Pierce. Those guys had aged. We weren't in the position of carrying the team every night. That frustrated all of us.

We got off to a rough start, going 10–21. But we were too talented to suck that bad. P, Joe Johnson, Deron Williams, and me—all coached by J Kidd. We started clicking and finished six games above five hundred. Got the sixth seed in the East. Matched up against Toronto in the first round. Went seven games and

*Sitting in front of Flip's empty parking spot at the Target Center shortly after the news of his death, 2015.*

won on the final play, with P blocking Kyle Lowry's last-second shot to give us a 104–103 win. We got Miami in the next round, and they took care of us in five games.

The next season was more challenging. P signed with Washington in free agency, and J Kidd left to coach the Bucks. Halfway through the year, I got a call from Flip. After serving as head coach for the Pistons and the Wizards, he'd been hired again as head coach for 'Sota in 2014 and brought on my big brotha Sam Mitchell as his assistant. Sam had been fired as head coach of the Raptors a few games into the 2008 season. That was some bullshit. Sam had been named Coach of the Year in 2006–07. And the next season he passed the great Lenny Wilkens as the winningest coach in Raptors history. He didn't deserve to get done dirty like that. Showed the kind of brains Flip had to bring Sam onto his staff. Brains and loyalty. Flip was a man I loved, the one I wanted to play for during my final stint in the league. I went back to 'Sota.

My knee was giving me trouble, so I only played five games for the T-Wolves that season. The next year, though, marked some major career milestones for me. I became the fifth player in league history to play at least fifty thousand minutes. I passed 26,000 points—only the fifteenth player to do that. And, most special, I passed Karl Malone as the all-time leader in defensive rebounds. But all that was marred because of what happened to Flip.

For some time, he had complained about this growth around his ear but never went to get it examined. When he went to check it out in August, they put him in the hospital and he never left. Sam took over as head coach, and Flip died of Hodgkin's lymphoma on October 15, 2015. He was sixty. I was never the same.

You don't expect a guy like Flip to die so young. That's because he had undying energy and undying optimism. In terms of basketball knowledge, he was one of the great teachers. In terms of understanding and loving his players, he was one of the great coaches.

A couple days after the news, I drove to the Target Center, down into the garage. I took a seat on the ground in front of Flip's empty parking spot, with his name on the wall. I couldn't believe he was gone. Still have a hard time believing it. He was there at that pre-draft workout in Chicago when I was in high school. He saw what few others could see. He took a chance on me. He believed in me. I'll never forget Flip. I cherish his memory.

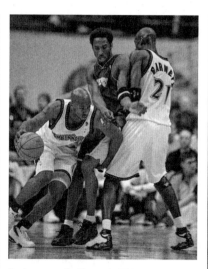

*Setting a screen for Shot against Kobean, 2001.*

# Screens

One thing I don't like about the way the game is played today is how players automatically switch on screens. I wouldn't even call 'em screens. All the screener does is make a move toward the defender and the switch comes. Screener doesn't even have to plant his feet.

Fuck that.

Where I come from, dude tries to set a screen on me, he better be rooted to the ground like an oak tree, cause I'm gonna try and fight through that shit. (Same goes for when I'm the one setting a pick. You get through a Ticket pick? Man, I'll give you my congratulations right

then and there.) I'm not gonna let the ball handler lose me that easily. I'm not gonna give them that advantage without putting up a fight. My teammates always knew that about me. They knew I was gonna stay home on my man and it was their responsibility to fight through the screen and stick with their man. Fighting through screens isn't easy. It's hard work. But it's worth it.

I feel the same about screens off the court. I'm talking about phone screens. Social media.

I understand its power to do good and its power to fuck you up. I understand there ain't no going back. It's the addiction of addictions. The planet is hooked. Today many use social media for righteous purposes, but for me, I gotta manage my phone. Gotta set limits. If not, phone reality replaces actual reality.

When Instagram came out, I thought it was cool. Back then, everyone wasn't on it. So I'd go on vacation and put some pictures on the Gram. Share pretty scenery with friends. But then the Gram became straight-up commerce and everyone and their mama was using it to sell or hustle or promote or pimp.

Today, if I'm in a room with my boys, I don't want them staring at their phones all evening long. If I go to a business meeting, I don't like the person I'm meeting to be checking email or texts every ten seconds. And even more importantly, if I'm on vacation, seeing an island I ain't ever seen before, I wanna be looking at the island, not trying to figure out how to make the coolest video of what I'm seeing.

I wanna be present.

Fucking with our phones or iPads, we're missing out on life. We're not experiencing the experience; instead we're experiencing the experience of recording the experience. To me, that's some dumb shit.

Life is to be looked at with our eyes. People are to be listened to with our ears. Emotions are to be felt with our hearts.

Phones don't have hearts. They may measure your heartbeat—and that's cool—but they can't replace the human ability to breathe in real life.

The other day a brotha I respect said he paid big money to get a good seat at an NBA game. Was tired of seeing the shit on TV.

"But I'll be goddamned," he said, "if I didn't spend most of my time looking at that big-ass screen over the court. Couldn't keep my eyes off the screen."

Screens have taken over the world. Screens everywhere you look. But when you do look at a screen, you ain't looking at life. You're looking at a reflection of life.

I'm tired of reflections. I'm tired of everyone jonesing out on these miraculous devices. The miracle ain't these devices. The miracle is life. And life, for all its heartaches and joys, is something I don't wanna miss.

## Malik Sealy

*see* **"Anything Is Possible!"**; Derrick Coleman; Escort; Learning; May 19, 2000; Kevin McHale; Showdown; Tattoos

## Shadowing

I practiced to prepare for games. When I fucked up in practice, I'd make those corrections and then apply them to the game. You can't do that if you don't practice at a high rate—a game rate—of intensity. During one practice, Doc got mad at my intensity. Said it was too much. He wanted me to take a couple of reps off. He wanted to sub me out for Leon Powe. But I didn't want out. I wasn't happy with my play. Eddie House had been kicking my ass. By being subbed out, I wouldn't have the chance to work through it and feel better about my game.

"Leon, you're in for KG," said Doc.

"Fuck!" I screamed and kicked one of the balls. I wouldn't let Leon sub me.

"Sub in for somebody else," I told him. And, just to be a dick, I sat on the floor—just to fuck practice up. Like, "You're gonna have to drag me off this bitch."

This wasn't the first time I pulled a tantrum like this. Doc and everyone knew they just had to wait a minute to let it pass, and then I'd stand up and get off the court. Which I did. But that day I came up with an idea. I still wanted to put my work in, so from the sidelines I pretended as if I was still in the game, in Leon's spot. Doe would bring the ball up, and Leon would come to set a pick. So I would make the same steps and set an imaginary pick. And when Leon rolled to the basket, I'd roll at the same time.

I called it "shadowing." At first, everybody looked over at me like, "What the hell is he doing?" They gave me those looks a lot. But Doc saw the beauty and intelligence of it. And so after that, we all started doing it. If you looked at our sidelines during scrimmages, you'd see two or three guys—whoever wasn't on the court—playing imaginary games. It probably looked silly to someone who didn't know what was going on. But it was serious business. Shadowing forced us to concentrate and utilize every single minute of practice.

## Shoes

When I was a kid, at first the only sneakers I could afford were fake Jordans from Payless. When I wore those joints to school, the kids nearly laughed me out. "Oh shit, look at those lame-ass kicks Kevin be wearing."

**Favorite Shoes**

1 Nike Garnett 3
2 Adidas Garnett 1
3 Jordan 11 Concord
4 Jordan 1
5 Air Force 1 (all-whites)
6 Timberlands
(wheat-colored)

"They ain't all that bad," said Bug. Bug always had my back. "I think they're pretty slick."

They weren't. They were lame-ass.

When you're young, status counts. When you get older, status counts even more. Friend told me about a record executive who had his shoes handmade in England at $1,200 a pop. His closet was lined with 125 pairs. Another cat is into cowboy boots. Alligator skin, ostrich skin, buffalo, calf, cowhide, elephant—you name it. I'm gonna guess his collection is worth seven figures. His whole identity—his self-worth—is tied up in boots. When you get some wisdom—and that takes forever—you realize status don't mean shit. But you're probably only able to say that when you get some status. Took forever to get to where I could rock sneakers with some status.

British Knights were the first brand-name shoes I got, though they weren't much cooler than those Payless joints. They were more than uncool; they marked me as being poor. I hated being marked.

Eventually, when I got good enough to get on teams, that mark went away. Or maybe not. Maybe that mark, because it's so deep, never goes away. Maybe we just cover it up.

I gotta believe that cool sneakers did cover some pain. Or at the very least they made me feel good. I also gotta believe that's true for millions of kids. What's interesting is that this phenomenon of worldwide shoe culture is built specifically on basketball shoes. Running shoes are big, and so are just plain casual shoes, but the driving force is basketball. Basketball shoes give you a bounce. A bop. A cool elevation. Basketball shoes also invite style. The best of them mirror the style of the player attached to the shoe.

This all crystalized in 1989 when I was thirteen. Word swept through the hood like a tornado. A kid had been killed for his Air Jordans. The red-and-black Air Jordans.

That was the moment. That's when the alarm rang. That's when one world stopped and another started. That turned out to be the number one selling shoe in the world, for any sport, for any athlete. Over a fuckin' million pairs sold.

Listen to me good: As a grown-ass man, I look back in horror at the violence. I look back in horror that a kid lost his life over a pair of sneakers. But that's me speaking now. Let me slip into the mindset I had as a kid hearing the news. That's the reality I need to share with you.

*What! What shoe is so bad that it's causing a killing?*

So me and my boys run down to the store, and there it is at Foot Locker, sitting high atop a plexiglass case, a beam of light shining on it.

It's the Holy Grail.

Then we ask what all kids ask, "How much is it?"

*One hundred twenty dollars!*

Ain't never heard of no shoe costing no $120.

Back then sneakers cost $30, $40, maybe $50. The price only added to the lure and legend.

Remember my man Eldrick Leamon, who died so young? Well, when he made a big street score, he bought Air Jordans for everyone in the hood. We were all wearing those joints, our hearts beating out of our chests, looking down at those bitches, walking slowly at first, then a little faster, then running, but no, not hooping, not about to take a chance of smudging those bad boys. The Air Jordans were far more than sneakers; they were a crazed obsession. Interesting—and important—that the shoes had no white on 'em. Just red and black. After the killing that made national news, Nike backed off and started making other versions. A white pair, a red pair, a black pair. But fuck those other versions. Nothing would replace the originals. The Holy Grail was sacred, sacred because blood had been spilt for it, sacred because it inspired a million worshippers.

This was when Nike was piggybacking and betting on that piggybacking. They were fixin' to jump on Jordan's back. They were taking him to Paris. They were turning his game highlights into commercials. They were putting him on soundstages and telling him, "Put on these shoes and then dunk. Put on these shoes and hit a three. Put on these shoes and just jump."

Who was dunking the ball like that before Jordan? Dr. J, that's who. But Jordan was a better Dr. J. Dr. J had a good

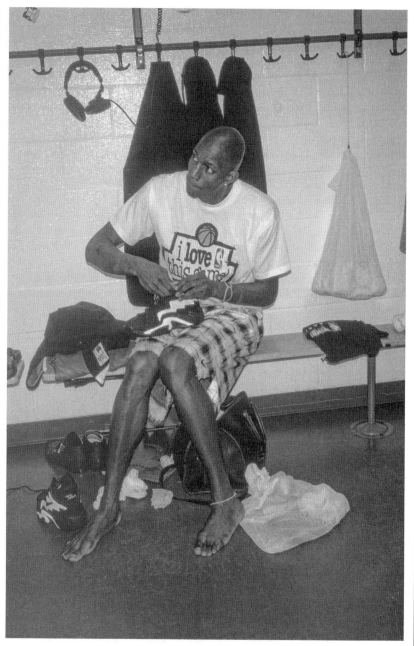

*Lacing up before a game, 1997.*

jump shot, but it wasn't no Jordan jump shot. Jordan was the script that all of us had to follow. He was the avatar. Mike was the mantra. And Nike was the corporate monster making it all happen.

When I entered the league as a nineteen-year-old, I went with Nike. I wanna say I ran to Nike, but the truth is that Nike ran to me. Naturally, I loved that. I quickly found myself wearing all sorts of Nike joints.

My first meeting with Nike was a signing event. But the second meeting, during my second NBA season, when the T-Wolves had a game in Portland, was about design. Ric Wilson, a true brotha, was my corporate contact. Loved Ric. Just one step out of the league, he worked under two other dudes: Steve Riggins and Howard White. Howard was the brotha who brought in Jordan. All these men were about Black excellence in business.

They took me on a tour of the Nike campus. A beautiful landscape of buildings. Then came the statement that blew me away:

"We're giving you your own shoe. Naming it Garnett 1."

Bug was with me during that meeting. Never will forget the look on his face. The look said, "Holy shit!"

Remember—this is fewer than two years after being expelled from Mauldin High.

Before this, I had premiered the Nike Jumpman. But the Jumpman was part of the Jordan brand. It was marketed under MJ's umbrella, a second tier to see if other players could sell sneakers. I was the first, but then came Eddie Jones, Jim Jackson, Jason Kidd, and Jamal Mashburn. I was

down with the Jumpman and played in those joints for a long time. At the same time, like every other brotha who's ever hooped, I wanted my own shoe. Far as I was concerned, the Garnett 1 was a milestone.

Another thing about sneakers that make 'em so attractive: they're fun. When you lace up your joints—whether you're four years old or forty—you're about to head out and have some fun. Which brings me to another reason I liked Nike. They put me on the Fun Police. The Fun Police was a series of commercials that helped launch my brand, even when the shoe wasn't mentioned. The Fun Police helped introduce me as a TV personality and, in some ways, something of an actor.

I might have been the main member of the Fun Police, but I wasn't the only one. My guys Tim Hardaway, Gary Payton, Jason Kidd, and Alonzo Mourning were on the force with me. The Fun Police had hoopers in the role of plainclothes cops making sure folks had a good time. But there's always a twist. In one commercial, for example, the Fun Police—me, Zo, and Hardaway—are showing people to their seats at a game. When a fancy rich couple shows us their courtside tickets, we send them to the nosebleed section. And then when three young Black boys show us their nosebleed tickets, we send them courtside. Justice prevails.

These little mini dramas became part of the pop culture. Hoopers as make-believe good-guy cops having fun; hoopers being heroes without even touching a basketball.

Downloading Nike culture was eye-opening. I saw the way they threw shit around. Try these Bo Jackson shoes. Try these Deion Sanders joints. Lace up them Agassis. It's all up and crackin', a merchandising machine that's running 24/7, a worldwide industry tapping into branding in a way I got to see up close and personal.

Enter Vince Carter. Vince was looking to get out of his Puma deal. This was happening in 2000 while we were on the Olympic team that won the gold medal. After our victory over France, Nike threw a party on a boat. Vince was there, and so was his agent. I could see that business was going down. Later, I saw that Vince didn't understand that as the first big-time athlete on Puma, Puma could take him global. Vince wanted Nike. Vince got Nike, but Nike never quite got Vince. They didn't do countless commercials on him. They didn't pump his brand like it could have been pumped.

I looked at all this. I reflected. I saw that when it comes to the shoe business, you gotta tread carefully.

I had big love for two Nikes in particular: the Garnett Air Flightposite 2, for which I wrote a script on the sole that gives thanks to South Carolina and Chicago. That meant a lot to me. Also was crazy for the see-through iridescent air bubble bottom and the contrasting colors of peacock blue and black. The Nike Air 3 Garnett was also dope, especially the one in Minnie green and a swath of snow white.

It wasn't all fun and games with Nike, especially when they introduced Shox, a new technology. Shox didn't work for me. Didn't like the way they felt on the floor. I also didn't like the way the sneaker looked.

The shoe sample I saw looked dumb as hell. Things came to a head at the 2003 All-Star Game in Atlanta. Nike threw a big party back in the dressing room. Cameras everywhere. Media going crazy. That's where Nike wanted to reveal the Garnett 4 Shox. But when they showed it to me, I couldn't fake my reaction. The shoe didn't excite me. So the Nike execs got on my agent about making me act like I loved the shit when I didn't.

When they kicked out the media, there was a shit show between Nike and my agent. The Nike suits were screaming that I gotta show love for the product, my agent was killing 'em with sarcasm, saying, "Oh yeah, my man's really gonna say he's loving the worst-looking shoe you ever turned out."

A lot of bread was involved, and I could have faked it. But to me a sneaker is like a painting. You start with a blank canvas. Then you pour your heart into it. It has to reflect your rhythm and sense of style. The Garnett 4 was clunky.

Sneakers are also like rap. They need a flow. The baddest rappers have their own flow. Same with the baddest shoes. In the beginning, Nike had me in on the creative process. But as time went by, they thought they knew my taste and went ahead with a model that that didn't even begin to mirror me. So I busted a move.

I left Nike with major respect for their engineering. Nike engineering is over the moon. Can't say they always used the best materials, but they taught me about materials. That helped when I made my next move.

I signed with AND1. That shocked a lot of folks. I did it for three reasons.

AND1 was open to my creative ideas. That came first. AND1 was also open to giving me what I considered a righteous equity deal. Back then, not even Jordan was getting more than 2 percent of sales. I thought that formula sucked. AND1 agreed. They paid me 20 percent. Because they were also building a brand, AND1 was open to my insistence that they use top-grade materials.

I took everything I learned from Nike and applied it to AND1. Nike product might not be the best, but their marketing is in a class all its own. With some exceptions, like Shox, they employ a beautiful aesthetic, almost like Apple, where the shit is smoothed out with a futuristic look. When it comes to sneakers, futurism is everything.

The sneaker sea is filled with sharks. But AND1 didn't have that vibe. They heard me out. At first, they were a little hesitant. The AND1 crew was made up of a bunch of Harvard boys wanting to be niggas. Even though I find that attitude annoying, I can't complain all that much cause that's the same attitude that's helped bring crazy wealth both to hoop and hip-hop. White kids feeling the creative energy of brothas. White kids responding to that energy and wanting to bite it off for themselves. That's the traditional American crossover, taking a Black product, whether it be music or sports, and crossing it over to mass market.

Sometimes the AND1 meetings could get testy.

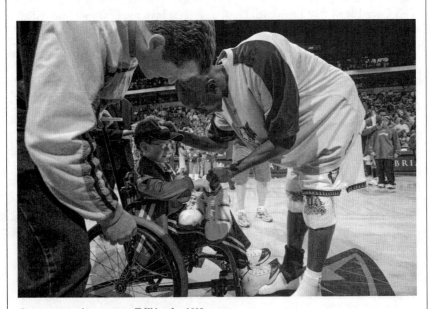

*Giving my game shoes to a young T-Wolves fan, 2005.*

They said, "We do street ball."

"I come from street ball," I said. "I know street ball, but I'm in the league and y'all gotta make shoes for the league." They listened. They followed my suggestions about putting in air bubbles, implementing a zigzag feel, a zipped-up accent, shit I had learned from the Nike lab and could now remix to where it reflected who I was.

At the same time, when I'm in a conference room with a group of cats who wanna be something they ain't, I'm uncomfortable. When white folks have to prove they're really down with Black folks, I back off. After a couple of years, I backed off AND1.

Next stop, Adidas. Fell in love with Adidas. Saw them like the Mediterranean. You pull up, jump into the warm water and the water's fine. Wasn't worried about no sharks. Adidas had their cool, but they lacked Nike's elegance. Adidas wanted to create what had already been proven. Wasn't interested in stepping out of the box. I was. I wanted next-level shit. But Adidas did have that hustle. Meanwhile, Nike was stepping on everyone and owning everything. Nike was the Roman Empire. Nike wasn't happy till they conquered the world.

At Adidas, the push-pull started all over again. Just like Ric Wilson was my man at Nike, Chris Persinger was my go-to guy at Adidas. I had to pound Chris to get more creative, more daring, and finally he did. I credit myself for making an opening that led to the Yeezys. It took a while, but I was also able to convince Chris to mix and match different athletes from different sports. Timmy Duncan and Tracy McGrady partnered with me at the start of the Adidas journey. I liked having Timmy, Tracy, Chaunce, Josh Smith, Derrick Rose, Dwight Howard, and myself in the same commercial. I liked how Adidas jumped on the team joint of having a gang of superstars jammin' together. But I still clung to the notion about crisscrossing different currents of the culture.

Adidas finally heard me and put James Harden, soccer player Lionel Messi, Pusha T, and some others around a big-ass table, chopping it up. They put me in a commercial with David Beckham where Kate Moss and Young Jeezy show up. Under the slogan "Celebrate Originality," we're having a blast.

When our contract was up in 2010, a cold wind hit me in the face. In the negotiations, Adidas got boisterous and assertive. They also came to me with half-assed promotional materials. Rather than looking fresh, the ads featuring me looked tired. I didn't appreciate that. I thought I had helped redefine their culture. I knew my worth. They tried to diminish my worth with little intangibles that bugged me. Previously, I'd seen how my commercials had become stagnated. I now saw that they did that to improve their bargaining position. All that pissed me off. I was over Adidas.

I moved on. Found me an Asian company. They had bought a lot of the Nike factories in China, kicked out Nike, and started turning out sneakers for consumers in that part of the world. That mainly meant small sizes. They'd never signed a player of any status, which gave me big leverage. I had the know-how and sophistication to help them design and manufacture for professional athletes.

Aesthetically we hit it off. I had some dope designs they were able to bring to life. The problem was the materials. They weren't up to par. They made more hires to better the quality. The sneakers improved. And I was feeling good about being heard. But even with those improvements, the shoes were killing my feet. I couldn't run up and down the court without feeling that something was wrong. Even though this firm did wonders for spreading my brand across Asia, once again I had to back off. I couldn't sell something I didn't believe in.

Final shoe chapter comes only a few years back, after my retirement from the league, when I returned to AND1. I signed on as a creative director and brand ambassador. A few months after AND1 gave me the gig, Jay-Z got named a creative director of Puma. I like to think I set a precedent.

AND1 was gonna roll out their Attack 2.0, Tai Chi, and Tai Chi Mixtape editions. I became their upper-tier representative. Part of my job was to glam up their shoe and also make sure the engineering was right. By then I had deep knowledge of the whole shoe process—from design concept to manufacturing to branding to marketing. I was also tasked with recruiting players to wear AND1.

That's a tricky process. Sometimes I went to a player and asked, "Do you care about the quality of the shoes?"

"I don't give a fuck. I just want my own shoe."

Might ask someone else the same question who'd answer, "I just wanna lot of money."

But some players did care about the integrity of the product and wouldn't stand for no class B sneaker.

At the time I had my own TV show on TNT, *Area 21*, where I got to interview everyone from WNBA players Sue Bird and Candace Parker to Ludacris and D-Wade. AND1 got to overreaching, telling me what I could and could not wear on the show. One day I'd hear, "We want you in a gray hoodie, Ticket." Next day I'd hear, "Wear a white hoodie, Ticket." Since it was my show, and I had my own sponsorship that had nothing to do with AND1, I told the shoe execs, "I can't believe we're even having this conversation." I moved on.

That was the end of my shoe career. At the same time, I see it starting again—and soon. Never have and never will lose my passion for sneakers. The shit separating you from the street, the leather or rubber or latex or whatever that lets you move on cold concrete or hard wood or wet grass or mud or brick is something more than a shoe. It's a statement.

## Showdown

May 19, 2004, was a big night. It was my twenty-eighth birthday and the four-year anniversary of Malik's passing.

The T-Wolves had beaten Denver in the first round—our first-ever playoff series win—and were facing a Game 7 against Sacramento in the semifinals. Malik was on my mind, just like he was on my mind every birthday. I wanted this one to be different. I wanted to win it for him. To do so, I'd have to beat Chris Webber.

I'm sitting in our Target Center locker room where I'm silently preparing myself.

*Battling C-Webb, my childhood idol, in Game 7 of the 2004 Western Conference semifinals.*

No way to cancel out my hype. Tonight I've got to find a balance. I've got to find the zone.

The place is thick with tension; crowd's in an uproar. I'm a little worried that Sam Cassell, since scoring forty points in Game 1, ain't right. His back and hip are hurting bad. I can see pain in his face every time he runs the court. But true to Sam's nature, he runs through the pain. He hangs in tough.

I'm loving my teammates. Spree and Sam, Trenton and Fred, Wally and Mark, Ervin and Gary, Derrick and Michael. I'm always loving my teammates. Always counting on 'em. Always encouraging 'em. Always needing 'em. But I also know that tonight this game is on me.

Right at the tip, I feel different. My first shots feel great. Defensively, I'm seeing things before they happen. My timing is impeccable. I feel like a boxer. As is often the case, I can't hear the crowd or even my coach. I can only see what I'm doing. Can see the rim. See the shot. Feel calmness in my wrists, calmness in my

*Celebrating my first trip to the Western Conference finals, 2004.*

shoulders. Slow down my heartbeat to where I'm not breathing hard.

At halftime we're up by nine. Kings make up eight of those points in the third quarter. Comes down to the final twelve minutes. I've been hitting, blocking, and rebounding like a fiend, but I'm not aware of my stats. Only the score.

We're up by three with 2.2 seconds to go. Target Center going nuts. Kings have possession of the ball—on their side of the floor. Everyone is standing. Every fan. Every player. Do or die for the Kings. Our team knows that they wanna get the ball to Peja Stojaković, their three-point shooting ace. I'm thinking: *Will I have a chance to foul so they can only shoot two free throws?* The Kings have no time-outs left, so they must get the ball in play within five

seconds. Legendary ref Dick Bavetta gives the ball to Kings guard Doug Christie to inbound. The five-second countdown starts. Trying to confuse our defensive set, the entire Kings team scrambles, running around like cockroaches when you turn on the light.

Christie accurately lobs the ball all the way across the court. I jump, but the brick is inches over my fingertips and falls right into Chris Webber's hands. *Oh shit!* I recover. Webb slightly pump-fakes and I take the bait, leaping as high as I can to deflect his wide-open shot. I miss the deflection. But thankfully, I leap high enough that my outstretched arms and upper body don't foul him. If I foul and his three-pointer goes in, we lose.

Right in rhythm, C-Webb launches a beautiful shot, perfectly targeted, perfectly arched. It falls in the cylinder . . . and . . . improbably, impossibly . . . it rattles out. C-Webb put just a little too much spin on the ball.

It's over. I wind up with thirty-two points, twenty-one rebounds—Malik's number!—and five blocks.

I'm shaking with joy and sending that joy to the spirit of Malik. I also make sure to go over and give C-Webb a long bear hug. I love this man. He inspired me to be who I am. Gotta let him know that.

I jump up on the scorer's table and throw my hands up to all the fans. But the victory proves bittersweet. After losing to the Lakers in the next round,

this twelve-year T-Wolves stretch will be over. I'll be leaving a city I've come to love.

# Silence

I hated to lose, but as the years have gone by, I see it's a lot more than that. I could deal with losing. I've lost hundreds of games in my life. It wasn't losing as much as it was *the way losing made me feel*. Losing made me feel worthless. Losing made me feel hopeless. Losing made me feel like that little kid trapped in my mother's house in Mauldin. Losing made me feel like I felt when my boys scapegoated me and I was expelled from school. Losing

*Taking a moment to myself before a game, 2011.*

brought me back to that day when Moms left Ashley and me at the baggage claim at Midway. Losing depressed me. And depression—deep-down, thick-fog, ain't-no-way-outta-this-bitch depression—is something no one wants to admit.

Rather than admit it, I say nothing. After losing a game or a series of games, I shut down. Don't ask me no questions. Don't talk to me. Don't even get near me. Lemme go hide in the corner cause I don't know how to articulate these feelings. And even if I did know, I don't wanna articulate. Don't wanna analyze or be analyzed. Just leave me the fuck alone and let me stew.

I've heard it said that depression is rage turned inward. Makes sense. The source of the rage might be something that happened to me as a kid or something that happened yesterday. Doesn't matter. On the court, I can express the rage in the force of my game. I can play like a man possessed. But off the court, where does the rage go? It goes inside. Then I put up the wall and push the world away. I go silent.

Obviously nasty remarks can wound the hearts of those you love. But sometimes silence can wound those hearts even worse. Passive aggression is still aggression. The only thing that helps is to have someone you can vent to. A brotha. A sista. A friend. A professional counselor. Keeping your fury inside your head makes it worse. Getting it out helps your mental health. That brotha, sista, or friend—if they're real ones—will understand that their job is just to listen to you, allow you to go off, and gently remind you to put things in perspective. The sky ain't falling. Your life ain't over. This too will pass.

Later I learned that losing tests your character. There's a lesson in every loss. If you fail to learn that lesson, the loss is even greater. But if you do learn the lesson, you're gonna have fewer losses in the future. One way or the other, learning to lose is fundamental.

# Skateboarding

*see* **Break Dancing; The Great Kabuki**

# Snoop Dogg

I know I said earlier I've got no desire to touch a basketball. The only exception I'll make is for Snoop. If Snoop calls and invites me to his compound to hoop and smoke a few blunts, I'm going. Snoop is not only a stone musical genius, he loves sports—watching and playing—and is one of my favorite niggas. But those games ain't nothing more than a few OGs having some fun. No 'bows are being thrown. No one's going nuts. And if truth be told, at this time of life we're more interested in smoking than hooping.

# *Sports Illustrated*

I gotta school the youngsters reading this book who don't know about *SI*. Back in the day, there was nothing bigger than

*My first* Sports Illustrated *cover, June 26, 1995.*

being on the cover. They put me on it at least ten times. I mentioned that first time when I was going to the draft. I was eighteen. Couldn't believe when I saw it on the newsstand. "Ready or Not . . ." the headline read. I know they meant *Was I ready for the league?* But that's not how I read it. I read it as *Was the league ready for me?* Nope, I thought. They have no idea what's coming.

# Latrell Sprewell

*see* **MV3**

# Springfield, Massachusetts

Home of the Basketball Hall of Fame.

I'm going in. I'm feeling like I should be more excited than I am. Not that I don't respect the institution. Not that I don't realize how few players get to experience the honor. Not that I don't like recognition.

But this class of 2021 is different. Three of us are going in, but only two of us are here. Timmy Duncan and I are here. Kob is gone. The absence of Bean changes everything. It's gonna be hard to feel joy or even happiness during the ceremony. Part of me wants to skip it.

They announced our admission in April, three months after Kob died. By then, it all seemed beside the point. I tried to see it in a positive light. Bean was being honored for all the right reasons. Timmy,

the anchor of a mighty dynasty in San Antonio, was getting his due. Kobean was an 18-time All-Star, me and Timmy 15-time All-Stars. The list of accolades is long.

I still have to figure out some speech. The speech I'd like to make ain't more than "I love Bean, I love Timmy, I love hoop, thank you and goodbye." I'll probably flower it up. I'll think of more shit to say.

But the truth is that I'd like to see the entire ceremony bathed in a long silence where we do nothing but remember the greatness of Kobe Bryant and all the good he gave the world.

# Dawn Staley

*see* **Rubber Band; WNBA**

# Suits

The summer I signed with the C's, we trained in Rome. That got me thinking about custom-made Italian suits. So I called up a designer and had him come measure all my teammates for suits. Not just the players, but the coaches, staff, interns, everyone. Even the cats who had no chance of making the team. I didn't do it for publicity. Did it to express my appreciation for being on this team and my excitement about the new season ahead.

When I became a vet with the T-Wolves, I bought new suits for all the

*Suited up, 2010.*

rookies. Did it to remind them that they were now grown-ass men who should look sharp and carry themselves like winners. Wanted to show them that it was part of being professional. For some rookies, the ones who didn't go high enough in the draft to afford to get all swagged out, this was their first suit.

In our dressed-down culture, dressing up—in the right place and at the right time—is the right move.

## Sheryl Swoopes

*see* **Rubber Band; WNBA**

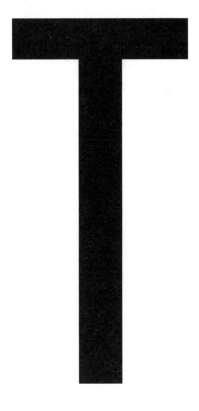

# T

Tattoos / Technical Foul / John Thompson /
Tough Guys / Trash Talk

# Tattoos

I like getting inked up. Ain't nothing about the process of customizing your body with art and words that doesn't appeal to me.

Props to AI for kicking off the craze. He was the one wanting to express his individuality in every way. To hell with what the world thought. Dennis Rodman was the other pioneer. Worm took it a whole lot further. Beyond the tats, he was pierced up from nose to lip to belly button. Muthafucka dyed his hair every color of the rainbow and liked partying in dresses and halter tops. Good for him. Go on and break the mold.

To me, tats say that no one owns us. Our bodies belong to us. It's our skin and we'll paint it up any way we want. Shout-out to cats like Chris Andersen who went wild. The big, colorful tat running across his neck says "Free Bird." He says it's the name of a Lynyrd Skynyrd song, but I take it as a metaphor that we're all free birds.

My ink has deep meaning for me:

"Rest in Peace MS2" of course refers to Malik Sealy and his number on the T-Wolves.

"21" is Malik's number when he played for St. John's, my number at Mauldin and in Minnie, and the number of years I played in the league.

Others speak for themselves: "Only God can judge me."

"Blood Sweat and Tears."

"Sky's the Limit."

"Ashley," for my baby sister.

A dragon.

A scorpion.

The Larry O'Brien championship trophy I won with Boston.

Inking up your body is an ongoing art project. I may get more. I'll let the course of my life decide what I want to commemorate.

It's a beautiful ritual. Pain's part of it. If you believe something deeply enough, you'll put up with the pain to have it engraved on your body. It's an act of affirmation. New tattoos give me new energy. They also confirm the fact that, as my mind and soul evolve, I can express that evolution on my skin. Nothing's static. Everything's growing. Everything's changing and rearranging. Changing and rearranging gives life fresh meaning.

# Technical Foul

*see* **Rasheed Wallace**

*John Thompson, 1999.*

# John Thompson

After Flip's firing and when the T-Wolves were at their lowest point, John Thompson caught me for a TV interview. Understand this: I loved John. Like practically every brotha who's hooped, I saw him as a father. His coaching success at Georgetown, his stewardship of players like Allen Iverson, Patrick Ewing, Alonzo Mourning, and Dikembe Mutombo; his becoming the first Black head coach to win an NCAA title; the way he backed up Bill Russell with the Celtics in the 1960s as a player in the NBA—everything about Big Ace spelled success.

John was a big man—6'10", 230 pounds—solid soul from head to toe. Even though an interview was the last thing I wanted—especially in light of Flip's leaving—I could never turn down John Thompson. That's how much respect I had for him.

He started out by saying he didn't want no political correctness from me. No problem. I ain't known for political correctness. John said he wanted straight answers. What were my feelings about Flip? I said Flip was a player's coach. Had nothing bad to say about Flip. Fact is, my teammates and I would run through a wall for Flip. Flip loved how I defied the rules when it came to scouting reports. The team would fine you if you didn't return the reports. I paid the fines in advance cause I never gave the reports back; I never stopped studying them. Flip had that same mentality. He was also a film freak. When it came to watching films of the games, Flip and I sat together for hours, going over every move. Because he had a coach's eye, Flip saw things I didn't see. Flip was my man, but Flip was gone, and right now I just had to focus on what was in front of me.

"How beat up are you, Kevin?" he asked.

"I'm beat up, John."

"You've been doubled-teamed, triple-teamed. You've been grabbed. You've been held. Give me the straight scoop. What is the status of your health right now?"

"I'm out there," I said. "I suit up every night. Banged up, hurt . . ."

"You play hard. You always play hard. What's driving you?"

"That I'm losing. I'm losing . . ."

I tried to hold back the tears, but it was no use.

"These are tears of pain," I said.

"Tears of pride," said John.

"Lotta pride. It's eating me up."

"Kevin, personally, you're doing as well as you did last year."

"This ain't golf. This ain't tennis. Ain't about me. It's about us. It ain't about what I'm doin'. Evidently what I'm doing ain't enough. I hate that I'm like this in front of you right now, man."

Tears kept flowing.

"No," said Big Ace. "I respect you for showing these emotions. I don't

disrespect you one bit today . . . you're putting the burden of this team on your shoulders, aren't you? Are you taking the full responsibility of this?"

"Got no choice. . . . I don't like showing emotion, man, cause it exposes you. You feel me?"

"Kevin, do you think what you're showing now is a sign of weakness?"

I was too choked up to answer.

"This is strength," said John. "You and I are going to get in a fight right now. You're showing strength. That's the thing that's so refreshing to me about you."

"I don't want to be like this, John. I'm a strong dude. And people watching this, I don't want them to think I'm weak. But I do give a lot. And it ain't cause I got to. See me. I came out the womb like this. This is how I am. You don't play ball cause you got to. You don't run sprints cause you got to. I don't have to put in extra shots cause I got to. I ain't gotta do none of that. This is me. This is how I'm built."

John switched to whether I regretted staying on all these years in Minnie. I said I didn't. I meant what I said. John pushed me further.

"Are you sure that isn't what bothers you so much? Because you feel part of it and you want it to change?"

"No, Big John. I just don't like to lose, man. Whatever we doing, I hate to lose. I hate to lose. That's my biggest problem. I can't accept losing. I won't ever accept losing. No one'll ever be able to call me a loser to my face."

When the interview and the camera was off, John embraced me.

"You did beautifully, son," he said.

Big John comforted my troubled soul.

When I went to Boston, I had his locker and wore his number 5.

Now he's gone, but his spirit isn't. His spirit lives inside me.

## Tough Guys

Big difference between a tough guy and a hard player. I played hard, but I don't consider myself a tough guy. The fact that I won't back away from a fight doesn't make me a tough guy. Every player in the league gotta be ready to fight. The whole league's about weeding out the weak. You ain't gonna survive NBA culture if you demonstrate even a sliver of weakness. The league's made of guys who've come out of their neighborhoods as superheroes. That neighborhood might be a college campus or a ghetto project. Doesn't matter. These brothas comin' in smokin' hot. They coming in with swag. They coming in with the support of their whole community. Soon as they arrive, they'll be tested, not only by their opponents but their teammates who worry about them taking their place. The competition is ocean deep and mountain high. You gotta play hard or you ain't playing at all.

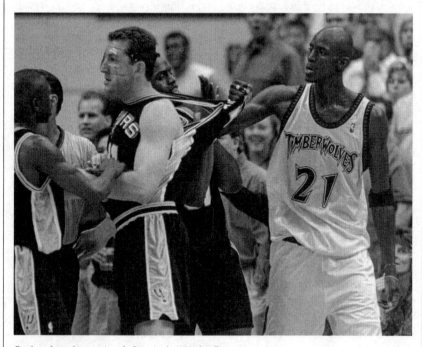

*Ready to throw down against the Spurs in the 1999 playoffs.*

Tough guys, though, are a category of their own. Best way to define them is this: Imagine being in a strange, crime-ridden city. Vacant lots. Rotting garbage on the street. Rats running loose. Sirens blaring. You don't know your way around. All you know is that niggas might be coming at you when you least expect them. You find yourself facing a dark alley. To get where you need to go, you gotta walk through that bitch. A black tomcat crosses right in front of you. Halfway down the alley you see five or six brothas who look like they be waiting for you. So the question is: As you enter the alley, who do you want to walk with you?

The answer is a tough guy.

I'm going with Charles Oakley.

I'm taking Kenyon Martin, one of the dopest people you'll ever meet.

I'm counting on Xavier McDaniel.

I'm asking Larry Johnson.

I'm rolling with fuckin' Otis Thorpe.

I'm needing Charles Barkley.

I'm looking to Dwight Howard.

I'm bringing Sam Mitchell.

I'm walking with Karl Malone.

I'm calling on Anthony Mason.

I'm with Zach Randolph.

Ain't going in there without Funk.

These brothas are about the business. These brothas are hitters. They ain't taking no shit. They ain't showing no fear. They in the trenches.

But it goes beyond recognizing their toughness. It's also, at least on the court, actually enjoying their toughness.

Every time I played Zach Randolph, for example, it was a bear fight. Same with Kenyon Martin.

In contrast, if I'm playing Rasheed Wallace or Timmy Duncan, it's a chess match. It's a clash of skill sets. Their offense will clash with my defense and vice versa. In the heat of battle, we figuring each other out.

Other players can't be figured out. Barkley, for example. Him and Olajuwon. They both unstoppable. In the paint, you won't match up with either of them.

There were other match-ups, though, that I looked forward to. Take Antonio McDyess. Always looked forward to going up against him. Knew I'd have a battle on my hands. Knew he'd bring out the best in me and vice versa.

I was blessed with teammates who did the same. Loved having Bobby Jackson on my team. Troy Hudson was dope. Me and Huddie had great chemistry. Trent Hassell. Brook Lopez. Zach LaVine. Andrew Wiggins. Rick Rubio. Leon Powe. Terrell Brandon. Doe. Nothing I like more than playing with guards, leaning on guards, learning from guards. So many hoopers with fresh skills and a clean understanding of how to win a dogfight.

If you gonna hoop at the highest level, you gonna wind up throwing a 'bow and breaking rules. That's the real culture of the NBA. Try and change the culture and the culture will chop you up like dog meat. Adapt to the culture and the culture will take you to another level of excellence.

Plain, in-your-face fact: You can't avoid physical punishment. You have big strong men running around a hardwood floor basically in their underwear. Ain't no real protection. Brotha slams you hard, throws you on your back. You ain't taking that shit lightly. You gonna do what you gotta do to get back. It's bone to bone.

# Trash Talk

Shout-out to Moms. My gift of gab came from her. She taught me how vocab, used wisely, can work to your everlasting advantage. And because I got that gift from Moms, and because I grew up in a household of women and developed a sensitivity around women's issues, I always followed Rule #1 of trash-talking: Never talk about a cat's mama or his girl. Never done that. Not even once. That's just a matter of respect. You can use your motormouth as part of your hardness—part of your strategy to control

**Favorite Trash-Talkers**

1 Gary Payton
2 Charles Barkley
3 Michael Jordan
4 Vernon Maxwell
5 Paul Pierce
6 Antoine Walker

*Gabbing against the Bobcats, 2009.*

the floor—but I've never seen the need to bad-mouth a loved one. I got limits. Everyone does, or at least should.

Rule #2 of trash talk: You gotta be able to back that shit up. Most cats who talk trash are garbage-bag players. Easiest way to shut them up is to just play the game. Show your dominance. And once they stop chirpin', that's when I know I got 'em.

That's Rule #3: Once you start talking trash, you can't ever stop. Ever. That's the worst thing you can do. You have to keep it up. Quieting down is backing down. Soon as that happens, it's over.

And that's it. Just those three rules. Other than that, anything goes.

Talking trash is important because every player has doubt. I saw it as my job to build up my opponent's doubt. If I do that, I'm at an advantage. And if you wanna win, you gotta get yourself all the advantages you can.

Most of the media stories about what exactly I said to a player in a trash-talk exchange are bullshit. The media couldn't hear what I was saying, so they made it up.

One story that's true, though, is the first time I went up against Steven Adams of OKC. I knew the dude was from overseas. I just didn't know where. And he knew I didn't know. So when I started going in on him, he said, "No English. Sorry." I laughed. Man, later I learned Steven Adams was from English-speaking New Zealand. Good one, Steve.

One thing most people don't understand about my trash talk is that as much as I was talking to other players, I was talking even more to myself. Self-criticizing, or self-motivating, or self-correcting. The entire game I'd be having a running conversation with myself. The key is making sure those conversations are instructive as opposed to destructive. It's about pumping yourself up, not tearing yourself down.

That's what I love about hoop. It allows and even encourages you to tap into that deep, primal shit. In any other context, if you're talking to yourself, people think you're crazy. But hoop permits you to express all those feelings and emotions in a way you never could out in the real world. Think about it: In what other profession is talking trash to your colleagues not only accepted but respected? Can you imagine going into your office and saying, "Yo, Bob, what the fuck was that presentation? That was dog shit, my man. That was straight trash. You gotta come stronger than that, son." You'd get fired on the spot.

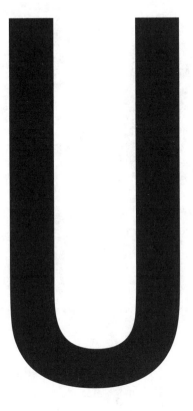

Ubuntu / Uncomfortable / *Uncut Gems* / Understanding /
United States Olympic Team / The University of KG

*Ubuntu at work during a 2010 playoff game against the Magic.*

# Ubuntu

Doc was all about creative motivation. Also creative language. What words you use. What words you don't use. Take the phrase "Boston culture." There's always been talk about Boston being a basically racist city. Of course Doc knew that, but Doc had his own way of dealing with it. He didn't bring up Boston culture or racism. He used one word, a word that captured our imagination: "Ubuntu." He introduced it as a concept from a South African language that embodied many meanings, but for Doc, the essence was *I can't be all that I can unless you're all that you can be.*

"Each of you," he said, "will have your version of Ubuntu. And that's fine. Let it live in your heart. Let it grow in your spirit."

Before each practice he went around the room asking each of us to explain Ubuntu.

I might say, "I am because you are."

P might say, "Teamwork."

Doe might say, "Sacrifice for the good of all."

Doc liked all the definitions. He liked the fact that Ubuntu got us thinking the right way. He saw it as a fraternity template. It was a circle where we all were equal. You need a defender, here's your defender. Need a shooter, here's your shooter. Doc could have said "Celtic Pride," and he did, in fact, remind us that our job was to bring back the glory of a storied franchise. But by putting the whole thing under the umbrella of Ubuntu, he reinvented our mission. It wasn't *We gotta do this for the city of Boston or the people of Massachusetts or the population of New England.* Ubuntu went beyond geography or race. Ubuntu was universal wisdom. Though it was ancient wisdom, to us it was new and vital and motivating. It was Doc's word. It became our word. And when the season got rolling, we all came together—team, family, friends, and fans.

# Uncomfortable

When I was on the court, I always wanted to make my opponents uncomfortable. That's how the old-school cats hooped in the '80s and '90s. They worked to make you feel uncomfortable as quick as possible. Trash-talked you. 'Bowed you. Did whatever it took to throw your ass off.

I learned that lesson from them. I saw making opponents uncomfortable as one of my main jobs. That job also entailed moving *myself* out of any comfort zone.

To progress, you gotta go through discomfort. The things you learn from discomfort are the same things you gonna need to get to the next level. That applies to all of life.

When I got to Boston, I sat down with C's owner Wyc Grousbeck. I wanted to get on the same page with Wyc early. If there was any discomfort, I didn't want it to work to my disadvantage. We both have strong personalities, but fortunately from the start he spoke to me with respect. I did the same. Later we got to know each other even better.

My main man in that ownership group was Jim Pallotta. We damn near became best friends. Jim was a gritty Italian kid who made it out of the North End. Gained lots of love by coming back to his hood and helping out the

*With Adam Sandler and LaKeith Stanfield in* Uncut Gems.

community. He finally bought into the Celtics, his lifelong dream. He wanted me to be a partner on his purchase of the Roma soccer team but, for reasons I never understood, David Stern blocked me. That didn't stop Jim from putting me into his deal when he came out with his own tequila.

Some owners don't even merit mention. Others, like Jim, merit praise.

# Uncut Gems

Besides my uncredited role in *Blue Chips*, I'd been in a movie before—*Rebound: The Legend of Earl "The Goat" Manigault*. Don Cheadle played the title character, the legendary Harlem street baller. Shot in Toronto my rookie year, the film had me playing the young Wilt Chamberlain. A small role, but a character I idolized. I was fascinated by the whole filmmaking process.

During my career, I'd made a boatload of commercials. The mechanics of doing them always interested me and gave me a chance to perform in front of the camera. The Fun Police was an example of that.

But the big fun didn't come along till a couple of years ago when the Safdie brothers, Josh and Benny, cast me in *Uncut Gems*, where Adam Sandler plays an out-of-his-mind Jewish jeweler/hustler/pussy hound hooked on hoop and gambling. As Howard Ratner, Adam gets hold of a rare stone that is supposed to give me—KG playing KG—the extra boost I need while the C's are playing Philly in the 2012 Eastern Conference semifinals. I was glad to take the role. After all, how bad can you really mess up playing yourself?

We got to shoot where no one had shot before—in New York City's Forty-Seventh Street Diamond District. That's because the Safdies' dad had worked there. The intensity of that block blew my mind. Cats with shaggy beards and long black coats carting crates of diamonds worth untold millions up and down the street like they're pushcarts filled with potatoes.

The movie belongs to Adam, who came on like Pacino on steroids. He tore up the part. I loved how the script never sugarcoated the characters. The Safdies told it like it is and let Howard Ratner be funky as fuck.

The work I put into the film was like the work I had put into hoop. Total focus. Hours of rehearsal where I lost track of time. I hung in cause the cast was so devoted. I wanted to match their devotion. I learned from everyone. Adam got into the head of Howie Ratner and never got out. LaKeith Stanfield, who I knew from *Atlanta*, Donald Glover's TV show, was a virtuoso with a huge range. Julia Fox, playing Ratner's mistress, was a natural.

I'm not sure I was a natural, but I did feel a sense of harmony among the cast—the way I felt during that championship season with Boston. Beyond bonding with the actors and feeling part of something bigger than myself, I got off on studying the production, the camera setups, the synergy with the producers and writers. Aesthetically, it took me to a different place.

The Safdies thought outside the box. They let their story go where it needed to go. It was funny, nasty, lighthearted, heavy-handed, comic, and tragic, all at the same time.

The experience helped push me into creating Content Cartel, a production company where my partners and I get to create and control uncompromised narratives about Black life. Like the NBA, Hollywood is a machine. Also like the NBA, newcomers can get fucked over. Hold on to your wallet. Hold on to your

dick. Someone wants to kick you in the balls and steal your story. I learned that the NBA can be rewritten. Same with Tinseltown. Rules gotta be rewritten, or else we're gonna be fed the same soap operas we've been fed forever.

Time for new stories, true stories, stories screaming to be told.

# Understanding

For athletes, "surgery" is never a word we wanna hear. In 2009, the year after the Celtics won it all, that word came up. For the first time in my career, I was dealing with a major physical issue: my knee.

**Favorite Commercials I'm In**

1 The Fun Police (Nike)
2 He's Got the Whole World in His Hands (Adidas)
3 20, 10 & 5 (AND1)
4 The Revolution Will Not Be Televised (Nike)
5 Edge Shave Gel, with Kareem

I didn't want to think about it because we had jumped off to a great start. Started the season 17–2. At that point we'd won nineteen straight games. We were setting records. All this time I'm determined to overcome this knee thing by using the methods I mentioned before. These are my ways of dealing with pain.

First, I see it as an out-of-body experience. Distance myself from it. It's there, I'm here. It's not me. It's just pain I can view from afar.

That approach flopped. No matter how hard I tried, I couldn't flex. Couldn't jump off that leg. Couldn't get outside of the pain. Truth is, I couldn't do shit.

Next approach was to breathe it in and then breathe it out. Inhale. Exhale. Watch it leave my body. Except it didn't. It stayed. And got worse.

Okay, time to face it. Talk to it.

"Fuck you," I said to pain. "Every other part of me is working. I ain't gonna worry about you."

"Yes, you are," pain answered. "You are cause you got no choice. I ain't going nowhere. And as long as I'm here, you ain't gonna play right. I'm gonna keep fucking you up."

"Then I'll slice you up."

"You talkin' surgery?"

"I'm talkin' surgery."

"You said you'd never do surgery."

"I said a lot a shit. But no matter what I might have said before, your ass is history."

My mind was made up. I was hurting so bad that I had to stop playing in February. I had to educate myself about the right surgical procedure. Meet with doctors. Hear them out. Explore options. And then go for it.

By May I checked into the hospital. I went under. Surgery went well. While recovering, I watched my team lose to Orlando in the conference semifinals.

That summer I came back cautiously but optimistically. Doubled my determination.

Some of the OGs in the league said, "You can be determined as you want, Ticket, but you ain't ever gonna be the same."

They weren't being mean. They were being real. Weren't trying to scare me. Were just trying to prepare me. I appreciated their candor.

I never was the same—never was as good as I had been pre-op—but I also have to say that doubling my determination got me another seven years of active play. Some of that play was excellent; some of it was just okay; but none of it was sad. I remained a happy warrior.

When I say it was determination that bought me more time, I need to explain what I mean. Determination was more than just *go out there and break your balls*. I was determined to study the nature of the calf. Memorize its muscularity. See how the operation had changed the structure. Learn to deal with this restructured body part. Take my time. Inch my way back in. Be smart. Learn the science and the anatomy. Listen to the trainers and then and only then hit the floor running.

I also learned to control my movements. I used my knowledge of the league to get around my limitations. I saw that knowledge is one thing and understanding is another. Knowledge won't always get you what you want. Understanding will.

# United States Olympic Team

*see* **Dunk; Euros; Shoes**

# The University of KG

It only lasted a couple of years, and there were only a few students. There wasn't any facility or buildings. Just a gym. And there was only one prof—me. But I loved the thing all the same. I loved becoming a trainer/teacher.

I left the game because my knees were shot. I had to quit or risk permanent injury. I had a long career but have often thought it might have been six or seven years longer had I played in the warm weather of California versus the freezing winters of Minnie, Boston, and Brooklyn. I hate cold and what cold does to my overall body condition.

No matter, by 2016, at age forty, I was through hooping. I didn't think much about teaching until Doc Rivers, then with the Clippers, asked me about one-on-one work with his players. Doc is someone I'm never gonna refuse.

My students were superstars Blake Griffin and DeAndre Jordan. Doc thought Blake was thinking a little bit too much—overanalyzing as opposed to reacting in real time. I gave him a script that I had used. When I went into a game, I'd studied everyone who might possibly be guarding

*Reviewing film with Jaren Jackson Jr. of the Memphis Grizzlies, 2019.*

me. I knew that every defender has his pluses and minuses. I knew how to avoid their strengths and attack their weaknesses. Knew that to the point where I didn't have to think about it; I just did it. My script was also about getting into the face of your opponent. I'm a big proponent of "Tear the fuckin' rim off." And when you do tear it off, tear it off like no one else can tear it off. Ain't no one can play with you. Ain't no one can keep up with you.

It's BG ingesting my belief on how to attack the rim. BG ingested all this and applied it the right way. His work ethic was strong. It was a pleasure working with him.

DeAndre Jordan, even with his titanic talent, didn't have enough belief in his offensive tools. So we worked on both those tools and his self-confidence. Ain't no one in the world who doesn't need encouragement, even a big like DeAndre. I love busting someone's ass during the heat of competition. But even more than that, I love supporting a brotha. DeAndre has a beautiful spirit on and off the court, and I still derive huge satisfaction in watching him improve his game year after year.

Word got around that I was willing to train and others came along like Jaren Jackson Jr. from the Grizzlies and the Bucks' Giannis Antetokounmpo, maybe the baddest boy since Bron. I'm not sure how much I added to a player with that much talent. Some of our training sessions were as much about psychological strategy as moves. It was dope to see that not long after our training, he got MVP. Credit to Giannis, not me.

In my personal time, I've worked with my boys Big Baby, Perk, and Leon Powe. Would go out and shoot with them and share my script.

After a lifetime of hooping, I didn't have any false modesty of how much I knew. I knew a lot. But I also knew enough to know that every player is unique. I didn't have any predetermined notion of how to make that player better, except to study him closely and see if I could do for him what coaches had done for me—find parts of his game that he might not consider a strength and turn those old liabilities into new assets.

Overall, those two years when I hired myself out as a trainer turned into a beautiful transition.

Vibrations / Video Games / Vulnerable

# Vibrations

I talked earlier about the Big Three and the importance of us being unselfish, but you don't want your playmakers to be completely unselfish. Ain't no such thing as a totally unselfish playmaker. There are gonna be games when somebody's got a hot hand and you want them to keep shooting no matter how many defenders the other team is running at 'em. Then there are gonna be games that come down to the last shot and you want a playmaker to put the team on his back. Even if you had enough time to swing the ball, you'd still want it in the playmaker's hands. You'd still want to ride or die with him when the game's on the line.

For the Celtics, sometimes that'd be P and sometimes that'd be Ray and sometimes that'd be me. And somehow, on any given night, without discussion or debate, we always knew who it should be. When you play the game for so many years, you start having telepathic relationships. Each game has its own vibrations. The flow of the game will tell you who should be getting that last shot. The game always knows best.

## Video Games

I love my games. Always have. Growing up, most of my friends couldn't afford a game system. We were always at the houses of the one or two kids who had a Sega or a Nintendo. When I signed with Minnie and moved into my crib, one of the first things I did was go out and buy every game system and a big-ass TV. Never forget the time we're playing *Madden 97*, and one of my boys throws up a Hail Mary as time is expiring. I'm up by a field goal and have my defense set up in Cover 4. One of his receivers comes down with the ball, and, fool that I am, I jump up, throw my controller at the TV, and crack the screen. I've had a lot of heartbreaking losses in sports, but that one's right up there. And speaking of right up there: one of my career highlights was making the cover of *NBA 2K9*.

I'm still a gamer to this day. I play everything—sports, shooters, stealth. What's amazing now is how you can be playing some guy on the other side of the world. It's great how games can bring people together.

But it can be unhealthy to stay inside for hours at a time and not get out and expose yourself to the world—to the danger and excitement. Especially for kids. You know who's outside? Older kids ready to whoop yo ass. But guess who else is outside? Potential girlfriends and boyfriends. New friends. People. The world.

*The Sega Genesis controller.*

It's safe inside. It's safe to be in front of the screen. But safety can be boring. I love my games. But I've never played a game more exciting than real life.

# Vulnerable

I had to learn that word the hard way.

As a kid, the idea of being easily hurt wasn't anything I wanted. I didn't want my heart crushed. I didn't want my feelings trampled on. I wanted to be tough. Wanted to grow three layers of skin. Wanted to get where you couldn't get to me. Wanted to be hard, not soft; unbreakable, invincible. Anything but vulnerable.

One of the big lessons of life is seeing the blessing of being vulnerable. That's the only way I learned what I had to learn. I could be fucked over just like anyone else. Just cause I was good at dunking a rock through a hoop didn't mean I didn't have a blind side. We all got blind sides. And the cats who are the blindest are those who see themselves as invulnerable.

As an elite athlete, it's easy to be arrogant. Friends and fans hype you up. Women are loving on you. You get money, fame, little kids worshipping you. When all that shit starts making you feel like God, watch out. You ain't God. You just another headstrong nigga cruising for a bruising. It's a rare brotha who won't get bruised. But, believe me, when the bruise heals, you'll be a lot stronger and smarter than before.

Antoine Walker / Rasheed Wallace / Way to Do Things Right /
Chris Webber / Weed / Kanye West / Whistling / The Wiggle /
Bill Willoughby / Ben Wilson / Wilt / WNBA / Wu-Tang Clan

*Arguing with official Jim Clark in 2001. (Yeah, I got ejected.)*

# Antoine Walker

*see* **Hot Dog; Kobe; Tyronn Lue**

# Rasheed Wallace

Trash-talking is one way to disrupt an opponent. Technical fouls are another. Sure, for most players techs are accidental. Cats get caught up in the heat of the moment and let their emotions get the best of them. But there are a select few who are methodical and understand that a precisely timed tech can change the momentum and ultimately the outcome of a game. Sheed was the best I ever seen.

He gave me a little bit of a rough time about not going to college when I first hit the league. Him and G Trent would both crack jokes about me, but I got their humor. It was cool. They wound up being two of my best friends. (Turned out that Sheed's mom and mine also became best friends.)

Sheed picked up 317 techs in his career, behind only Karl Malone and Sir Charles. I'm number seven on the all-time list with 176. My man also has the record for most techs in a season with 41—which breaks down to a tech every other game. Of course not all of Sheed's techs were intentional. Early in our careers, the refs were a lot more hands-off. If they thought you were crossing the line, they'd pull you to the side

and tell you to cut the shit. Man to man. And only if you kept at it would you get T'd up. Later in our careers, though, the officials got more involved. Got quicker with the whistles. That was especially true after the 2004 "Malice at the Palace" brawl between the Pistons and Pacers, which spilled into the stands. After that, the league really cracked down on player behavior. Started treating us like children.

Sheed was in the middle of that brawl. Rushed right in and tried to break it up. People always call him a hothead, but that night he was trying to keep it cool. Sheed understood the temperature of a game better than anyone. He controlled the thermostat. And he did that through techs or even ejections. (His twenty-nine career ejections will be one of the toughest NBA records to beat. That's twice as many as anyone else.) If his team wasn't bringing the energy, he'd get a tech to fire them up. If the other team was going on a run, he'd get a tech to slow the game down. He was such a talented player, but his ability to use the ref's whistle to manipulate the game was among his greatest skills. I consider Sheed a mirror image of myself, but better because he had the advantage of college.

As brothas, he and I share many of the same interests and passions. When it came time to go on TNT with *Area 21,*

*Me and Rasheed before Game 1 of our 2008 playoff series against Detroit.*

Sheed joined me as a cohost. The brotha is also a music man. Can DJ his ass off. Every day I thank Jehovah God for the man I call Ra-Booger.

## Way to Do Things Right

I'm about to boast, so I better stop and be careful. Your ego's your best friend who also wants to kill you. You need your ego to compete, accomplish, and get shit done. But if you don't watch it, your ego will eat your ass for lunch.

I like that my ego is strong, and I like that my ego wants to tell you that probably my biggest victory in my career wasn't the All-Star Games, or MVP, or Defensive Player of the Year. The biggest victory was keeping my nose clean, keeping my head down, and focusing on my profession. Nothing but going out

there, busting my ass, and hooping best as I could. Ain't saying that there weren't nasty confrontations on and off the court. I did more than my fair share of trash-talkin'. But I never held grudges. I focused on the game and figured out the way to do things right.

## Chris Webber

*see* **Duke vs. Michigan; Learning; Showdown**

## Weed

Been smelling weed since I was a kid playing outside in the yard on a Saturday night while my uncles and aunts were inside listening to Al Green.

Weed, though, never really interested me. I was always interested in staying in shape. Didn't want nothing that would slow me down or stunt my growth in any way. When I got into trouble in high school and was put on parole, I was super strict about avoiding drugs, both in Mauldin and Chicago. If I was riding in your car and you were holding, I'd jump out. When I got in the league, I never failed a single drug test. That's because I didn't smoke my first joint until 2004, and only then because I was nervous about my upcoming marriage. A friend said a little weed might mellow me. After that, if I did indulge, it was always off-season. Wouldn't let anything get in the way of staying in shape.

During my early years in the NBA there was lots of coke. Cats were tooting regularly, and the league knew it. The league saw the culture falling apart and laid down the law. That was a good thing since coke, in my view, separates you from your soul. Coke is some nasty shit. I never did it.

In the league, I know players who've used weed to improve themselves. Whether it mellowed out cats who were too hyper, or whether it gave them a new perspective, the right joint can put you in the right frame of mind. Just be careful. It's tricky. But it's worth investigating.

I started investigating cannabis years ago. I saw it as an investment opportunity. I jumped on the bandwagon early on and am glad I did. I learned that cannabidiol—CBD—is the component that makes up 40 percent of the plant. It has tons of medicinal uses. The worldwide market for CBD, in everything from oils to candy, is exploding. CBD doesn't get you high. THC is the element that gets you high. If you don't wanna mess with your mind, ingest CBD products. If you like messing with you mind, find the joint with the CBD/THC combination that will swing your mood in the direction you wanna go. CBD works for me. It's a healer and a calmer. It also adjusts my dyslexia. Because I see written words backwards, I can get spoken words jumbled up in my mind. Weed helps straighten that shit out.

Our culture is finally recognizing the positive properties of well-cultivated cannabis.

Times changed and sports have to change with those times.

There was a time when baseball players got silly drunk and the MLB looked the other way. There was a time when cigarette smoking was considered cool. Hollywood promoted those cancer sticks in practically every movie they made. Actors—especially in love scenes—smoked their asses off.

Cats liked coke cause coke jacked up their egos. But then coke led to the pipe and crack, and crack did more damage than maybe any drug in human history. But when the government conflated coke with weed, the government showed its ignorance. Weed did more than survive the anti-drug wars. Weed prevailed because weed proved it's for a lot more than partying. It's for managing pain, just to mention one of its benefits.

I've heard about cats, now in their seventies, going to the penitentiary for possession of a single joint back in the 1960s. The prosecution of pot users has a long, ugly history. We gotta rejoice about living in a time when that kind of uninformed thinking is—at least among the open-minded—a thing of the past.

Last word on weed: Cats I know who appreciate pot know how to grow it. Growing it requires not only knowledge but tender loving care. No different than developing an athlete. I think of Dell Curry cultivating his gifted sons Steph and Seth into elite hoopers, Richard Williams cultivating his gifted daughters Serena and Venus into elite tennis players. You give the right attention. You give the right nourishment. You seek the right balance. You make it a priority. You never stop monitoring the progress. And then you let nature takes it course.

When I was a little kid, Stevie Wonder put out an album called *Journey Through the Secret Life of Plants*. It talked about how plants can feel. He said that a seed is a star. A seed can take us to heaven. When we cultivate seeds in the right way, life blossoms. Love blossoms. The world becomes a better place.

# Kanye West

*see* **Japan; Kenny G; "King Kunta"**

# Whistling

*see* **Illmatic**

# The Wiggle

Another term for "adapting" or "adjusting." The wiggle is one of the secrets to getting through life.

# Bill Willoughby

*see* **Isolation; One-and-Done**

# Ben Wilson

Ben Wilson had been shot to death in the Go twelve years before I arrived in the city, but his myth never died. On the streets, his fame never faded. He was a legend, larger in death than in life.

He grew up on the South Side of Chicago. Went to Simeon Vocational High School. By the time he was a sophomore, he'd made varsity. By his junior year, ESPN was calling him the best in the country. Everyone was comparing him

*Ben Wilson, 1984.*

to Magic. Everyone was saying he could out-magic Magic. No one had seen such a slick skill set on the part of a floor general.

To be shot at age seventeen during a street scuffle in the city of Chicago in the cracked-out '80s was hardly news. God only knows the number of brothas and sistas, mamas and daddies, and grandmamas and granddaddies who lost their lives to killer cops, killer drugs, killer demons that have haunted—and still haunt—this country. We stop and pray and breathe in the millions of tragedies that we don't even know about.

When we do know about one—especially one that involved maybe the greatest hooper of his generation—the pain gets personal. I could have been Ben Wilson. I could have been any of the fallen brothas whose future was filled with hope. That I got to live out a dream ain't something I can take credit for. Take the wrong street, take the wrong turn, make a move too soon or too late—I could have done any of those things. That I didn't ain't no cause for self-celebration. I was careful, but you can be careful as fuck and still get crushed.

# Wilt

It was as if God had come to the game.

It was the All-Star Game in Cleveland, the one where I met Biggie. At the Saturday night skills competition events, I looked in the stands and there he was.

The man was massive. His body was broad enough to occupy three chairs. He was slumped down, legs crossed, relaxed, but completely in command.

He illuminated the arena. All eyes on Wilt. Dressed in black, black headband, black cutoff shirt so you saw his massive arms, black jeans, black designer slip-ons, four or five gold chains. He was a magnet, women running over to where he was seated at half-court, him waving and smiling and commanding the food vendors and the fans to bring him this and bring him that. Signing autographs. Talking to the media. Orchestrating everything. In charge. In command.

I couldn't help myself. I had to go over to shake hands.

I came on like a groupie.

"Excuse me, Mr. Chamberlain," I said. "Just wanted you to know that I'm a huge fan."

"Why, thank you, young fella. Where you from?"

"South Carolina."

"Oh, I thought you were a Chicago kid."

"Went to high school in Chicago."

"Well, I love your game. Keep working. Get stronger. Build up those skills. Don't let nobody tell you you can't do nothing. Know what I'm saying?"

"Yes, sir. What you say means a lot to me, Mr. Chamberlain."

"Take care of the rookies. Take care of the younger generation. That's what's up."

"I hear you."

"Keep giving."

"I'm giving you respect, Mr. Chamberlain, cause without you there wouldn't be me."

"Enjoy the weekend. There'll be a lot more weekends like this in your future."

And with that he reached out his hand to shake mine. His hands went all the way up to my forearms. Biggest hands I'd ever seen.

*Wilt, 1959.*

"Don't wanna take up any more of your time," I said.

He smiled and turned his attention to another bunch of hot women heading his way. I know in his book that he claimed to have bedded thousands of ladies. That night showed me he was telling the truth. He generated an electricity, a bigness of spirit and charisma I ain't ever seen before.

Wilt was a giant. King of the court.

# WNBA

Got deep into the WNBA in Minnie. Bought season tickets to the Lynx and loved going to the games. Female athletes inspire as much as men. Maybe more because they've had to break down iron barriers. Breaking down those barriers meant building up a work ethic like no other. That work ethic led to them mastering the game. They haven't gotten the credit, they haven't gotten the bread, they haven't gotten the respect they deserve.

I watched Cynthia Cooper-Dyke tear it up for the Comets down in Houston, four championships, three-time leading scorer in the league. Loved watching Coop go to the hoop. Chamique Holdsclaw. My idol Dawn Staley. My dear friend Candace Parker. The great Sheryl Swoopes. The list goes on. Hall of Famers.

*The New York Liberty play the Indiana Fever under the lights at Arthur Ashe Stadium in Flushing Meadows, New York, 2008.*

Olympic gold-medal winners. Women who have showed us that no matter how much we honor Brotha James Brown, JB might have made a mistake singing "this is a man's world."

Four years ago, ahead of the curve, the Minnesota Lynx were rocking shorts that said "Change Starts with Us: Justice & Accountability." They were bringing light when dark deaths started mounting up all over the country. The New York Liberty started up an annual Unity Day to bring focus on social injustice. They were down with Black Lives Matter early, strongly, and unapologetically.

I don't just follow women in hoop, but women in all sports. Mia Hamm in soccer. Venus and Serena in tennis. Danica Patrick racing cars. Maybe because I got a strong moms. Maybe because I was raised up in a household of ladies. I know that the power of women is a force for good. I also know that women have been closed down, blocked out, and have suffered the scorn of a male-controlled society.

My question is simple: What the fuck do we men think we're accomplishing by suppressing women in any area of life?

# Wu-Tang Clan

Ain't Nuthing ta Fuck Wit.

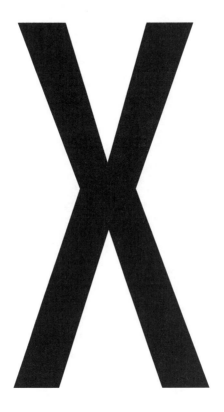

Malcolm X / X's and O's

# Malcolm X

When we were kids, Moms's Jehovah's Witnesses connection had us downplaying birthday parties. Maybe that's why it took me so long to learn that I shared May 19 birthday with Malcolm X.

My realization came, appropriately enough, in Harlem. Happened after I was in the league for a while. Me and my boys were shopping at Dr. Jay's. Manager was nice enough to close up the store for us so we could shop in peace. One woman was in there with her three kids, counting her pennies to buy them clothes, and I was more than happy to pick up the tab. Things like that always brighten everyone's day. She couldn't have been more gracious. Then we bought some things of our own. By the time we walked out, word had gone out and the street was mobbed. Seemed like a thousand people were waiting to greet me. It was all good, all love.

"You always welcome up here in Harlem, KG."

"Great to see you, Ticket."

I was thanking the brothas and sistas left and right when one old-school cat came up to me and said, "You do know that you and Malcolm share a birthday?"

"Malcolm who?" I asked.

"Malcolm X."

That stopped me cold. "For real?"

"Yeah, dawg," he said. "You doin' shit out of the spirit of Malcolm. Be conscious of your power, man."

"Wow," was all I could say.

"Peace be unto you," he said before walking on. He didn't have no rings on, no labels. Just a brotha out there in the street with everyone else.

Had a huge impact on me. Thought back to those times in Chicago when I'd get caught up in some gangbangin', trash-talkin' crossfire and was able to speak with a boldness that got me and my boys out of harm's way. Where did that velocity and

*Malcolm X, 1964.*

directness come from? I thought of how I'd sometimes talk with a certain tone that would amaze even me. Times when I spoke up for my friends or my teammates or my family. The very thought that I could be channeling even a little slice of the spirit of someone as game-changing and brave as Malcolm X was humbling. May 19 became a more important date.

It's not about religion or politics but, for me, it's about what Malcolm X stood for as a Black man—and a towering member of the human race. He spoke truth without fear. No one was gonna shut him up. He spoke truth without compromise. No one was gonna twist his words. His words rang with clarity. His words expressed the depth of his pride. His words reflected his sense of self-worth. He spoke for the oppressed in his own unique and powerful way.

He was the man who said, "Stumbling is not falling."

The man who said, "There is no better teacher than adversity. Every defeat, every heartbreak, every loss contains its own seed, its own lesson on how to improve your performance next time."

Another jewel: "Early in my life, I had learned that if you want something, you better make some noise."

The jewels kept coming: "You can't separate peace from freedom because no one can be at peace unless he has his freedom."

And maybe the brightest jewel of all: "If you're not ready to die for it, put the word 'freedom' out of your vocabulary."

Words spoken by a man who woke up a spirit in Black America that will never fall asleep again.

# X's and O's

Fascinating and fun to draw up plans. Figure out strategy. Learn the science. Map out the plays. Anticipate what's gonna happen next. Learn your literacy about

*Doc with the clipboard during the 2008 finals.*

traps. Think it all through. During a time-out, study these calculations, cause these calculations are based on past experience and deep knowledge. But the minute you step on the court, while those X's and O's are flitting around your brain, your brain better respond to the reality you're facing. That reality might render those X's and O's useless. That reality might mean you gotta throw out the playbook and let your instincts take over. Those instincts can not only win a basketball game, under certain situations in a world where danger is forever lurking, they can save your life.

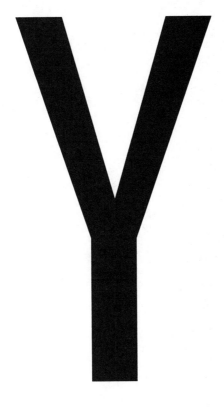

Yoga / Youth

# Yoga

It took me a while. I'd see folks twisted up like pretzels and think, *What's the point?* I grew up fighting and clawing and wrestling brothas to the ground. Then when I went from Minnie to Boston I looked for new worldviews. Figured it was time to change up.

Yoga is all about breath. Consciousness of breath. It's about the organic union of all your parts. A joining together of elements that maybe once were warring.

Have those warring elements inside me found peace? I'm not sure.

I am sure that there are other ways to tone your body and chill your mind than benching three hundred pounds. Not that I'm against lifting. Weights strengthened me. I like the business of pushing through pain. I like the feel of flesh on metal. I like running and swimming. I stay in shape with all kinds of modalities.

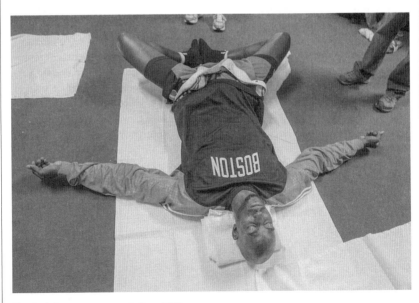

*Focusing before a preseason game in Rome, 2007.*

As a kid, I knew one modality. Go for it. Fight for it. Grab it. Choke it. Then fight, grab, and choke even harder. Never thought twice about breath. Took me a long time to see a wider world where you can honor your past, not regret a thing, and still realize that your past took place in a tiny province. Greenville had its own culture. The dream back then was to marry your childhood sweetheart, move to Charlotte, Charleston, or, if you were lucky, Atlanta. Go to college. Get a nine to five. Have kids. Live through your past. Wind up catching cancer or diabetes. And die. A dark dream.

There were rays of hope like Orlando Jones, who went to Mauldin High a decade before me and came to Hollywood where he became a comic, got into the cast of *MADtv*, and wrote for *A Different World*. We knew certain brothas and sistas had found a way out. But what was our way? Our way was to try harder and harder and then even harder. Nothing about stopping to breathe.

Goes back to my rant to Coach John Thompson during that TV interview about how I hated losing. I saw losing as a curse. The cure to the curse was winning. Winning is great, and in this Western culture of ours, the need to win is implanted in our brains at birth. But the drive to win, as fruitful as it might be, also has another side. It can be a sick obsession to the point where nothing else

counts. That sick obsession can crush your soul. And when that happens, winning turns into losing.

Yoga brought me the idea that the mind needs rest and the body needs ongoing readjustment. It opened me and surprised me cause, truth be told, I didn't even know that I was closed down.

# Youth

Don't got no generational prejudice. Different times, different cultures, different hoopers. The stars who came before me will always remain legends. Same as those who played with me. Maybe more so for those who've come after. MJ was Dr. J 2.0. LeBron was MJ 2.0. Giannis may well turn out to be LB 2.0. Zion Williamson could become Giannis 2.0. And some kid who has just been born could one day develop into Zion 2.0.

And so it goes. We learn more, we train better, eat better, invent new moves, find ways to last longer. I appreciate these young hard-goers. I feel their hunger. Fresh blood. Fresh energy. The league thrives on renewal and reinvention.

It's an art form, and art forms rely on originality. I loved the experience of watching my art form being transformed before my very eyes by players who grew up at different times and in different ways.

Zero Fucks / Zero Tolerance

# Zero Fucks

I give zero fucks about anything that's not true.

Zero fucks about people who don't like me.

Zero fucks if you don't like my music or playlist.

Zero fucks if you don't like my shoes.

Zero fucks about downloading, copying, and looking to better the moves of everyone from Bill Walton to Patrick Ewing to Chris Webber to Arvydas Sabonis to Robert Horry to Bill Russell. I went through every big in the league, took something from each of them, and tried to 2.0 it. I did it cause that's what creativity is. I did it with gratitude to all those magnificent athletes whose journey inspired mine. But I did it with zero fucks.

Zero fucks if you start judging. Only one who should be judging is Jehovah God. The rest of us are humans who should be looking to open our hearts and deepen our souls.

# Zero Tolerance

For hate.

For racism.

For sexism.

For ageism.

For discrimination of any kind.

For whiners and moaners and complainers.

For noneffort.

For playing the pass-the-blame game.

For noncharacter.

For anyone who stifles creativity.

The other night I had a dream where I came to some city in America where I was directed to a room. Inside, Malcolm X was talking to Huey Newton. Martin Luther King Jr. was talking to Marcus Garvey. All real ones in this room. All trading off ideas. All saying the same thing: We need to take our OG superpowers and spread it throughout the land. We need to take a stance and protect and promote the folk dying to come alive, dying to live and learn and give and get their just rewards.

We need to stay on the case and raise everyone up, especially those who are lost and looking to save their lives. We need to feed these folk. We need to supply them with food that nourishes mind, body, and spirit.

And we need to start today.

# Acknowledgments

David Ritz thanks Kevin, for his big heart and positive spirit; Sean Manning, for brilliant editing; David Vigliano, great agent; Daniel Voll, great friend; Mike Marangu, great teammate; Herb Powell; Joanna Parson; Nico Ager; my wife, Roberta; family, friends, and God, endless source of creative energy and boundless love.

# Image Credits

111 Reuters / Mike Segar /
Stock.adobe.com
114 Keith Torrie / *NY Daily News*
Archive via Getty Images
117 Reuters / Tim Shaffer /
Stock.adobe.com
121 Reuters / Reuters Photographer /
Stock.adobe.com
124 Brian Babineau / NBAE via Getty
Images
126 Reuters / Reuters Photographer /
Stock.adobe.com
127 NBA Photos / Boston Celtics
128 John Croft / *Star Tribune* via Getty
Images
131 Reuters / Sue Ogrocki /
Stock.adobe.com
135 Tim Chevrier / NBAE via Getty
Images
136 Manny Millan / *Sports Illustrated*
via Getty Images
143 Bill Baptist / NBAE via Getty Images
145 Andrew D. Bernstein / NBAE via
Getty Images
148 Reuters / Danny Moloshok /
Stock.adobe.com
155 Imagn © *The Greenville News*-USA
TODAY NETWORK
157 Jerry Holt / *Star Tribune* via Getty
Images
158 Jerry Holt / *Star Tribune* via Getty
Images
159 Reuters / Reuters Photographer /
Stock.adobe.com
162 Reuters / Reuters Photographer /
Stock.adobe.com
168 Imagn © MCT
169 Judy Griesedieck / *Star Tribune* via
Getty Images
172 Jeffery A. Salter / *Sports Illustrated*
via Getty Images

173 Jesse D. Garrabrant / NBAE via
Getty Images
178 Brian Bahr /ALLSPORT / Getty
Images Sport
183 Clarence Davis / *NY Daily News*
Archive via Getty Images
189 Everett Collection /
Courtesy Everett Collection /
Stock.adobe.com
190 Reuters / Brian Snyder /
Stock.adobe.com
193 Imagn © *The Greenville News*-USA
TODAY NETWORK
194 Reuters / Brian Snyder /
Stock.adobe.com
199 Reuters / Rebecca Cook /
Stock.adobe.com
200 Reuters / Brian Snyder /
Stock.adobe.com
203 Reuters / Reuters Photographer /
Stock.adobe.com
206 Lisa Blumenfeld / Getty Images
207 Reuters / Aaron Josefczyk /
Stock.adobe.com
208 Reuters / Mike Segar /
Stock.adobe.com
209 NBA Photos / Boston Celtics
210 Reuters / Adam Hunger /
Stock.adobe.com
212 Reuters / Reuters Photographer /
Stock.adobe.com
214 Elsa / Getty Images
224 Reuters / Ray Stubblebine /
Stock.adobe.com
226 Reuters / Brian Snyder /
Stock.adobe.com
229 Stephen Dunn / Staff / Getty
Images Sport
234 NBA on TNT: Courtesy and
© Turner Sports, Inc.
236 Author's Collection

237 Reuters / Reuters Photographer / Stock.adobe.com

241 David Sherman / NBAE via Getty Images

244 David Sherman / NBAE via Getty Images

247 Reuters / Reuters Photographer / Stock.adobe.com

248 Melissa Majchrzak / NBAE via Getty Images

249 Reuters / Max Whittaker / Stock.adobe.com

251 David Walberg / *Sports Illustrated* via Getty Images / Getty Images

253 Reuters / Adam Hunger / Stock.adobe.com

258 Reuters / Reuters Photographer / Stock.adobe.com

260 Reuters / Reuters Photographer / Stock.adobe.com

262 Reuters / Chris Keane / Stock.adobe.com

266 Jesse D. Garrabrant / NBAE via Getty Images

268 Netflix / The Hollywood Archive / PictureLux / The Hollywood Archive / Alamy Stock Photo

272 Joe Murphy / NBAE via Getty Images

278 JR Moreira / Stock.adobe.com

280 Craig Lassig / AFP via Getty Images

282 Reuters / Adam Hunger / Stock.adobe.com

284 *Chicago Tribune* photo by Ed Wagner Jr. / TCA

286 Everett Collection / Courtesy Everett Collection / Stock.adobe.com

287 Reuters / Keith Bedford/ Stock.adobe.com

291 Everett Collection / CSU Archives / Everett Collection / Stock.adobe.com

292 Reuters / Adam Hunger / Stock.adobe.com

297 Jesse Garrabrant / NBAE via Getty Images

300 Jim McIsaac / Getty Images